The Apocrypha: A Guide

GUIDES TO SACRED TEXTS

The Apocrypha

A Guide

MATTHEW GOFF

OXFORD
UNIVERSITY PRESS

OXFORD
UNIVERSITY PRESS

Oxford University Press is a department of the University of Oxford.
It furthers the University's objective of excellence in research, scholarship,
and education by publishing worldwide. Oxford is a registered trade mark of
Oxford University Press in the UK and in certain other countries.

Published in the United States of America by Oxford University Press
198 Madison Avenue, New York, NY 10016, United States of America.

CIP data is on file at the Library of Congress

ISBN 9780190060749 (pbk.)
ISBN 9780190060732 (hbk.)

DOI: 10.1093/9780190060770.001.0001

Paperback printed by Marquis Book Printing, Canada
Hardback printed by Bridgeport National Bindery, Inc., United States of America

For Liam

נַפְשׁוֹ גֶּחָלִים תְּלַהֵט וְלַהַב מִפִּיו יֵצֵא
בְּצַוָּארוֹ יָלִין עֹז וּלְפָנָיו תָּדוּץ דְּאָבָה

De gustibus non est disputandum—or as Tristram Shandy puts it, "there is no disputing against Hobby-Horses." This project has been my hobby horse for the last couple of years. It was a rewarding and enjoyable pursuit. The project prodded me to learn more about texts which I already knew something about. I often had much to learn about their reception. On numerous occasions I turned to friends and colleagues for guidance. Among many others, I thank Jordan Henderson, Francis Macatangay, Annette Yoshiko Reed, Dylan Burns, David Edwards, Martin Kavka, Karina Martin Hogan, Yonatan Binyam, François Dupuigrenet Desroussilles, and Sonia Hazard. Writing for a general readership was an unexpected challenge that I found rewarding and important. I am especially grateful to the students at Florida State University, undergraduate and graduate, who read drafts of chapters and let me know when they couldn't follow along: Alana Zimath, Mason Pullum, Emily Olsen, and Tommy Woodward, among others. Special thanks go to the students in my Spring 2024 class, "The Lost Books of the Bible." They essentially 'beta-tested' this book for classroom use. It sparked their interest in the Apocrypha and the volume is better as a result. I benefited from the expertise of librarians at Strozier Library, in particular Adam Beauchamp, Rachel Duke, Malcolm Shackelford, and the people at Special Collections and Archives; I am grateful for their help. My wife Diane's reading of drafts was also crucial. The comments of the anonymous reviewer were of great benefit. I thank Steve Wiggins at Oxford for inviting me to write for the Guide to Sacred Texts series. He, along with others at Oxford, especially Brent Matheny, aptly helped turn my manuscript into a book. While any errors are my own, I am delighted to have benefited from so many fellow-laborers and associates in this great harvest of our learning, to quote Tristram Shandy again.

Contents

1

Introduction

"The Bookes Called Apocrypha"

This book is about texts which are in the Bible—sort of. In these
writings a dragon blows up, somebody throws his own guts at
people, and bird poop makes someone else go blind. While many
people have never heard of these books, they were in the Bible for
centuries—and for millions of people still are. There is a venerable
tradition of referring to these texts collectively as the "Apocrypha."
This is a Latin word (and a Greek word) which means "hidden
(things)" (the singular form is "apocryphon"). The term has often
signified not books with "hidden" or esoteric knowledge, but rather
ones that should be rejected—"hidden away." The word "apocryphal" is used today for stories that people mistakenly believe to be
true. Stories about Bigfoot are apocryphal. Stories about the Loch
Ness Monster are apocryphal. How several strange and interesting
biblical books came to be classified as apocryphal is part of the
story this book tells.

This book is not written for biblical scholars, who know quite a
lot about these texts. It is written for people who want to learn more
about them. To that end, it provides a concise introduction to the
"lost books" of the Bible for a non-specialist audience (some more
specialized introductions are listed at the end of this chapter). Each
chapter focuses on a specific book, examining its core themes and
ideas, the cultural and historical context of its composition, and its
later reception. These books were not written as a single group of
texts called the Apocrypha. While the Bible is often revered as a

The Apocrypha: A Guide. Matthew Goff, Oxford University Press. © Oxford University Press 2024.
DOI: 10.1093/9780190060770.003.0001

fixed, unchanging text, the story of the Apocrypha illustrates that the contents of the Bible have varied a great deal.

The GEM and Beyond: The Texts Covered in This Book

Many in the English-speaking world have regarded the King James Version (KJV) as the most authoritative rendering of the Christian Bible. The original version of the King James, published in 1611, does not have two sections, like most Bibles today, but three—the Old Testament, the New Testament, and between them, the "Bookes called Apocrypha." The books of this latter section were in the Bible—but in neither the Old nor the New Testament. The "Bookes called Apocrypha" of the King James Bible include the following texts, in this order:

1 Esdras
2 Esdras
Tobit
Judith
The Rest of Esther (the "Additions" to Esther)
The Wisdom of Solomon
Ben Sira (Ecclesiasticus)
Baruch, along with the Letter of Jeremiah
the "Additions" to Daniel (The Prayer of Azariah and the Song of
    the Three Jews; Susanna; Bel and the Dragon)
The Prayer of Manasseh
1 Maccabees
2 Maccabees

This is not a small amount of material. Together these books in size rival the New Testament. Other early Protestant Bibles also had an Apocrypha section. Martin Luther's famous German translation of the Bible, the Wittenberg Bible of 1534, has one. The Wittenberg Apocrypha is similar to but not the same as the KJV Apocrypha. 1 and 2 Esdras are in the Apocrypha of the King James, for example, but not the Wittenberg Bible. Luther's Apocrypha also has a different order, beginning, for example, with Judith rather than 1 Esdras.

The inclusion of an Apocrypha section in the King James Bible was in accordance with the official position of the Church of England at that time. The Church's Thirty-Nine Articles (1571) stipulated its tenets and doctrines. The sixth article lists the books that constitute scripture. After the books of the Old Testament, it enumerates "other books." Though it does not refer to them as the Apocrypha, these "other books" match exactly the texts of the King James Apocrypha, in the same order found there.

The organization of this book follows that of the Apocrypha in the King James Bible. This decision highlights that there is a long-standing tradition that the Bible includes many of the texts covered in this book—not just for Catholics or Eastern Orthodox but Protestants as well.

The King James Bible was designed to support the reign of King James I, who ruled England from 1603 to 1625. The KJV's ornate presentation of biblical material, which is spectacularly evident from its title page, sought to evoke the grandeur of the English monarchy. The original edition of the King James Bible includes a letter from the translators to the reader in which they praise scripture, among many other metaphors, as "a treasury of most costly jewels, against beggarly rudiments." The KJV's table of contents page graphically likens scripture to a jewel (see Figure 1.1). The first letter of the title of the first book of the Old Testament is enlarged and richly decorated—a "G," from Genesis. The first letter of the title of the first book of the second section, the Apocrypha, is depicted in the same manner—an "E," from 1 Esdras. So too the first letter of the title of the first book of the New Testament—an "M," from the gospel of Matthew. Together the books of the Bible

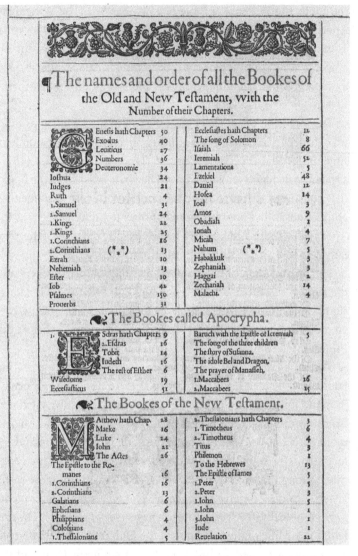

Figure 1.1 The table of contents page of the first edition of the King James Bible (1611).

Image courtesy of the Florida State University Libraries, Special Collections and Archives.

comprise a "GEM." The King James Bible extols scripture in a way that would be impossible without the Apocrypha.

A more hesitant posture toward the Apocrypha, however, is also evident in the King James Bible. Its richly decorated title page states that what follows is the Holy Bible "conteyning the Old Testament, and the New," without mentioning the Apocrypha. King James himself took a dismissive view of this section. He said some of the apocryphal books are "like the dietement of the Spirit of God, as an Egg is to an Oyster." That is, they are inherently different from scripture, as common food (egg) is from gourmet fare (oyster). An intense dislike toward books in the Apocrypha, as we shall see, was not limited to King James.

This book covers more texts than those in the Apocrypha of the King James or Wittenberg Bibles. After the King James sequence of 1 Esdras to 2 Maccabees, the present volume has four chapters which cover, respectively:

Psalm 151
3 Maccabees
4 Maccabees
1 *Enoch* and *Jubilees*

These books are not in the Catholic Old Testament. Consequently, early Protestant Reformers did not move them into the Apocrypha. The term "apocrypha" can encompass more texts than those in the KJV. There are many, many more ancient writings, Jewish and Christian, than those in the Bible. Many of them could be and have been classified as apocryphal. Books like Psalm 151 or 3 Maccabees are the tip of the iceberg.

I decided to cover in this book all the texts in the Apocrypha section of the *New Oxford Annotated Bible* (NOAB), a leading and widely available study edition. I regularly assign this Bible in my introductory courses to the Old Testament/Hebrew Bible. This book can also be read along with the *SBL Study Bible*, which includes the same compositions as the NOAB. The present volume can serve as a companion piece while people read the texts for themselves. The NOAB Apocrypha covers more texts than the classic Protestant Apocrypha because it includes books which were and/ or are considered part of the Old Testament (more on this below). Of the texts discussed in this book, only *1 Enoch* and *Jubilees* are not in the NOAB. I added them because in my experience students enjoy learning about these poorly known texts.

The Many Canons of Christian Scripture

"Scripture" and "canon" are overlapping but not equivalent terms. "Scripture" denotes texts that form the basis of a religious community's beliefs and practices. The word "canon" signifies a fixed, established list of books that a group considers scripture. The terms "apocrypha" and "canon" often function as different sides of the same coin. The word "apocryphal" has often been used derisively by people who sought to denigrate books that in their view should not be regarded as scripture. To appreciate how the term has been deployed, one needs to understand what is canonical.

While there are different forms of Judaism (i.e., Reform, Conservative), all Jewish communities have the same Bible—the Tanakh. This term is an abbreviation that expresses the threefold structure of the Jewish Bible: Torah, Prophets (*Nevi'im*), and the Writings (*Khetuvim*). All the books of the Tanakh, which include well-known texts such as Genesis, Isaiah, and the Psalms, are in the Old Testament, but often in a different order.

While all Christian communities today have an Old Testament, they do not all have the same Old Testament. Their scriptures are different primarily with regard to the books early Protestants moved from the Old Testament into the Apocrypha. These differences can be represented by Table 1.1.

INTRODUCTION   7

Table 1.1 The Books in This Volume and Their Canonical Status

	In the Jewish Bible (*Tanakh*)	In the Protestant Apocrypha (King James)	In the Catholic Old Testament (the Deutero-canonical books)	In the Orthodox Old Testament (the *Anagignoskomena* books)		
				Greek	Russian	Ethiopian
1 Esdras		X	X*	X	X	X
2 Esdras		X	X*		X	X
Tobit		X	X	X	X	X
Judith		X	X	X	X	X
Esther with the "Additions"		X	X	X	X	X
The Wisdom of Solomon		X	X	X	X	X
Ben Sira		X	X	X	X	X
Baruch and the Letter of Jeremiah		X	X	X	X	X
Daniel with the "Additions"		X	X	X	X	X
The Prayer of Manasseh		X	X*	X	X	X
1 Maccabees		X	X	X	X	***
2 Maccabees		X	X	X	X	
Psalm 151				X	X	X

(*continued*)

Table 1.1 Continued

In the Jewish Bible (*Tanakh*)	In the Protestant Apocrypha (King James)	In the Catholic Old Testament (the Deutero-canonical books)	In the Orthodox Old Testament (the *Anagignoskomena* books)		
			Greek	Russian	Ethiopian
3 Maccabees			X	X	
4 Maccabees			X**		
1 Enoch					X
Jubilees					X

* Books placed in an appendix in the Sixto-Clementine Vulgate Bible (1592), which is no longer used.

** There is a tradition in the Greek Orthodox church of including 4 Maccabees in the Bible as an appendix.

*** The Ethiopian scriptural tradition includes a different group of indigenous Maccabean texts, 1–3 Maqebeyan.

While none of the books in this chart are in the Jewish Bible, they are all, as the rest of this book will discuss, Jewish texts written in antiquity. The Catholic and Orthodox forms of the Old Testament have more books than the Tanakh. The Protestant Old Testament, by contrast, has the same books as the Jewish Bible if one excludes the Apocrypha, as is now the norm. The books traditionally considered Apocrypha in the Protestant tradition are referred to in Catholicism as Deuterocanonical and correspond to what the Orthodox tradition calls the *Anagignoskomena*, a Greek term that means "those (books) which are read." As discussed below, all three terms derive from their usage over a thousand years ago by early Christian authors.

Differences in scripture between Protestants and Catholics do not fully explain the canonical diversity evident in the chart. Some books in the Orthodox Old Testament are not in the Catholic Old Testament, such as 3 Maccabees or Psalm 151. "Orthodox" is an umbrella term that encompasses several distinct national churches (i.e., Coptic, Greek, Russian, Ukrainian). They do not all have the same Old Testament. 2 Esdras is, for example, in the Russian Orthodox Bible, not that of the Greek Orthodox. The Ethiopian Orthodox church, one of the oldest Christian communities in the world, is the only church whose Old Testament includes *1 Enoch* and *Jubilees*. The diversity among Christian churches regarding their scriptures reflects different crystallizations of the pluriform and variegated nature of the ancient Jewish scriptures which they inherited.

The Forgotten Greek Bible and the Pluriform World of Ancient Jewish Scripture

It is a common opinion that an accurate and authentic translation of the Old Testament should be made from the Hebrew. Its books were indeed written in Hebrew. But prioritizing Hebrew as the basis for the Old Testament, while a reasonable position, can obscure a key point—the linguistic world of early Christianity was predominantly Greek. Christians in antiquity generally did not encounter scripture in Hebrew, but in Greek.

Ancient Jewish scribes in Egypt translated their scriptures into Greek. This primarily took place during the Hellenistic age (323–31 BCE), a time when for many Jews, like other peoples, Greek was the main language. The Greek scriptures they produced are collectively known as the "Septuagint." Often abbreviated as "LXX," this name derives from the Latin word for "seventy" (*septuaginta*) and comes from early Christian authors discussing the Greek Old Testament in Latin. According to legend, the Septuagint was made by seventy-two translators who independently each produced the same text. This assertion is not historically accurate but nevertheless conveys that ancient Greek-speaking Jews highly regarded their scriptures.

The Septuagint includes Greek versions of Hebrew texts that are in the Jewish Bible, such as Genesis or the Psalms. It also has books translated in antiquity from Hebrew (or Aramaic) into Greek but the Semitic original is lost. This is the case, for example, with 1 Maccabees and parts of Baruch. As discussed in their respective chapters, modern textual discoveries have brought to light the lost Semitic versions of some of these texts (e.g., Ben Sira, Psalm 151, Tobit). The Septuagint also has texts that were not composed in Hebrew or Aramaic but rather in Greek (e.g., 2 Maccabees, the Wisdom of Solomon).

The Septuagint attests versions of biblical texts that are different from the Hebrew. For example, while the standard version of Genesis 2:2, translated from the Hebrew, states that God rested on the seventh day, in the LXX the verse says that he rested on the sixth. The Septuagint versions of Daniel, Esther, and 1 Esdras contain extensive expansions and revisions not in the Hebrew Bible (see Chapters 2, 6, and 10). If you are interested in reading the Septuagint, I recommend the *New English Translation of the Septuagint* (see the end of this chapter).

The ancient Jewish Greek scriptures were not preserved in rabbinic Judaism. They became the Christian Old Testament. The books of the New Testament were written in Greek and, when they quote older scriptures, they are quoting Septuagint texts. Our oldest complete manuscript of the Hebrew Bible is the Leningrad Codex, so named because it is housed in St. Petersburg, Russia (formerly Leningrad). When the Old Testament is translated from the Hebrew, this is normally the manuscript that is used. The Leningrad Codex is a medieval text made in Cairo, Egypt, in 1008 CE. Sometimes called the Masoretic text (MT), its text was standardized in late antiquity by rabbis who were textual scholars known as the Masoretes.

Our manuscripts of the Septuagint, by contrast, are much older. Our oldest manuscripts of the Greek Old Testament are three codices from the fourth and fifth centuries CE—Codex Vaticanus, Codex Sinaiticus, and Codex Alexandrinus. A codex is a bound volume that is a precursor to the modern printed book. There is significant diversity among these ancient Christian codices in terms of the books they contain. They all have familiar texts such as Genesis or Isaiah. They also include several books in the Old Testament that are unfamiliar to many today (see Table 1.2).

Most of the variety among these Septuagint codices occurs with respect to books that have no analogue in the Hebrew Bible. These works comprise the bulk of the texts which later became the Protestant Apocrypha.

The period when ancient Jewish scribes translated their scriptures into Greek (roughly the third century BCE to the first century CE) overlaps with when the texts examined in this book were written (third century BCE to the late first/early second century CE). Most of them became books of the Septuagint. They provide an important vantage point from which to assess how Jews in the Hellenistic age understood scripture. While the books of the Pentateuch (the first five texts of the Old Testament) were likely translated into Greek in the third century BCE, others were translated later, in varying and different styles, suggesting that their translation was a gradual, sporadic process rather than a single, organized effort. It's not clear that Greek-speaking Jews before the common era even called their scriptures "the Septuagint" or thought of it as a single book. The Christian codices of the Septuagint, as we have seen, show that even by the fourth century CE there was no uniform agreement as to what books comprise the Septuagint.

The Jewish writings composed in the Hellenistic period that are preserved in the Septuagint were produced by people who considered scripture important. These texts present themselves as in continuity with older scriptural traditions. Some of them cite verses of older books. Tobit 2, for example, cites the book of Amos.

Table 1.2 The Books in This Volume and Ancient Septuagint Manuscripts

	Vaticanus	Sinaiticus (not complete)	Alexandrinus
1 Esdras	X		X
2 Esdras			
Tobit	X	X	X
Judith	X	X	X
Esther with the "Additions"	X	X	X
The Wisdom of Solomon	X	X	X
Ben Sira	X	X	X
Baruch	X		X
The Letter of Jeremiah	X		X
Daniel with the "Additions"	X		X
The Prayer of Manasseh			X*
1 Maccabees		X	X
2 Maccabees			X
Psalm 151	X	X	X
3 Maccabees			X
4 Maccabees		X	X
1 Enoch			
Jubilees			

* The Prayer of Manasseh is in Alexandrinus as part of a larger text called the Odes, a collection of hymns.

Many of these works engage themes in older scriptural texts. The Wisdom of Solomon, for example, offers a lengthy exposition of the Exodus story. These texts also attest early designations for scripture. The prologue to the book of Ben Sira mentions the "law and the prophets and the other books of our ancestors," which is similar to the threefold structure of the Bible that becomes standard in later Judaism (Torah, Prophets, and Writings). 4 Maccabees refers instead to the "law and the prophets," a designation also found in 2 Maccabees and the New Testament, without reference to a third category. 2 Maccabees also attests a different description, in its claim in chapter 2 that Nehemiah founded a library and collected books about kings, prophets, and other writings attributed to David, without mentioning the Torah.

While the Hellenistic-era Jewish descriptions of scripture vary, none of them include the word "Bible" (which is itself a Greek word meaning "books"). In the Judaism of the Hellenistic age, scripture was not envisioned as a closed-off canon of texts. On the contrary, in this era reflection about the past of ancient Israel, as recounted in scriptural texts, could generate new scripture. For example, 2 Kings 17 describes the destruction of the northern kingdom of Israel and the exile of its people to Assyria, in the eighth century BCE. The book of Tobit, likely written in the third century BCE, tells the story of one of the northern Israelite families exiled to Assyria. The books examined in this volume conceptualize scripture as a loose corpus of texts whose contents could change and expand.

An analogous conception of scripture is evident in the Dead Sea Scrolls. They comprise about 930 Hebrew and Aramaic texts discovered in the mid-twentieth century near the Dead Sea, in territory seized in war by the state of Israel from Jordan in 1967. Found in caves near a site called Qumran, most of the scrolls were written from the second century BCE to the first century CE, roughly the same period as the texts discussed in this volume. They are the fragmentary remains of writings produced by an ancient Jewish sect sometimes called the Essenes, but the scrolls refer to its members as

"the sons of light" and the "*yaḥad*" (the Hebrew word for "unity").
They venerated scripture. The sons of light fervently believed that
interpreting and studying these writings were foundational for correctly following God.

The Dead Sea Scrolls include many fragments of scriptural texts.
They comprise our oldest material evidence for these writings.
Some are basically in line with the later Masoretic text, which became the standard form of the Hebrew Bible. They also include a
rich abundance of variant versions and expansive rewritings. To
take one example of many, fragments of the book of *Jubilees* were
found at Qumran. This composition is a retelling of Genesis and
part of Exodus. It makes the incredible assertion that it is a transcript of the revelation Moses received on Mount Sinai. *Jubilees*,
an alternative version of Genesis and Exodus, claims to be a kind
of scripture—that it has the status of revealed literature. Several
other Qumran texts are previously unknown works that purport
to be written by authoritative figures from Israel's past (a technique scholars call pseudepigraphy), such as Enoch, Levi, and
Amram (Moses's father). This accords with a core point evident
in the Apocrypha/Deuterocanonical literature—that engagement with older scriptural stories about Israel's past could produce new texts set in that past. The Dead Sea Scrolls, along with
the writings examined in this volume, offer an impression of how
Jews conceptualized scripture in the Hellenistic age—that it was
a pluriform, multivalent body of texts. They could be revised and
rewritten, and interpretation of them could lead to the creation of
new writings. There was scripture. But there was no canon.

Canonical, Those Which Are Read, and
Apocryphal: Early Christian Taxonomies
of Scripture

Both Christianity and rabbinic Judaism, which developed after
the turn of the common era, formed canons of scripture. Judaism

emphasizes the centrality of Hebrew scriptures, the Tanakh. The Mishnah, an important compilation of teachings by rabbis compiled in the third century CE, discourages the reading of "the outside books" (*ha-sefarim ha-ḥitsonim*). While no rabbinic text offers a comprehensive list of these writings, the expression denotes books "outside" the canon. One tractate (*Sanhedrin*) of the Babylonian Talmud, another foundational rabbinic text, explains that "the outside books" include Ben Sira and the writings of heretics (*minim*; a term that can refer to Christians). Opposing the reading of such texts was a way to prioritize the canon of the Hebrew Bible. The Septuagint has versions of books that are also in the Hebrew Bible, such as Genesis, and books which are not, such as Ben Sira. While our main textual evidence for the Septuagint are early Christian manuscripts, its Greek texts preserve the more expansive view of scripture that was operative in the Hellenistic age described above in a way that the Hebrew Bible does not. This difference, the "extra" books in the Greek Bible that are not in the Hebrew Bible, became a touchstone for early Christian leaders who sought to define and control what constituted their scriptures.

Early Christians presumed the authoritative status of books in the Septuagint. Numerous early Christian authors, as discussed in the following chapters, wrote in Greek and cited books in the Septuagint which are not in the Hebrew Bible as scripture, including Tobit, Ben Sira, and the Wisdom of Solomon. Tertullian (ca. 155–220 CE), one of the first Christian authors to write in Latin, even refers to Enochic writings as "scripture."

One can also discern among early Christians, as among the early rabbis, a shift away from the earlier, more expansive conception of scriptures. Some Christian leaders discouraged the reading of particular books. They often described them as "apocryphal." With the term they sought to claim that some books are mistakenly considered scriptural. Such texts, they contended, can lead to deviant forms of Christianity. Irenaeus, a second-century bishop of Lyon (in what is now France) who fervently opposed forms of Christianity he considered heretical, attacked, for example, in his

Against Heresies the "apocryphal and spurious scriptures" of one group, the Marcosians, claiming that its members wrote them to "bewilder the minds of foolish men." A bitterly negative usage of the term "apocrypha" is also clear in the sixth-century *Gelasian Decree*, attributed to Pope Gelasius I (r. 492–496). It lists accepted books of the Old Testament, including several of the texts in the Septuagint not found in the Hebrew Bible, such as Tobit and Judith. It then provides a lengthy list of many other works, some of which are extant, such as the *Testament of Job*, condemning them as "apocryphal." The authors of apocryphal books, the *Gelasian Decree* asserts, should "be damned in the inextricable shackles of anathema forever."

In the fourth century Christianity became an official religion of the Roman Empire, after the conversion of the emperor Constantine in 312 CE. An extensive network of bishops and churches developed. Christian leaders used their social power to establish a kind of orthodoxy—a formalized set of tenets and practices grounded in a canon of scripture that helps define Christianity. The condemnation of some writings as "apocryphal" was an important part of this "orthodoxizing" process.

One possible reason the emergent orthodox Christians used the term "apocrypha" in a negative sense is that Christians they considered heretical were employing the word in a positive way. The Nag Hammadi texts are a corpus of writings written by Egyptian monks in the fourth century that were discovered in the 1940s. They provide crucial testimony into lost forms of Christianity which the creators of orthodox Christianity despised. These writings are in the Coptic language, the traditional language of Egyptian Christianity (which remains the religion of a minority community in Egypt today), and were translated from Greek. One Nag Hammadi text known as the *Apocryphon of James* claims that it is a "secret book" (*apocryphon*), which God revealed to James and Peter. The term "apocryphon" here denotes that this composition purports to contain heavenly, esoteric knowledge.

The *Apocryphon of James* also illustrates the modern scholarly tendency to use the same word ("apocryphon") as a title for ancient books which resemble books in our Bible but are different from them. Nag Hammadi texts like the *Apocryphon of James*, while authoritative and important for some ancient Christians, became forgotten. Early Christian leaders successfully attacked the beliefs of Christians they derided as heretics and undermined the legitimacy of the authoritative texts upon which they based their views.

One of the most important proponents of orthodoxy in the fourth century was Athanasius, a bishop in Alexandria, Egypt. One letter by him (*Festal Letter 39*) is the earliest surviving Christian document that lists the texts which became the standard books of the New Testament. The letter also stipulates that the Old Testament consists of twenty-two books, so that their number corresponds to the twenty-two letters of the Hebrew alphabet. Athanasius enumerates these books, which are texts also in the Hebrew Bible such as Genesis and Exodus, and he describes them as "canonized." This reflects an effort to police the boundaries of the Christian canon by limiting it to books that accord with Jewish scripture, a perspective that conveniently excludes "secret" books such as the *Apocryphon of James*. This mindset promoted the view that Christian scripture should reflect the fact that Christians are the proper custodians and interpreters of originally Jewish scriptures.

Athanasius endorses other books aside from the ones in his category of "canonized" texts. He places others, which he also lists, in a second category—"those (books) which are read." It is not clear that Athanasius considers them part of the Old Testament, but he endorses these books as good for people who "want to be instructed in the word of piety." His books "which are read" are texts in the Septuagint which have no analogue in the Hebrew Bible—the Wisdom of Solomon, Ben Sira, Esther, Judith, Tobit, and also two Christian texts, the *Didache* and the *Shepherd of Hermas*. The Greek for "those (books) which are read" is *anagignoskomena*. This became the designation in the Eastern Orthodox tradition for the Apocrypha/Deuterocanonical literature. While it was not necessarily Athanasius's intent, his distinction between the "canonized" books and those "which are read" helped delineate a hierarchical conception of Old Testament scripture—that the former books have a higher status than the latter. By this measure, books in the Old Testament which correspond to texts in the Jewish Bible have more value than those which do not—the "extra" writings of the Septuagint. The books "which are read" came to comprise a secondary category of scripture—of lesser value than Athanasius's "canonized" books but scripture nevertheless.

Athanasius has a third category, reserved for the worst kind of books—"apocryphal." Like Irenaeus, he despises apocryphal writings as "an invention of heretics" composed to deceive people. He is furious, for example, that some people revere Enochic writings: "Who has made the simple folk believe that books belong to Enoch even though no scriptures existed before Moses?" Athanasius was a bishop in Egypt and actively opposed various kinds of Christians there. He was an enemy of the kind of Christianity represented by the Egyptian Nag Hammadi texts. Understanding this helps explain a shift during this time in the meaning of the term "apocrypha." It is increasingly used less by Christians in the positive sense of a book containing "hidden" or secret knowledge (like the *Apocryphon of James*) and more in a negative sense—books which should be "hidden away" and emphatically not considered Christian scripture.

Athanasius programmatically lays out a hierarchical taxonomy of texts: canonized, books "which are read," and apocryphal. The canonized are the most important and apocryphal the most reviled. The books "which are read" occupy an ambiguous middle ground in early Christianity, valued but with a secondary scriptural status.

Other influential early Christians likewise sought to define the Old Testament by correlating it to the Hebrew Bible of Judaism.

Cyril, a bishop in Jerusalem in the fourth century, for example, stipulates in his *Catechesis* that the proper Old Testament has twenty-two books, and that they "have nothing to do with the apocryphal writings." He also states that other books have a "secondary" (Gk. *deuteros*) status. This designation likely denotes the texts of the Old Testament that are in the Septuagint without analogue in the Hebrew Bible, in accordance with the texts Athanasius described as "those (books) which are read."

The earliest evidence for portraying Jewish scripture as a set of numbered books is from the late first century CE. The Jewish historian Josephus in his *Against Apion* states that the Jews revere twenty-two books. In the same period, 4 Ezra recounts Jewish scripture as having twenty-four books, along with seventy other esoteric texts reserved for the wise (see Chapter 3). Twenty-four becomes the standard enumeration of the books of scripture in rabbinic Judaism. The discrepancy between the twenty-two and twenty-four counts is often attributed to ambiguity as to whether Ruth and Lamentations should be considered separate texts or extensions of, respectively, Judges and Jeremiah. In both Josephus and 4 Ezra, the numbers 22/24 likely correspond, as Athanasius would later observe, to the twenty-two letters of the Hebrew alphabet. This correspondence suggests that for Josephus and 4 Ezra the enumeration of books may have not been understood literally but typologically. To say at that time that the scriptures comprise twenty-two books may not have denoted a simple listing of twenty-two books but rather that all things can be said in scripture, in the twenty-two letters of the Hebrew alphabet. This would accord with the conception of ancient Jewish scripture already delineated— that in the Hellenistic period it is a broad and expansive textual category, not a fixed number of books.

The most extreme early Christian articulation of the view that the Old Testament should correspond to the Jewish Bible is from Jerome (ca. 347–420 CE). In the Catholic Church he is the patron saint of translators, with good reason. He was hailed in his own day as a great biblical scholar. He was an expert in Latin and Greek, and he learned Hebrew, a rarity among Christians at the time. In Bethlehem, Jerome translated the Christian scriptures into Latin over the course of many years (ca. 390–405). His translations became the basis of the Vulgate, the Latin Bible which was for centuries the Bible of western Christendom.

Jerome was guided by the principle of *hebraica veritas* ("Hebrew truth"). This is a more stringent formulation of the opinion that the books of the Old Testament should match those in the Jewish Bible. Jerome insisted that the Old Testament should be translated *from* Hebrew. This perspective undercuts the venerable Christian tradition of revering scriptures in Greek. Jerome's *hebraica veritas* questions the status of the books in the Septuagint not found in the Hebrew Bible.

Jerome in his famous Helmeted Prologue (*Prologus Galeatus*), his preface to Samuel and Kings, observes that the Jewish Bible can be considered to have twenty-two or twenty-four books, which he lists, in their threefold order in the Tanakh (Torah, Prophets, and Writings). He then writes:

> This prologue of the scriptures can function as a helmeted preface for all the books, which we are converting from Hebrew to Latin, so that we are able to know that whatever is outside of these should be removed into the apocrypha. Therefore Wisdom, which commonly is inscribed "of Solomon" (= Wisdom of Solomon), and the book of Jesus son of Sirach (= Ben Sira), and Judith, and Tobit, and the Shepherd (= the *Shepherd of Hermas*) are not in the canon.

For Jerome, Old Testament books translated from Hebrew to Latin are "helmeted" in the sense that they are protected and endorsed. They are in the "canon," and not unlike Athanasius's twenty-two "canonized" books, he relates them to the letters of the Hebrew alphabet. He distinguishes these writings from Old

Testament books not in the Jewish Bible which should be "removed into the apocrypha." What does "apocrypha" mean in this context? Athanasius describes roughly the same books not as apocryphal but as "those which are read."

It is entirely possible that for Jerome, like Athanasius, "apocrypha" denotes non-scriptural books, but that he had a more expansive sense of "apocrypha" than Athanasius. In this reading, Jerome is saying that only books in the Jewish Bible should be in the Old Testament. This reading would accord with his conviction that Old Testament texts should be translated from the Hebrew. So understood, Jerome wanted in effect to extend Athanasius's conception of "apocryphal" books to encompass the books of the Septuagint without analogue in the Hebrew Bible (books in his "which are read" category). By this measure, those books should not be considered scripture at all.

Consistent with this interpretation, elsewhere Jerome displays a dismissive view toward books he considers apocryphal. In one of his letters (*Epistle 107*), he advises a young woman (named Laeta) to read biblical books such as the Psalms and Proverbs. But she should "avoid all apocryphal writings," he writes, because errors were introduced into them. He does not specify what these writings are, but they likely include the Septuagint, and he is implying that Greek translations of scripture are deviations from Hebrew verity. He acknowledges that apocryphal texts may contain some positive qualities but "it requires infinite discretion to look for gold in the midst of dirt." Such a negative view of apocryphal books leaves little room for anything considered apocryphal to remain in the Old Testament.

Jerome, however, is not consistent. In his preface to the books of Solomon, he describes the texts of the Old Testament that are in the Septuagint but not the Hebrew Bible much more positively: "just as the church reads the books of Judith and Tobit and the Maccabees, but does not receive them among the canonical scriptures, so also let her read these two volumes (the Wisdom of Solomon and Ben

Sira) for the edification of the people, not for the authoritative confirmation of ecclesiastical doctrines." Here Jerome does not dismiss these books as "apocryphal." He distinguishes them from "canonical scripture" and does not want church doctrine based on them. He affirms, however, that they should be read for moral edification. This fits nicely with Athanasius's category of books "which are read" (*anagignoskomena*). It also accords with the larger corpus of scriptures evident in the Septuagint, with the provision that its books without analogue in the Tanakh have a secondary scriptural status. In keeping with this view, he did translate some of the Old Testament books which are in the Septuagint but not the Hebrew Bible into Latin, such as Judith, but he did so reluctantly and under pressure from others.

Efforts by early Christian leaders to restrict the canonical bounds of the Old Testament were not successful. Many, as we have seen, advocated for a shorter Old Testament whose books match those in the Jewish Bible. Others, such as Augustine (354–430 CE), the well-known theologian from North Africa, endorsed the larger Greek canon. The surviving Greek codices of the Old Testament from the period, Vaticanus, Sinaiticus, and Alexandrinus, all attest the larger canon, despite their variety. They include books that are not in the Hebrew Bible.

Jerome's translations formed the basis of the Vulgate Bible which dominated the Middle Ages. But his *hebraica veritas* did not. Over time, almost all the books of the Septuagint were translated into Latin and became part of the Vulgate, including those not in the Hebrew Bible. The larger canon evident in the Septuagint, not the smaller canon of the Hebrew Bible, forms the basis of the Old Testament in the Catholic and Orthodox traditions.

The failure of Christianity to adopt the shorter canon akin to the Hebrew Bible as its Old Testament despite the persistent advocacy of influential Christians for this position suggests an implicit conception of canon that is defined primarily by its center, not its periphery. The Old Testament was understood primarily in terms of its core texts, which correspond to major books in the Jewish Bible (e.g., Genesis or Isaiah), not by efforts to rigidly police its canonical boundaries. The books examined in this volume continued to have an odd, ambiguous existence on the edges of the canon, simultaneously devalued and endorsed.

Despite the ambiguity regarding the Old Testament books that are in the Septuagint but not the Hebrew Bible, there is agreement among early orthodox Christians regarding the term "apocrypha"—that it denotes condemned books which should be radically distinguished from scripture. By this measure, "biblical apocrypha" is an oxymoron, a nonsensical phrase. It is perhaps not surprising that the early Protestant decision to create a new section of the Bible called the Apocrypha proved to be controversial.

The Rise and Fall of Biblical Apocrypha

The Protestant Reformation developed in western Europe during the sixteenth century as a critique of the tenets and practices of Catholicism. Framing themselves as restorers of an original Christian piety that had over time become corrupted, the Reformers made a sharp distinction between scripture and tradition, considering the former good and the latter bad. *Sola scriptura* (scripture alone) became their rallying cry.

The Reformers created a new section of the Bible, the Apocrypha, to which they moved books of the Old Testament that are in the Septuagint but not the Hebrew Bible. The earliest evidence for this arrangement is a four-volume edition of the Septuagint produced by Johannes Lonicerus, an ally of Luther, in Strasbourg (1524–1526). Their radical decision to create a third section of the Bible was based on their study of early Christianity, in particular the writings of Jerome. The *hebraica veritas* Jerome championed, while a fringe opinion in his day, was taken up by the Protestant Reformers. There was a polemical edge to their efforts to valorize

Hebrew as a language of Christian scholarship. This move sought to displace Latin as the dominant medium of the Bible, as part of their attack against the Catholic Church.

The early Protestant Reformers can be understood as implementing what Jerome recommended in his Helmeted Preface a thousand years earlier—that Old Testament books not extant in Hebrew should be "removed into the apocrypha." But Jerome never called for a new section of the Bible, much less one called the "apocrypha." As discussed above, he likely meant that any books deemed apocryphal should not be considered Christian scripture.

Luther and his colleagues are reasonably understood as adopting a "canonical" reading of their beloved Jerome. They read him in a way that smoothed out contradictions to construe his disparate writings as offering a unified message. The title page of Luther's Apocrypha section illustrates the importance of Jerome for them: "Apocrypha. These books are not held equal to Holy Scripture but are useful and good to read." This echoes the earlier views of Jerome on these writings. Creating a new section of the Bible called "Apocrypha" for books considered to have secondary scriptural status that people should nevertheless read blends together two different Hieronymian (Jerome-ian) statements: his call in the Helmeted Preface for the Old Testament books in the Septuagint without analogue in the Hebrew Bible to be "removed into the apocrypha" and his statement in his preface to the Solomonic books that they have a lower status but are good to read. Positing this would also explain why they called this new section of the Bible the "Apocrypha," even though the term traditionally denoted books that should not be in the Bible at all.

Like Jerome, Luther wrote prefaces to many biblical books. His prefaces give us an impression of his views on the books of the Apocrypha. Some of them he clearly liked. 1 Maccabees, with its account of fighting oppressive powers with God on your side, fired him up to continue his struggle against the Catholic Church (see Chapter 12). He says the book of Judith is "holy." Other books he despised. He was especially critical of 2 Maccabees, because of its importance in Catholic teachings (consult Chapter 13). Like the early Christian creators of orthodoxy, the early Protestants attacked not only their opponents but also their scriptural books. But even in the case of 2 Maccabees, while Luther says it should be thrown out of the canon, he leaves it to the "pious reader" to decide the question of its status. Despite the centrality of the Bible in his thought, Luther at times seems surprisingly uninterested in policing the canonical boundaries of the Old Testament. Now included in a new Apocrypha section, its books remained both devalued but affirmed as worth reading, just as they had been long before the Protestant Reformation.

The Protestant restructuring of the Bible did not go unchallenged. The Council of Trent (1545–1563), an official Catholic response to the Reformation, affirmed the divine status of all books in the Catholic Old Testament. An Eastern Orthodox synod which convened in Jerusalem in 1672, led by the Patriarch Dositheos II, likewise affirmed the larger Septuagint-based Old Testament canon, by endorsing the integrity of the Catholic Bible. (This position does not reflect the variety regarding scripture among different Orthodox churches that has already been observed.)

The Catholic Church did however acknowledge that some Old Testament books have a kind of "secondary" status. Catholics began to refer to the texts in the Protestant Apocrypha as the "Deuterocanonical" books of their Old Testament. This appellation is attributed to the Catholic theologian Sixtus of Siena (1520–1569). He emphasized that "deutero-" conveys not that some Old Testament books have a lesser scriptural value, but that they are among the last biblical texts to have been written. But his terminology accords with the fact that the books of the Old Testament which the Protestants placed in the Apocrypha long had a secondary status. Sixtus's "deuterocanonical" designation resonates, for example, with the claim by Cyril of Jerusalem, discussed above, that some scriptural books have a "secondary" (*deuteros*) rank.

The creation of an Apocrypha section was also controversial among Protestants, particularly in England. As we have seen, it was the official position of the Church of England for the Bible to have an Apocrypha section. Radical Protestants broke with this mainstream tenet. They viewed the books in the Apocrypha as unwanted Catholic books in their Bibles.

The Apocrypha became a "wedge" issue. How people came down on it became a way to articulate difference between Protestants and Catholics, and between mainline and radical Protestants. The Puritan polemicist John Vicars, in his tract *Unholsome Henbane Between Two Fragrant Roses* (1645), likens "the most vile and vitious Apocryphal-writings" to a noxious weed (henbane) which besmirches two roses, the Old and New Testaments. He demanded that the Apocrypha "be utterly expunged and expelled out of all Bibles whatsoever." The long-standing ambiguity regarding books on the margins of scripture became a casualty of the ideologically charged, partisan atmosphere of early modern England.

Moreover, the formation of the Apocrypha as a single unit made its books easier to remove. In 1615 George Abbot, the Archbishop of Canterbury, threatened that printers who did not include the Apocrypha in the King James Bible would be imprisoned for one year—an indication that some printers were doing just that.

The Puritans' disdain for the Apocrypha is recognized and lampooned in a bawdy ballad from the first half of the seventeenth century, "Off a Puritane" (in modern English, "Of a Puritan"). It begins:

> It was a puritanicall ladd
>   that was called Mathyas
> & he wold goe to Amsterdam
>   to speake with Ananyas.
> he had not gone past halfe a mile,
>   but he mett his holy sister;
> hee layd his bible vnder her breeche,
>   & merylye hee kist her.

"Alas! what wold the wicked say?"
quoth shee, "if they had seene itt!
my Buttocckes thé lye to lowe: I wisht
appocrypha were in itt!"

The Puritans were well-known, like evangelicals today, for their strict moral teachings. This ballad portrays them as hypocrites, as if the ones who complain the most about the immorality of others are the most debauched. The ballad spoofs the centrality of the Bible in the Puritans' moral crusades. Here a Bible plays an important role in a couple's erotic exploits. When a man (Mathyas; Matthew) comes across a female in his community while traveling, they have sex. During their coitus, he puts a Bible underneath her, as if it were a kind of "sex pillow." Thinking of the book this way explains why she complains that her bottom is too low ("my Buttocckes thé lye to lowe"; this also suggests what kind of sex they are having). The woman wishes she had a larger book beneath her, as if the sex would be better if her buttocks were higher. If only her Bible had the Apocrypha! The ballad acknowledges the Puritan disdain for the Apocrypha by suggesting that it had for them extra allure, as forbidden books.

Because of the importance of the Puritans in the early settlement of North America by white Europeans, Bibles without the Apocrypha became normative in the United States. The first Bible printed in New England, published in Cambridge in 1663 in the Algonquin (Massachusett) language for missionary purposes, does not include the Apocrypha. The first English Bible printed in the United States, published in 1782 in Philadelphia, likewise does not have the Apocrypha.

While the hard-line, anti-Apocrypha view eventually won out among Protestants, it was still common for the King James Bible to include the Apocrypha until the nineteenth century. The British and Foreign Bible Society (BFBS) was formed in 1804. Its mission was to make Bibles available to the poor in Europe and people throughout the world. The American Bible Society (ABS) was founded in 1816, along similar lines as the BFBS. These societies promoted the mass production of cheap Bibles. This gave them a material incentive to exclude the Apocrypha, which many Protestants were inclined against anyway. In 1826 the BFBS announced, after much internal squabbling about the issue, that its Bibles would no longer include the Apocrypha. The ABS adopted similar measures in 1828. Advances during that century in printing technology made the large-scale mechanical production of identical Bibles possible. The global ambitions of Protestant Bible societies helped standardize the exclusion of the Apocrypha.

Still, even in the nineteenth century the Apocrypha did not completely disappear. It was common, for example, for households to have a "family Bible," a large tome in which information about births, deaths, and marriages in the family was recorded. As monumental editions of the Bible, size mattered. Their scale symbolized their value as an anchor point throughout the generations of a family. To give them heft, family Bibles would have, along with the text of the Bible, numerous illustrations, and encyclopedic essays on biblical topics. They could also include the Apocrypha. In this context, its books had value primarily as filler material.

As Protestantism became dominant in the modern West, the Apocrypha became less controversial. Its books were condemned less and increasingly forgotten. It has long been normative for Protestant Bibles not to include the Apocrypha. Many today have no idea such books were in the Protestant Bible for a long time, and for millions of other Christians, still are. The inclusion of the Apocrypha into a single section, a measure designed in part to make them available for people to read, ironically made it easier for its books to be removed and subsequently forgotten. These writings are nevertheless a pleasure to read, as are all the texts examined in this volume. I think if more people knew about these texts, they would enjoy reading them. This book is designed to help.

Guide for Further Reading

Coogan, Michael, et al., eds. *The New Oxford Annotated Bible with Apocrypha.* 5th edition. New York: Oxford University Press, 2018.

DeSilva, David A. *Introducing the Apocrypha: Message, Context, and Significance.* Grand Rapids, MI: Baker Academic, 2018.

Hawk, Brandon W. *Apocrypha for Beginners: A Guide to Understanding and Exploring Scriptures Beyond the Bible.* Emeryville and New York: Rockridge Press, 2021.

Klawans, Jonathan, and Lawrence M. Wills. *The Jewish Annotated Apocrypha.* New York: Oxford University Press, 2020.

Law, Timothy Michael. *When God Spoke Greek: The Septuagint and the Making of the Christian Bible.* New York: Oxford University Press, 2013.

McKenzie, Steven L., et al. *The SBL Study Bible.* New York: HarperCollins, 2023.

Pietersma, Albert, and Benjamin G. Wright, eds. *A New English Translation of the Septuagint.* New York: Oxford University Press, 2007.

Wills, Lawrence M. *Introduction to the Apocrypha: Jewish Books in Christian Bibles.* New Haven, CT: Yale University Press, 2021.

2

Exile? What Exile?

The First Book of Esdras (3 Ezra)

Few readers of scripture bother to read the book of Ezra. With its long lists of names and detailed accounts of obscure events, reading it does not generally strike people as a white-knuckle ride. But the composition is a major, if problematic, resource for a crucial period of the history of Israel: roughly 550–450 BCE, which covers the end of the Babylonian exile and the re-establishment of Judah as part of the Persian Empire. Ezra, together with the book of Nehemiah, recounts how Judah reconstituted itself by rebuilding Jerusalem and the temple, and by renewing the people's commitment to the Torah. These books are problematic as historical sources because they contain obvious chronological problems.

Another book offers a similar but quite different account of the early post-exilic period. This composition is entitled 1 Esdras. It is read even less frequently than the books of Ezra and Nehemiah. An early form of the composition was likely written in the second century BCE. Though forgotten by many, 1 Esdras remains a book of the Bible in the Eastern Orthodox tradition. This form of the Old Testament contains *two* versions of how Judah established its society after much of its leadership was exiled in Babylonia (Ezra-Nehemiah and 1 Esdras). This situation is analogous to the books of Samuel and Kings vis-à-vis 1–2 Chronicles, which offer two different accounts of the monarchic history of Israel and Judah; 1–2 Chronicles extensively reworked an early form of Samuel-Kings. It's a point debated among scholars, but it appears that 1 Esdras similarly revised a now lost text that was similar to Ezra-Nehemiah.

The Apocrypha: A Guide. Matthew Goff, Oxford University Press. © Oxford University Press 2024.
DOI: 10.1093/9780190060770.003.0002

1 Esdras presents post-exilic Judah under the leadership of Zerubbabel and Ezra as restoring an ideal level of piety that was achieved under King Josiah before the exile. The book emphasizes their accomplishments in a way that erases the historical significance of the exile and the destruction of the temple.

Nomenclature and Canonical History

1 Esdras and Ezra-Nehemiah have had different titles in different scriptural contexts. Two of the oldest manuscripts of the Christian Bible (the Greek Septuagint), Codex Vaticanus and Codex Alexandrinus (fourth–fifth centuries CE), include two books entitled, respectively, 1 and 2 Esdras (actually, Esdras A and B). "Esdras" is the name "Ezra" in Greek; "Ezra" is its Latin form. The subject of this chapter is 1 Esdras; 2 Esdras (Esdras B) comprises a Greek translation of Ezra and Nehemiah, presented as a single book. "2 Esdras" is also the title of another book sometimes called 4 Ezra, which is examined in the next chapter. That text is explicitly attributed to Ezra, which is not the case in 1 Esdras, although this is implied by its title. The nomenclature of these books can be confusing. Table 2.1, which includes some material discussed not here but in the following chapter, will hopefully provide some clarity.

The Vulgate Bible includes Ezra and Nehemiah, which are in the Hebrew Bible. Jerome (fourth century) did not translate 1 Esdras, which is not. In keeping with his view that books in the Christian Old Testament should be translations of Hebrew texts (*hebraica veritas*), he took a derisive stance toward this composition. He presented Ezra-Nehemiah as a single book and wrote in his preface to it that no one should "take delight in the fantasies found in the apocryphal third and fourth books" (i.e., 1 and 2 Esdras). By the Middle Ages it became increasingly common for Latin Bibles to treat Ezra and Nehemiah as separate books. They were often titled 1 and 2 Ezra (1 Ezra = Ezra; 2 Ezra = Nehemiah). The Vulgate also

Table 2.1 The Varying Nomenclature of Ezran Books

	Jewish Bible (Tanakh)	Septuagint	Vulgate	Ethiopian Orthodox Old Testament	Russian Orthodox Old Testament (Slavonic)
Ezra Nehemiah	Ezra-Nehemiah (regarded as a single book)	2 Esdras (Ezra-Nehemiah as one book)	I Ezra II Ezra	3 Ezra (Ezra-Nehemiah as one book)	Ezra-Nehemiah (as one book)
1 Esdras	Not present	1 Esdras	III Ezra	2 Ezra	2 Ezra
2 Esdras	Not present	Not present	IV Ezra 3–14 (= 4 Ezra) IV Ezra 1–2 (= 5 Ezra) IV Ezra 15–16 (= 6 Ezra)	1 Ezra (only ch. 3–14)	3 Ezra (only ch. 3–14)

over time began to include 1 Esdras. The book is, for example, in the Gutenberg Bible, the first printed Bible (1455) and a version of the Vulgate. It eventually became common for this composition to be included after 1 and 2 Ezra, which thus came to be called 3 Ezra (or sometimes 3 Esdras); 1 Esdras can still be referred to as 3 Ezra.

The Council of Trent (1545–1563), in response to the Protestant Reformation and its reconfiguration of the Bible, promulgated a list of the books that comprise the official canon of Catholic scripture. 1 Esdras was not on the list. Nevertheless, Catholic Bibles produced after Trent have often included this composition. Pope Clement VIII (r. 1592–1605) published in 1592 a revised version of the Vulgate known as the Sixto-Clementine Vulgate. This edition has an appendix placed after the New Testament that consists of 1 and 2 Esdras, and the Prayer of Manasseh. The appendix's preface explains that the texts were added "lest they should perish completely." Catholic Bibles no longer include the Clementine appendix. For many readers of scripture, 1 Esdras did unfortunately "perish completely."

The Catholic Church's ambiguous attitude toward 1 Esdras, both denying its canonical status and printing Bibles that include it, helps explain why the early Protestant attitude toward the composition was also mixed. Not unlike Jerome, Martin Luther despised the book. According to his *Table Talk*, he wanted to throw the book in the Elbe River. In his preface to Baruch, he explains why he did not include it in the Apocrypha section of his Bible: "I very nearly let it (Baruch) go with the third and fourth books of Esdras, books which we did not wish to translate into German because they contain nothing that one could not find better in Aesop [the famous Greek author associated with animal fables] or in still slighter works." The first edition of the King James (1611), by contrast, has 1 Esdras. As the first book of its Apocrypha section, the composition's title is key for how its table of contents page presents the books of the Bible as a kind of jewel ("GEM"; "E" is from 1 Esdras), as discussed in Chapter 1.

1 Esdras has traditionally not been a focal point of Christian exegesis. One exception has been the praise of truth in its story of the three bodyguards (3:1–5:6). Augustine (fourth century) quotes a verse from 1 Esdras in his *City of God* ("above all things truth is victor"; 3:12) and understands this phrase to prophesy Christ. Cyprian, a bishop of Carthage (third century), interprets the praise of truth in 1 Esdras similarly. He connects language in 1 Esdras 4 (e.g., "Truth endures and is strong forever") to Jesus's claim in the gospel of John, "I am the truth."

The Dead Sea Scrolls do not include any fragments of 1 Esdras. Ezra and Nehemiah are also not prominent in this corpus. They include only three small fragments from an Ezra scroll and nothing from Nehemiah. Josephus's history of Jewish tradition (*Jewish Antiquities*), written at the end of the first century CE, uses 1 Esdras more as a source for his account of the post-exilic period than Ezra-Nehemiah. There is no other example of unambiguous Jewish engagement with 1 Esdras for a thousand years. *Yosippon*, a medieval reworking of Josephus's writings into Hebrew, shows familiarity with the work. It includes, for example, a version of its story of the three guards.

1 Esdras: The Basics

1 Esdras begins with a grand display of public piety. King Josiah (r. 640–609 BCE) leads a large Passover ceremony at the temple. He gives out 30,000 lambs and kid goats for the people to sacrifice. The composition is consistent with 2 Kings and 2 Chronicles, which describe Josiah as a zealous advocate for the veneration of God in Jerusalem. According to these biblical books, he eradicated other sites of worship and removed statues of other deities from the temple in Jerusalem.

The pious king inexplicably attacks the Egyptian pharaoh Necho while he passes through Judah to fight in Mesopotamia. Josiah's ill-conceived aggression results in his death. This, 1 Esdras 1 emphasizes, is followed by a string of weak and impious kings in Judah. The priests pollute the temple with sacrilege and the people ignore the prophets. This collapse of piety culminates in the invasion of Judah by King Nebuchadnezzar and the Babylonian army. They destroy Jerusalem and force many Judeans into exile. They steal holy vessels from the temple and raze it to the ground.

Not spending much time on the exile itself, 1 Esdras 2 begins with the Persian king Cyrus announcing that it is over. In 539 BCE he conquered the Babylonian Empire; 1 Esdras purports to quote an edict by Cyrus, as do the book of Ezra and 2 Chronicles, which allows the exiled Judeans to go home and bring the vessels taken by Nebuchadnezzar with them. Judah is reconstituted not as an independent monarchy, but as part of the Persian Empire. The first wave of exiles returns in the days of Cyrus, led by a Judean official named Sheshbazzar.

Some people in Judah oppose the returnees' desire to restore Jerusalem and the temple. They include the Samaritans, a community in northern Israel that does not accept the centrality of the Jerusalem temple. These opponents write a letter to the Persian king, who is now not Cyrus but Artaxerxes (a chronology of Persian kings is given below). Their document portrays Jerusalem as a rebellious city and argues that if the returnees' construction plans are realized, the Persian Empire may lose the region. The king agrees to halt rebuilding efforts in Jerusalem.

The story of the three bodyguards follows. This tale is unique to 1 Esdras. Darius, who is now understood as the king, holds a grand banquet for the nobles of his vast empire, as Persian kings also do in Esther 1 and Daniel 5. Afterward, three of the king's bodyguards propose a contest: each is to answer the question, "What is the strongest?" They hope that Darius will reward the guard with the best response. They write down their answers and put them under the king's pillow. Upon reading their statements, Darius takes them seriously, as if it were important for the well-being of the empire to know what the strongest thing is. He summons many nobles before whom the guards are to offer speeches on this question. The first explains that wine is the strongest, since it can overwhelm anyone, rich and poor alike. For the second guard, a king is the strongest, because many people follow his commands, whatever they are. The third proclaims that the strongest of all is in fact women. Men are powerful, he reasons, but they will do anything for a woman. Apame, a royal concubine, he points out, takes Darius's crown off his head and puts it on her own. She even slaps him and the king lets her. A famous painting by Hendrick Goltzius (1558–1617) depicts Apame's brazen behavior. The third guard additionally affirms, as mentioned above, that truth is the strongest of all.

One can easily imagine Darius becoming furious at the third guard, whose speech emphasizes that the king allows himself to be publicly humiliated. On the contrary, Darius considers this guard the wisest (suggesting that he enjoys being demeaned by women and men alike). The third guard is none other than Zerubbabel. According to 1 Chronicles 3, he is the grandson of Jehoiachin, the last legitimate Davidic king to sit on the throne in Jerusalem. In the prophetic books of Haggai and Zechariah, which are also set during Darius's reign, Zerubbabel is the governor of Judah, and his support for rebuilding the temple is critical; 1 Esdras makes in a different way the same point. The story of the three guards offers a unique etiology for the construction of the second temple. As a reward for his speech, the king grants Zerubbabel one wish. He asks Darius to honor his vow to rebuild the temple and return the temple vessels. No other scriptural text mentions such a vow. In any case, the king agrees and lifts the ban on its construction.

A second wave of returnees arrives in Judah. They begin work on the temple, laying its foundation and resuming sacrifices. They celebrate their achievements with much fanfare, accompanied by trumpet blasts, cymbals, and shouts of joy. The noise attracts the opponents of the temple, who again manage to halt construction. In response, Haggai and Zechariah whip up support to rebuild it. In the prophetic books attributed to them, they also encourage its construction. Darius, as requested by two local officials in Palestine, initiates a search in the imperial archives for Cyrus's edict that supports the rebuilding of the temple. It is found and Darius urges that construction be resumed to fulfill Cyrus's decree. This explanation of Darius's support differs from that of the earlier story of the three guards; there he endorses the temple's construction to honor the request of Zerubbabel.

The last section of 1 Esdras centers on the figure of Ezra (fifth century BCE). With the support of the Persian king Artaxerxes (probably Artaxerxes I), Ezra zealously promotes observance of the Torah in Judah. He leads a third wave of returnees there. Upon arriving, Ezra is horrified to learn that the Judeans have been marrying people from other ethnicities. Ezra begins an intolerant policy of annulling mixed marriages on the grounds that they are not in accordance with the Torah (cf. Deut 7). He forces many couples to separate. 1 Esdras presents the people as supporting Ezra's divorce policy because they want to follow the Torah. A celebration follows which centers on Ezra reading the law by the temple, and 1 Esdras ends with Judah affirming that it is a Torah-observant community.

Different Editions of the Same Story: 1 Esdras vis-à-vis Ezra-Nehemiah

Even a cursory comparison of 1 Esdras with Ezra-Nehemiah demonstrates that they are very similar. At times they have the same text, virtually word for word. Their close relationship can be expressed with Table 2.2.

Table 2.2 1 Esdras Vis-à-vis Ezra, Nehemiah, and 2 Chronicles

1 Esdras	Corresponding Passage	Content
1:1–24	2 Chron 35:1–19	Idealized piety under King Josiah
1:25–58	2 Chron 35:20–36:21	Decline, exile, and destruction
2:1–15	Ezra 1:1–11	King Cyrus's decree and return from exile
2:16–30	Ezra 4:7–24	Correspondence with King Artaxerxes to block temple construction
3:1–5:6	None	The three guards in King Darius's court
5:7–46	Ezra 2:1–70; Neh 7:7–69	List of returnees from exile
5:47–73	Ezra 3:1–4:5	Construction of the temple is resumed and then blocked.
6:1–7:15	Ezra 4:24–6:22	Construction of the temple is completed.
8:1–9:55	Ezra 7:1–10:44; Neh 7:73–8:12	Ezra's leadership

As noted, 1 Esdras and Ezra-Nehemiah are different editions of the same basic story. Scholars have long debated if 1 Esdras reworked Ezra-Nehemiah, or if Ezra-Nehemiah revised 1 Esdras. The Dead Sea Scrolls illustrate that scribes in the late Second Temple period could either reproduce texts in a relatively strict manner or make extensive changes. This pluralistic textual environment counters simplistic assessments of whether 1 Esdras or Ezra-Nehemiah came first. The precise nature of the lost Semitic text which 1 Esdras translated into Greek cannot be fully ascertained. Neither can the precise form of Ezra-Nehemiah in the late Second Temple period. Multiple, varying versions of both compositions were possible. 1 Esdras and Ezra-Nehemiah, which later became standardized, are remnants of that lost ancient Jewish textual diversity.

1 Esdras and Ezra-Nehemiah draw in distinctive ways on a common body of traditions about Judah after the exile. Ezra-Nehemiah is itself a reconfiguration of older textual materials, designed to accord with a format in which lists of returnees are structurally significant. The book of Ezra begins with Cyrus's decree for the Judeans to return. Then follows a long list of returnees in Ezra 2. Virtually the same list occurs in Nehemiah 7, even though it is set about a century later than when the list appears in Ezra. The repetition of the list functions as a framing device that defines Judah's multigenerational response to Cyrus's decree. The material in between delineates a thematic sequence, Temple–Torah–Jerusalem: it highlights the construction of the temple (Ezra 3–6), Ezra's harsh Torah-based reforms (Ezra 7–10), and Nehemiah's rebuilding of Jerusalem (Nehemiah 1–7).

While the text underlying 1 Esdras cannot be fully recovered, it must have been similar to Ezra-Nehemiah. This lost work, it can be inferred, was in Hebrew and Aramaic. So is Ezra-Nehemiah. While most of Ezra is in Hebrew, its correspondence with Persian officials is in Aramaic (4:7–6:18; 7:12–26). This is apt since it was the administrative language of the Persian Empire. In 1 Esdras 2, the letter to the Persian king Artaxerxes twice mentions a person named Beltethmus. Each time, his name follows that of Rehum, an opponent of the temple. In the version of the letter in Ezra (ch. 4), there is no one named Beltethmus. Rather, Rehum has a title, be'el-te'em, Aramaic for "royal deputy" (lit. "master of the decree"). The Greek translator, whose base text must have been very similar to the letter in Ezra 4, misunderstood Rehum's title as a name, inadvertently creating a new individual (Beltethmus). Similarly, 1 Esdras 9 mentions someone named Attharates. But in the corresponding text in Nehemiah 8 no one has that name. In the Hebrew, Nehemiah's title is hattirshatha ("the governor"). In 1 Esdras 9, this word was mistranslated as a person's name. This chapter also, unlike Nehemiah 8, never mentions Nehemiah (more on this issue below). Parts of the text that 1 Esdras translated into Greek were in Hebrew and others in Aramaic.

In some specific instances it can be determined that 1 Esdras revised textual materials that closely resembled passages in Ezra-Nehemiah. Ezra 5:14 states that Cyrus took temple vessels which Nebuchadnezzar stole and handed them over to Sheshbazzar, to return them to Jerusalem. The corresponding verse in 1 Esdras (6:18) has essentially the same text, but Cyrus gives the vessels to *two* individuals, Sheshbazzar and Zerubbabel. The next verse in 1 Esdras, however, as in Ezra, has the verb in the singular, as if one person, not two, returns them. Moreover, both passages shortly thereafter affirm that Sheshbazzar brings the vessels back, without mentioning Zerubbabel. 1 Esdras likely attests here a scribal intervention, the addition of Zerubbabel's name to a verse that accords with one in Ezra. Moreover, as is evident from the story of the three guards, 1 Esdras strives to emphasize Zerubbabel's role in post-exilic Judah. It would fit with the editorial priorities of the composition to add a reference to him. It cannot be established, however, if such revisions occurred when the text was translated into Greek of if they were already in the Semitic text that was translated.

Understanding 1 Esdras as revising a base text similar to Ezra-Nehemiah also allows readers to appreciate how the composition highlights the figure of Ezra. Nehemiah 8:1 states, "they told *the scribe* Ezra to bring the book of the law of Moses." The corresponding text in 1 Esdras (9:39) reads, "they told Ezra *the chief priest and reader* to bring the law of Moses." Unlike the book of Ezra, 1 Esdras presents Ezra as the high priest, the most important sacerdotal official of the temple. The composition also emphasizes Ezra's connection to the temple by specifying that the assembly at which he reads the Torah takes place before the east gate of the temple. The version of the event in Nehemiah 8 never mentions the temple. There he reads the Torah by the Water Gate, which was not a scandal but an entryway into Jerusalem on its eastern side. Describing Ezra as a "reader" highlights his public reading of the Torah. In Haggai and Zechariah, Zerubbabel is associated with Jeshua son of Jehozadak. These books describe Jeshua as the high priest, whereas 1 Esdras only states that he is a priest. The Zerubbabel-Jeshua pairing is attested in 1 Esdras, but the composition accentuates instead Zerubbabel and Ezra, although they never appear together in the work. This editorial decision stresses two major aspects of the Judaism of the post-exilic Persian period, when the Davidic kingdom no longer existed. Emphasizing Zerubbabel highlights the Davidic tradition, which, independent of the monarchy, becomes important for the later development of messianism. Stressing Ezra is a way to emphasize the high priesthood, an office which becomes politically powerful in the post-exilic era.

Some revisions in 1 Esdras help us date the composition. In the book of Ezra, the province of the Persian Empire that includes Judah is called "the Province Beyond the River," referring to the Euphrates River in Mesopotamia (now Iraq). 1 Esdras consistently updates the name of the province to "Coele-Syria (or just Syria) and Phoenicia," an expression also in 1–2 Maccabees. This became the name of the province when Judah became part of the Seleucid

Empire in 198 BCE. The Greek translation of 1 Esdras was likely produced after this date.

Interpreting 1 Esdras as having reworked a text similar to Ezra-Nehemiah allows readers to identify not only changes to specific texts, but also more extensive forms of editorial activity. The story of the three guards can be understood as an older tale incorporated to form part of a narrative about the construction of the second temple. In 1 Esdras the letter written to King Artaxerxes by opponents of the temple occurs soon after the first returnees arrive in Judah. In Ezra the letter comes later (ch. 4), after the foundations of the temple have been laid. It is likely that in the text that 1 Esdras revised, the letter was in the same location as it is in Ezra, and that 1 Esdras relocated it earlier in the story. This possibility, while not provable, is suggested by the fact that the sequence of events in the two compositions in general matches (as illustrated by the above chart), except for the letter. Placing the letter, written by opponents of the temple's construction, after the first exiles' return accentuates the immediacy of the opposition they faced.

Where's Nehemiah?

While at times they closely match, one should not assume that the Semitic text which 1 Esdras revised was exactly the same as Ezra-Nehemiah in its present form. This issue is particularly relevant regarding Nehemiah. In the book of Nehemiah, he is a Judean and chief cupbearer to Artaxerxes I. The king commissions him to go to Judah and fortify the city of Jerusalem. The book of Nehemiah recounts his efforts, which focus on improving the city's outer walls. While 1 Esdras emphasizes the figure of Ezra, Nehemiah is almost completely absent. Ezra-Nehemiah contains a large bloc of Nehemiah material between Ezra's discriminatory marriage policy and his public reading of the Torah (Neh 1–7). A key question, which cannot be decisively answered, is if 1 Esdras omitted some or all of these Nehemiah texts. The reverse scenario is also possible; that is, 1 Esdras may attest an older, non-Nehemiah version of the narrative, to which another scribe later added Nehemiah material, leading to the form of the text in Ezra-Nehemiah. Elements of 1 Esdras demonstrate that Ezra could exist in the late Second Temple period independent of Nehemiah. Ezra is important in later compositions, such as 2 Esdras, without any connection to Nehemiah. Other texts roughly contemporary with 1 Esdras include Nehemiah without reference to Ezra (2 Macc 1–2; Ben Sira 49). In an ancient Jewish context, it was not necessary for Ezra and Nehemiah traditions to be combined, as is the case in Ezra-Nehemiah.

In any case, without any version of Nehemiah 1–7, in 1 Esdras Ezra's state-mandated divorces, which bring Israel into compliance with the Torah, culminate with his public reading of the law. The Torah ceremony smoothly follows the divorces. Together the two scenes emphasize that under Ezra's leadership Judah affirms its commitment to the Torah.

One possibility that would suggest (not prove) that the scribes who produced 1 Esdras removed Nehemiah material relates to the fact that Nehemiah is primarily known for rebuilding parts of Jerusalem. While 1 Esdras does mention the reconstruction of the city, its focus is much more on the rebuilding of the temple. An editorial decision to leave out Nehemiah's civic achievements would be consistent with this theme.

Obscuring the Exile and Returning to a Pre-Exilic Ideal: King Josiah at the Temple

Some of the most interesting textual adaptations in 1 Esdras have nothing to do with the books of Ezra and Nehemiah. As mentioned above, 1 Esdras begins with Josiah leading Passover. In 2 Chronicles a description of the king's pious activities that is

itself an extensive reworking of an earlier iteration of his reign in
2 Kings; 2 Chronicles 35 has a nineteen-verse account of Josiah
celebrating Passover, whereas 2 Kings 23 devotes only three verses
to this topic. 1 Esdras appears to adapt a form of the narrative in 2
Chronicles. Both texts tell the same basic story and have many of
the same details. In 2 Chronicles 35 and 1 Esdras 1, for example,
Josiah distributes the same astronomical number of lambs and kid
goats for sacrifice (30,000). But 1 Esdras 1 has some modifications.
It explains that Josiah, by deciding to fight Necho, rejected the
advice of the prophet Jeremiah. This detail is not in 2 Chronicles
35—or the book of Jeremiah—and likely constitutes an exegetical
addition. The king's attack on the pharaoh, so understood, is not
simply a tactical blunder. It is the beginning of a larger decline of
piety in Judah which results in the destruction of the temple and
the exile.

   1 Esdras is framed by celebrations at the Jerusalem temple. Its
first image is Josiah leading a Passover ceremony at the temple, in
accordance with the Torah. The last scene of the composition is
Ezra reading the Torah at a large and joyous assembly at the temple.
In 1 Esdras, Josiah, a Davidic king who promoted the Jerusalem
temple as the only legitimate site for worshipping God, represents
a pre-exilic ideal of piety that is regained after the exile by the high
priest Ezra, with both the temple and Judah's devotion to the Torah
fully restored.

   Yet 1 Esdras gives scant treatment to the exile itself. At the end
of chapter 1 they go into exile, and at the beginning of chapter 2
Cyrus ends it. The book of Ezra, by beginning with Cyrus's decree, construes the end of the exile as a major fulcrum point,
the beginning of a new age (the "post-exilic" period). In several texts examined in this volume, such as Baruch, the exile is
an epochal era, serving as clear evidence that Israel is sinful and
has disobeyed God, forcing him to punish his people; 1 Esdras,
by contrast, does not stress the exile but rather continuity between pre-exilic Josiah and post-exilic Ezra. The composition's

de-emphasis of the exile may constitute an effort to deny or refute its significance.

1 Esdras and Ezra-Nehemiah as Bad Historiography?

There are different but significant historical inaccuracies in 1 Esdras and Ezra-Nehemiah. This is particularly clear with respect to the chronology of Persian kings, which is given in Table 2.3.

As mentioned above, the book of Ezra begins with Cyrus ending the exile, and in chapter 4 opponents of the temple successfully lobby the king to support blocking its construction. They make this request to him in a letter. Their letter is dated not to the reign of Cyrus, but that of Xerxes (Ahasuerus, the Persian king in the book of Esther), and the document itself claims to be even later, since it is addressed to Artaxerxes, who ruled a century after Cyrus. According to the end of chapter 4, the opponents who wrote the letter brought work on the temple to a halt until the reign of King Darius. This claim is chronologically problematic since he died long before Artaxerxes became king.

Table 2.3 The Chronology of Persian Kings (sixth–fifth centuries BCE)

Cyrus	559–530
Cambyses	529–522
Darius	521–486
Xerxes I	485–465
Artaxerxes I	464–424

Though 1 Esdras does not date the letter written by opponents of the temple to the time of Xerxes, it is described, as in Ezra, as written to Artaxerxes. As mentioned above, the letter is now even earlier in the story, just after Cyrus's decree and the arrival of the first returnees in Judah. The temple opponents responsible for the letter, according to chapter 2, block its rebuilding until the second year of Darius (520 BCE). This produces the same chronological problem just observed in Ezra (Artaxerxes ruled after Darius). Josephus in his account of this period discerned this inaccuracy and corrected it. In his history the letter is addressed not to Artaxerxes but Cambyses, who did rule between Cyrus and Darius. There is a Talmudic tradition of solving this chronological problem by positing that Cyrus, Darius, and Artaxerxes are all names of the same king—Darius. This solution has the added appeal of suggesting that Ezra was in Jerusalem at the important moment when the second temple was built. (Ezra 6 states that happens during the reign of Darius, and Ezra 7 that Ezra went to Jerusalem during the reign of Artaxerxes.)

After 1 Esdras 2 states that temple construction was blocked until the second year of Darius, the story of the three guards begins. One could reasonably assume that the tale begins in this year. It obviously takes place during his reign. But later (the end of chapter 5), when construction of the temple is halted again, it is not resumed until the reign of King Darius, as if the second stoppage occurred *before* he became king.

The historical problems in 1 Esdras and Ezra-Nehemiah are easy to criticize. But it is not clear that the scribes who produced these texts operated with the same chronology of Persian kings available to scholars today. Throughout his writings, for example, Josephus uses different chronological formats for Persian history. Moreover, the scribes responsible for 1 Esdras and Ezra-Nehemiah were, as we have discussed, willing to revise their source material to highlight specific themes and ideas; this was more important to them than chronological consistency in the sense that it is for historians today.

The Story of Darius's Guards, Greek Banquet Culture, and the Date of 1 Esdras

The story of the three guards is the most entertaining part of 1 Esdras. While strictly speaking its contest does not occur during a banquet but after one, the tale is shaped by Greek banquet culture. A staple of Greek aristocratic life, banquets could be accompanied by a rich array of dinner entertainment, including songs and drinking games (such as *cottabus*, in which one attempts to throw the leftover wine from their cup into a bowl without spilling a drop). They could also include various contests involving speeches, poetry, music, or riddles. Posing a question that guests would make speeches on and try to outdo one another was typical fare. Athenaeus's *Deipnosophistae* (*The Learned Banqueters*) is a compendium of knowledge about ancient Greek banquet culture, written in the third century CE. At times its accounts of banquets are quite similar to the contest in the story of the three guards. Athenaeus, for example, recounts that three young women from the Aegean city of Samos, at a feast for the god Adonis, would expound on the same question animating the 1 Esdras tale: "What is the strongest of all things?" One says iron and the second a blacksmith. The third woman, giving an impression of how bawdy these feasts could be, asserts that the strongest thing of all is the penis. If someone sticks his penis up the blacksmith's ass, she continues, it makes him groan. A penis can overpower the man who can manipulate metal, making it the strongest of the three.

Moreover, the speeches of the three guards, about wine and how women make powerful men swoon, would be fully at home in the rhetorical contests of Greek banquets. The guests in general were drunk, influential men. The Greeks also imagined the Persians deliberating important state affairs in the way depicted in the story. According to Herodotus (fifth century BCE), before Darius took power a council was convened at which three individuals took turns arguing what form of government their state should have.

The first man proposed a kind of democracy, the second oligarchy, and the third, who is Darius himself, advocated for monarchy. This is the system that was chosen, with him as its king. As in the story of the three guards, the third speech trumps the previous two.

The familiarity with Hellenistic banqueting culture in 1 Esdras accords with the likelihood that the composition was produced after 200 BCE. This time frame, mentioned above, is suggested by the text's use of the phrase "Coele-Syria and Phoenicia." Though perhaps not in the same textual form that we have today, the Greek text of 1 Esdras was written in the second century BCE or perhaps somewhat later. Its underlying Hebrew-Aramaic text, which was translated into Greek, is obviously earlier, but a precise date of composition cannot be established for it. As for where 1 Esdras was composed or translated, the evidence does not point clearly to one specific locale.

A second century BCE date for 1 Esdras would situate its translation and revision of a text similar to Ezra-Nehemiah to the period when texts of Daniel and Esther were being reworked and translated into Greek. Many of the Dead Sea Scrolls, which include extensive revisions of texts, were also written in this same general timeframe.

Conclusion

1 Esdras and Ezra-Nehemiah are two different editions of the same basic story about the return of exiles to Judah. While the exact nature of the Semitic text that 1 Esdras translated into Greek cannot be recovered, its core outline of events must have been close to Ezra-Nehemiah. Some passages essentially match each other, word for word. Comparison of the two highlights the distinctive character of 1 Esdras. The composition emphasizes the role of Zerubbabel in the construction of the temple and highlights Ezra as a high priest. The book ends on a triumphant note, with the people of Jerusalem

celebrating their commitment to the Torah, which Ezra reads at the temple before them. The emphasis in 1 Esdras on continuity between the pre-exilic and post-exilic worship of God at the temple effectively neuters the exile of any historical significance. With the temple built anew and the people devoted to the Torah, Ezra's leadership restores a level of piety that Josiah achieved before the destruction of the temple and the exile.

Guide for Further Reading

De Troyer, Kristin. "1 Esdras: Structure, Composition, and Significance." Pages 367–78 in *The Oxford Handbook of the Historical Books of the Hebrew Bible*. Edited by Brad E. Kelle and Brent A. Strawn. New York: Oxford University Press, 2020.

Fried, Lisbeth S., ed. *Was 1 Esdras First? An Investigation into the Priority and Nature of 1 Esdras*. Atlanta: Society of Biblical Literature, 2011.

Talshir, Zipora. *1 Esdras: From Origin to Translation*. Atlanta: Society of Biblical Literature, 1999.

3

The Death of the Eagle and the Return of the Torah

The Second Book of Esdras (4 Ezra)

Second Esdras, also known as 4 Ezra, confronts the trauma of losing the Jerusalem temple. The armies of the Roman Empire destroyed it in 70 CE as part of their brutal suppression of a Jewish revolt against their dominion over Palestine. They honored this devastation with a triumph, a traditional Roman way to celebrate a military victory which involved parading captured enemy leaders through the city. The emperor Domitian (r. 81–96 CE) memorialized the triumph with the Arch of Titus, a large archway which can still be visited in Rome today. It depicts soldiers hauling away treasures from the temple, including a large menorah (lamp). The Jerusalem temple was for Jews the holiest place on earth. Its loss was a crisis on a scale that is difficult to imagine. 4 Ezra, probably written in Palestine around 100 CE, engages this tragedy. So do two other Jewish texts from the period, *2 Baruch*—which has much in common with 4 Ezra—and the *Apocalypse of Abraham*, and the event is poignantly recounted by Josephus.

In 4 Ezra, Ezra is bitter and asks God difficult questions. He also illustrates the resilience of Jewish traditions in the wake of trauma. God gives the Torah anew to Ezra, restoring it for Israel. The composition reimagines Judaism without its temple by centralizing the observance of the law. 4 Ezra teaches that the end of history is at hand, not unlike the New Testament book of Revelation, which was also written circa 100 CE and likewise wrestles with the

The Apocrypha: A Guide. Matthew Goff, Oxford University Press. © Oxford University Press 2024.
DOI: 10.1093/9780190060770.003.0003

dominion of Rome. These themes of Torah observance and imminent eschatology resonate, respectively, with rabbinic Judaism and Christianity, neither of which existed at the time in the forms they do today. 4 Ezra suggests that some Jews in the late first century CE reinvented their traditions in the crucible of national trauma in ways that resonate with and differ from what became rabbinic Judaism and Christianity.

2 Esdras: Some Basics

Ezra and Nehemiah are books of the Hebrew Bible. 1 Esdras and 2 Esdras are books of the Septuagint ("Esdras" is the name "Ezra" in Greek). 1 Esdras is the subject of the previous chapter. The 2 Esdras of the Septuagint is not 4 Ezra but a Greek translation of Ezra and Nehemiah, regarded as a single book. The text on which this chapter focuses is not in the Septuagint. In the Vulgate, Ezra was often entitled "1 Ezra" and Nehemiah "2 Ezra." It became common later in the Middle Ages for the Vulgate to include the two other Ezran books, after 1 and 2 Ezra. The titles 3 and 4 Ezra (or 3 and 4 Esdras) reflect this arrangement, although the ordering and names of the four books vary in the manuscript record. A chart at the beginning of the previous chapter summarizes how the names of these books change throughout varying scriptural traditions.

The text generally known as 2 Esdras comprises sixteen chapters. The term "4 Ezra" denotes the oldest section of 2 Esdras, chapters 3–14. Those chapters constitute the originally Jewish text from circa 100 CE. Chapters 1–2 and 15–16 are separate compositions that became attached to 4 Ezra through its transmission primarily in Latin. Other ancient versions of the book, such as the Armenian or the Ethiopic, have only chapters 3–14. 2 Esdras consists of three texts that over time became one text. Appreciating this gradual process explains why some Latin manuscripts attest a different sequence: chapters 3–14, chapters 15–16, and then the text of chapters 1–2. Scholars generally refer to chapters 1–2 as 5 Ezra, chapters 3–14 as 4 Ezra, and chapters 15–16 as 6 Ezra. Some Latin manuscripts entitle 5 Ezra "the second book of the prophet Ezra," and this heading for the first of these three texts may be why the composition as a whole became known as 2 Esdras.

4 Ezra was originally written in a Semitic language, most likely Hebrew. It was translated into Greek in antiquity. The earliest citation of 4 Ezra is in Greek, in the *Stromateis* written around 200 CE by Clement, a bishop of Alexandria. But no ancient manuscripts of the composition in Hebrew or Greek exist (except for a small Greek fragment of 2 Esdras 15). 4 Ezra is in neither the Septuagint nor the Dead Sea Scrolls. Its absence from those corpora, both composed before the failed Jewish uprising (ca. 70 CE), coheres with the view that 4 Ezra was written after that event. Most modern translations of the text are based on the Latin.

In terms of genre, 4 Ezra is considered an apocalypse. In contemporary culture this term denotes the cataclysmic end of the world. This meaning derives in no small part from several ancient Jewish and Christian texts, such as Daniel or Revelation, which recount eschatological events. This is why biblical scholars understand "apocalypse" as denoting a genre of ancient Jewish and Christian literature which purports to reveal secrets about the world and the end of history. This description, as we shall see, fits 4 Ezra well.

The content of 4 Ezra falls into seven distinct units:

1. 3:1–5:20
2. 5:21–6:34
3. 6:35–9:25
4. 9:26–10:59
5. 11:1–12:51
6. 13:1–58
7. 14:1–48

The first three are dialogues between Ezra and the angel Uriel. In the fourth, the midpoint of the book, Ezra encounters a weeping woman who turns into a city. The fifth and sixth units are eschatological visions about, respectively, a three-headed eagle and a man from the sea who breathes fire. In the seventh unit Ezra renews the scriptures of Israel. The seven sections together delineate Ezra's transformation, from a distraught skeptic to a leader who reestablishes the covenant.

Today 4 Ezra is neither in the Jewish canon nor in the Old Testament of most Christian communities. It is, however, in the Bible of the Ethiopian Orthodox Church, one of the oldest Christian churches, where it is known as 1 Ezra. It is also a biblical book in the Russian Orthodox tradition and in that tradition is called 3 Ezra. The authenticity of 4 Ezra was disputed in antiquity. Jerome hated the book. In his preface to Ezra-Nehemiah in the Vulgate, he asserts that one should not be inclined to the "fantasies" of the "third" and "fourth" books of Ezra. Jerome did not translate 4 Ezra and boasted in his *Against Vigilantius* that he never read it. His disdain may have been sparked by the book's strange and highly eschatological content, along with his dismissive attitude toward any Old Testament book that could not be traced back to a Hebrew text. Ambrose of Milan, a bishop and contemporary of Jerome, had a much more positive view of the composition. He regarded it as a genuine text written by Ezra and cited it extensively.

For much of the Middle Ages most copies of the Vulgate did not include 4 Ezra, except in Spain. Two important early bishops in Spain, Priscillian of Avila (fourth century) and Isidore of Seville (seventh century), thought highly of the book, suggesting its popularity there is long-standing. Language from 4 and 5 Ezra is prominent in the Mozarabic rite, a mode of Catholic liturgy practiced in early medieval Spain; the Requiem Mass (the liturgy for the dead) of the Roman rite also incorporates material from 5 Ezra.

5 and 6 Ezra (2 Esdras 1–2 and 15–16) survive mainly in Latin. Both are considered Christian texts, and their association with 4

Ezra attests late antique and early medieval interest in the book in a western Christian milieu. 5 Ezra is dated to the second or third century CE. It depicts Ezra as a prophet who rebukes Israel for rejecting God and proclaims that a new people will appear. They are told to await their shepherd and the end of the age. It concludes with Ezra having a vision of the Son of God rewarding this people with immortal life, placing crowns on their heads and palm fronds in their hands.

6 Ezra is also a work of eschatological prophecy. It provides a vivid account of upheavals which signal that the end is near. "Fire and hail and flying swords and floods of water" will destroy cities, including Babylon, and also mountains and forests. Corpses will pile up on the ground like dung. God is furious that his people are being killed. This may refer to persecution endured by early followers of Jesus. The "dragons of Arabia" shall fight the Carmonians. Carmania is a region of Iran (today called Kerman). This likely alludes to wars that took place in the 260s CE in the eastern Roman Empire between Odaenathus (Odainat), an Arabian king based in Palmyra (Syria), and Shapur I, a king of the Persian Sasanian Empire. 6 Ezra was probably written in the third century CE.

The Christian transmission of 2 Esdras is evident in 4 Ezra itself. It is the only Old Testament book that attests the name of Jesus. In the Latin, 4 Ezra 7:28 states that "my son Jesus" shall be revealed. In other ancient versions, such as the Armenian or Syriac, this verse states that the messiah will be revealed, a common expectation in late Second Temple Judaism, without mentioning his name. Christian scribes in a Latin milieu changed an existing reference to a messiah by adding Jesus's name. Many Latin manuscripts are also missing a large section of chapter 7 (vv. 36–105).

Several other texts, mainly Christian, demonstrate engagement with 4 Ezra. They include the *Greek Apocalypse of Ezra*, the *Apocalypse of Sedrach* ("Sedrach" is likely a corruption of "Ezra"), which is in Greek, and the Armenian *Questions of Ezra*. These texts cannot be dated precisely. But they depict in various ways Ezra debating with an angel or God, a major element in 4 Ezra. In *Sedrach*, for example, Ezra ascends to heaven and contends with God over Adam's transgression and its consequences, a prominent theme in 4 Ezra. Ethiopian Jews (the Falasha) have preserved another Ezran text, the *Apocalypse of Ezra*, which is likewise concerned with the fate of the righteous and the wicked.

Ezra, Historical Fantasy, and Trauma

4 Ezra is attributed to Ezra. According to the books of Ezra and Nehemiah, he was a scribe and priest who around 400 BCE aggressively implemented harsh Torah-based policies in Judah. He mandated, for example, the divorce of mixed-race couples to force the community to cohere with the ethnic exclusivism of Deuteronomy. 4 Ezra, however, is set earlier. The Babylonians destroyed the temple in 586 BCE. The work purports to be written thirty years after this event, in the mid-sixth century (556 BCE), while Ezra is in Babylon among the Jews exiled there. The books of Ezra and Nehemiah focus on his activities after he returns to Judah.

4 Ezra recounts the Roman destruction at one remove. The Babylonians obliterated the first temple, which was later rebuilt and then demolished by the Romans (70 CE). These violent events are separated by over six centuries. But they are conflated in Jewish memory. Rabbinic literature teaches that both acts of destruction occurred on the same day of the year, a claim also made by Josephus; both losses are mourned on the same day in the Jewish liturgical year (Tishbe Av; the 9th of the month of Av). The book of Revelation also merges Rome and Babylon. It envisages a woman who rides a dragon with seven heads as the cruel ruler of the world. According to chapter 17, she represents a city (Rome) and her name is "Babylon the great, mother of whores and of earth's abominations."

4 Ezra merges Rome and Babylon to offer a kind of alternative history. According to 4 Ezra, the second temple was *never built*. The book takes place before it was constructed (516 BCE) and emphatically states that Ezra lives close to the end of history. 4 Ezra engages the Roman destruction of the second temple by imagining Ezra reeling from the loss of the first temple. The temple was the center of the world according to Jewish tradition. With its destruction, how Jews understood the world and their religious traditions was shattered. 4 Ezra constructs a kind of historical fantasy to confront a loss that is too profound to name, to talk about it without talking about it. By imagining the world ending before the second temple was built, it was never destroyed.

The trauma Jews faced should not be solely understood in terms of the destruction of the temple. Afterward, Rome minted coins that memorialized its victory over Judah. These coins, which were in circulation throughout the empire, read *Iudaea capta* ("Judah captured") and depict Judah as a forlorn, dejected woman (see Figure 3.1). Whereas Jews had been paying a half-shekel tax for the upkeep of the Jerusalem temple, the emperor Vespasian after 70 CE forced them to pay instead the *fiscus iudaicus* (the "Jewish tax"), which supported the temple of Jupiter Capitolinus, a major temple in Rome devoted to the god Jupiter (Zeus). That 4 Ezra begins thirty years after the destruction of the Jerusalem temple—a key reason scholars date the composition to 100 CE—suggests that the trauma which the composition engages includes the loss of the temple and the officially sanctioned forms of humiliation that followed it.

Why Did God Give Us Understanding?
A Sad Man Argues with an Angel

4 Ezra begins with Ezra lying on his bed, fraught with anxiety. He reminds God that he loved Abraham and made a covenant with

Figure 3.1 Roman coin produced to commemorate the suppression of the Jewish Revolt (66–70 CE). Obverse: image of Emperor Vespasian. Reverse: depiction of Judah as a mourning woman (cf. 4 Ezra 10). Reads: IUDAEA CAPTA ("Judah captured").
Image courtesy of Classical Numismatic Group, LLC (http://cngcoins.com).

Israel. But God did not remove the "evil heart" from Israel, which made Adam disobey him. All humans have an evil heart because of Adam's transgression. The human condition, Ezra laments, prevents us from following his covenant. We can but only disappoint God and he punishes us for it. Writing at roughly the same time, Paul's letters also critique the viability of the Torah as the means to salvation.

The evil heart (Latin *cor malignum*) is an iteration of the Hebrew *yetzer ha-ra*, the evil inclination. In the Dead Sea Scrolls and rabbinic literature this *yetzer* is understood as an inherent attribute of the human being that compels one to do evil. In 4 Ezra, as in the New Testament writings of Paul, Adam's disobedience in the garden—both ignore Eve—reverberates throughout history. *2 Baruch* adapts this Adamic motif to stress individual responsibility rather than a design flaw in the human condition, asserting that each of us has become their own Adam.

Ezra cannot reconcile humankind's evil heart and God's covenant with Israel. If the evil heart prevents Jews from obeying the
Torah, what value does the covenant have? Moreover, rather than
receive special treatment from God, recent history suggests the
opposite. He sees the humiliation of Zion and the prosperity of
Babylon (Rome). Like Job, Ezra is unable to justify the ways of God
(an issue scholars call theodicy).

Ezra's questions trigger a response from heaven and a fascinating
theological debate ensues. An angel named Uriel arrives to make
sure Ezra understands one thing: you don't understand anything.
He asks him to weigh fire and measure wind, both impossible for
Ezra. Uriel argues: if you can't understand basic things about the
world, what makes you think you can fathom the way of God?
Ezra becomes even more dejected. He laments that it would have
been better not to have been born than to suffer without understanding why.

Uriel emphasizes that this age is quickly approaching its end.
The current moment and its travails are to be understood within
the larger context of God's plan guiding history. It is *supposed* to
be a time of sadness, evil, and upheaval. This characterization of
the present is common in apocalyptic literature. It is a powerful
answer to Ezra's poignant questions. The current dominion of evil
becomes a sign that its overthrow is imminent. The humiliation of
Zion does not refute that God is in control, but rather means that
everything is going according to plan. So understood, this age must
simply be endured until its ordained end. Then, at the final judgment, God will allocate rewards and punishments, respectively, to
the righteous and the wicked.

Uriel does not stress the evil heart but another core aspect of the
human condition—pregnancy. To understand the end-times, he
recommends that Ezra speak with a mother. A pregnant woman
knows her term will reach a decisive end characterized by intense
pain and travails that will result in new life. But she does not know

when exactly her "end-times" will begin. The earth, Uriel contends, is like that woman. He also uses an agricultural metaphor to explain the coming judgment, as does the book of Revelation—human evil is growing, as seeds do into plants, and there is an appointed time for the harvest. The evil is not yet ripe. But it will be soon.

As the dialogues progress, Ezra receives eschatological knowledge. While things are bad, they will get much worse. In the next stage of history, the angel tells him, women will give birth to "monsters" (children with abnormalities), the sun will shine at night, and blood will drip from wood (ch. 5). After the birth pangs of the end-times, the heavenly Jerusalem will appear (ch. 7). All those who survive the tribulations will see the messiah, who will rejoice for four hundred years and then die. This form of messianic expectation is quite different from that of New Testament texts, which are roughly contemporary with 4 Ezra. Then, after seven days of primeval silence, the dead will be resurrected, so that all people who ever lived may face judgment. They face two opposing fates, the pit of torment and the paradise of delight.

Ezra urges God not to focus on the sins of his people but on those who serve him in truth. He promotes a national or communal conception of salvation in which the righteous of Israel can help spare the rest of the community from destruction. Uriel stresses instead salvation at the level of the individual. The vast majority of people, he contends, are destined to be punished. This fills Ezra with pathos. The angel urges him to think about the righteous, who are few, rather than the wicked, who are many.

Mother Zion, the Weeping and Heavenly City

In terms of Ezra's progress, the fourth episode of 4 Ezra (9:26–10:59) is critical. Uriel asks him to spend seven days in an uninhabited area called Ardat. He is to eat nothing but the flowers that grow there. Some readers have suspected that the flowers have hallucinogenic properties, because Ezra has strange visions in this field.

After the seven days, Ezra encounters a woman lamenting her son, who died on his wedding day. Ezra reminds her of the anguish of Zion, "the mother of us all," and urges her to "be consoled because of the sorrow of Jerusalem." When confronted with another person's pain, the cause of his own anguish, the devastation wrought by Rome, becomes a basis for consoling that other person. The tragedy that has befallen Israel is so profound—what is one family's loss by comparison? National trauma, Ezra suggests, helps make a loss suffered by a single family more endurable because it is a shared, communal experience.

It turns out to be quite odd that Ezra urges the woman to remember Mother Zion, the personification of Israel. She is Mother Zion! The woman responds to Ezra's consolation by transforming into a city. Uriel appears but there is no debate. Ezra does not argue with the angel but stresses that he does not understand. Uriel discloses heavenly knowledge to him, which angels often do in apocalyptic literature. The encounter with the woman was a vision, which he interprets for Ezra. Uriel explains that the woman is Mother Zion, and her son is Jerusalem. The city's "death" (its destruction by Rome) so understood is part of a larger divine plan that Ezra is beginning to understand. Seeing Zion's full glory is a reward for Ezra being distraught over the mother's pain. The vision likely inverts the imperial propaganda of the *Judaea capta* coins and their humiliating depiction of Judah. The heavenly truth, the vision counters, is that the sad woman will become a glorious city. Her transformation also resonates with the New Jerusalem, eschatological paradise in the form of a city, as described by the book of Revelation.

The Downfall of the Three-Headed Eagle and the Messiah's Lethal Breath

Uriel tells Ezra to enter the visionary city and learn much there. The imaginary Jerusalem is in a sense where Ezra experiences two vivid eschatological visions, the eagle vision and the man of the sea vision (11:1–12:51; 13:1–58).

An eagle with twelve wings and three heads rises out of the sea and conquers the world. One wing rules over the whole body of the eagle and then disappears, replaced by another. The middle head also vanishes and the one on the right devours the head on the left. A lion rebukes the eagle, which is then killed with fire.

Ezra is troubled and confused by what he sees, as is Daniel after his visions. Also like the book of Daniel, an interpretation of the vision is revealed to Ezra along with the vision itself. The eagle vision describes the eschatological downfall of Rome. The eagle is an imperial symbol of Rome. Its wings represent specific kings, although not all of them can be identified with confidence. Its three heads likely symbolize the three emperors of the Flavian dynasty who ruled the empire during the period that concerns 4 Ezra (ca. 70–100 CE)—Vespasian, Titus, and Domitian. Vespasian and then his son Titus oversaw the Roman destruction of Judah. The Flavian interpretation of the eagle heads is suggested by 4 Ezra 12:26. This verse explains that the head which disappears will be fulfilled by a king who dies in agony on his bed. According to the Roman historian Suetonius (late first–early second centuries CE), Vespasian died of a bowel illness in 79 CE, struggling to get out of bed while experiencing severe diarrhea (he wanted to die on his feet).

4 Ezra 12 identifies the eagle as the fourth beast of Daniel 7. This vision was produced during the Maccabean revolt (second century BCE), and in Daniel this beast signifies the Greco-Syrian Seleucid Empire whose policies triggered the conflict (see Chapter 12). 4 Ezra offers a different understanding of the Danielic vision. For 4 Ezra it becomes, as in Revelation, the lens for understanding the current moment as the end of history. Daniel 7 stresses the power and destructiveness of the fourth beast and teaches that this turmoil will be followed by the final reckoning, when God will judge and destroy the beast with fire. But Daniel 7 never states what kind of animal it is. 4 Ezra's eagle vision fills out that picture. The book

of Daniel also asserts that its visions are to be sealed for a future time. 4 Ezra, not unlike Revelation whose beast likewise draws on Daniel 7, presents itself as that future time. The Ezran eagle vision purports to fulfill the Danielic vision of the end-times. The lion, a symbol of Judah, represents the Davidic messiah, a figure not explicit in Daniel 7.

The eagle vision claims to reveal the divine plan guiding history in which the current crisis should be understood. The eagle was supposed to gain power. Its might, so understood, marks the beginning of the end, the final stage of history before the revelation of the messiah. This perspective subverts Roman imperial ideology. The *Judaea capta* coins convey that the defeat of Judah demonstrates the power of the empire. But according to the eagle vision, Rome's dominance is itself evidence that its demise will happen soon. Rome may run the world, 4 Ezra teaches, but God orchestrates history.

Seven days later Ezra has another vision (ch. 13). A man rises from the sea. He flies throughout the air and lands on a large mountain. A great throng of people rushes to attack him. Fire shoots out of his mouth, incinerating them. This vision is also divinely interpreted. The man is the messiah and he stands upon Mount Zion. The interpretation stresses the vastness of the sea. The messiah's aquatic origins denote his incomprehensibility and transcendence (the sea imagery differs from that of the eagle vision). While the reference to Rome is less explicit than in the prior vision, the man of the sea vision is very much about Rome. It draws on the Gog and Magog tradition to understand the final stage of history (in different ways, so do Daniel and Revelation). Recounted in Ezekiel 38–39, Gog and Magog represent a massive army of various Gentile (non-Jewish) peoples who attack Jerusalem from all directions, resulting in a large battle at which God defeats them. The attacking armies signify "all the nations" in the Ezran vision, an allusion to Gog and Magog. Rather than subvert a Roman symbol (the eagle), the man of the sea vision utilizes a traditional Israelite motif to conceptualize Roman power as an expression of Gentile violence that is intimidating but ultimately futile. With different imagery, here too the dominion of Rome is a sign of its impending downfall.

The messiah is more explicitly a violent figure here than in the eagle vision. Fire also destroys the eagle, but there it is not associated with the messiah. The interpretation of the vision identifies the fire as symbolizing the Torah. The law denotes the word of God uttered against the wicked, enunciated via messianic violence. In the background of the fire-breathing messiah is, undoubtedly, Isaiah 11. That chapter contains an enigmatic prophecy that a future Davidic king will strike the earth with the "rod of his mouth" and slaughter the wicked with the "breath of his lips." Imagining fire spewing out of a messiah's mouth is one way to understand how he kills the wicked with his breath. Revelation 19 provides another solution. There Jesus leads a heavenly army against the beast and his armies (another Gog and Magog scenario) and he kills them with a sword. He does not wield the sword with his hands. Rather, it comes out of his mouth. Some people back then thought a lot about the messiah's lethal breath.

Ezra as a Second Moses: The Renewal of the Torah after the Loss of the Temple

The seventh and final unit of 4 Ezra establishes that the transformation of Ezra is complete, from a grief-stricken cynic to the one who leads Israel into its post-temple future. He no longer challenges God with his own understanding of events. The Babylonian Talmud (tractate *Qiddushin*) imagines the evil inclination, which is compatible with the evil heart of 4 Ezra, as a lethal poison that spreads throughout the human body, while also asserting that God provides its antidote, the Torah. 4 Ezra 14 does something similar. It describes the Torah as burnt up and lost in a world of darkness. Ezra volunteers to receive revelation and write down the law.

God agrees. Ezra is to be secluded with five other scribes for forty days. He also offers moral leadership to Israel. Before leaving, he assembles the people and urges them to "discipline your hearts," a reference to their evil hearts, in order to attain new life after death. Re-establishing the law makes that possible. After drinking a liquid that tastes like fire, Ezra is filled with understanding. He speaks continuously, day and night, for the entire forty days, as the scribes write it all down. Ezra restores the Torah. He is a second Moses.

But Ezra writes more than Moses did. After the forty days, ninety-four books have been written. That's a lot! Twenty-four are for Israel and seventy just for the wise. That these books are for the "wise" denotes that they are to be read by Jewish intellectuals and scribes rather than Israel as a whole. The "wise" may also be an early reference to rabbis, but one that is quite different from their presentation in rabbinic literature. The term "wise" (Heb. *hakham*) can be a title for authoritative teachers in rabbinic texts. But in rabbinic writings the "wise," unlike 4 Ezra, are very much not praised as custodians of esoteric books.

4 Ezra 14 is one of the earliest attestations of the trope that Jewish scripture comprises a set number of books, a topic also discussed in Chapter 1. The twenty-four books denote the Hebrew Bible. That it contains twenty-four books would become the standard count in rabbinic Judaism. In rabbinic tradition, Ezra is likewise hailed as a second Moses who restored Torah after the Babylonian devastation of Jerusalem.

But 4 Ezra thematizes scripture in ways that diverge from rabbinic Judaism. In that tradition, there is an awareness that other ancient Jewish writings exist. But they are sharply distinguished from the Hebrew Bible and reading them is discouraged. The Mishnah calls them the "outside" books, and this remains a Jewish term for apocryphal, non-canonical texts. 4 Ezra 14, by contrast, imagines Jewish scripture as more expansive than the Hebrew Bible. The seventy additional books signify a vast esoteric corpus of writings. The composition does not disclose the identity of these books, which remain enigmatic. The Renaissance humanist Pico della Mirandola (1463–1494) argued that they were the mystical writings of Kabbalah. They may denote "outside books," such as *1 Enoch, Jubilees,* or 4 Ezra itself. In any case, these seventy books are important but, not unlike salvation itself in 4 Ezra, only for the few, whereas the twenty-four are for all Israel. 4 Ezra does not make clear if the seventy books are necessary to achieve salvation, whereas the twenty-four are. 4 Ezra urges that the seventy books are to be preserved, but in a way that does not challenge the centrality of the Torah.

The number seventy may not denote a list of specific books. This number in ancient Judaism can denote totality. Genesis 46, for example, lists seventy family members to convey that Joseph's entire family unit relocates to Egypt. So understood, the seventy books signify not actual texts but an additional revelation that is more extensive than but compatible with the Torah. In 4 Ezra 14, Ezra volunteers to write down not only the law but also "everything that has happened" since the beginning of history. The seventy books may analogously denote an esoteric revelation of God's entire plan for history, from creation to judgment. *Jubilees* similarly imagines Moses on Sinai receiving both the Torah and a revelation of the entire scope of history, a trope 4 Ezra 14 alludes to.

In most ancient versions of 4 Ezra 14, although not the Latin, after Ezra renews the scriptures he ascends to heaven and attains a blessed afterlife. This suggests it was an authentic element of the chapter that fell out of the text in its Latin transmission. His ascension emphasizes his exceptional status. Ezra is one of the few people who escape death.

The Strange Early Modern History of 4 Ezra

Before concluding, some attention should be devoted to the odd career of 4 Ezra in the early modern period. It grew in popularity, in part because of its inclusion in the Gutenberg Bible (1455), a version of the Vulgate that was the first Bible produced by a printing press. 4 Ezra also plays a role in the "discovery" of the Americas. Christopher Columbus's opinion that it would be possible to travel westward to India from Spain was shaped by 4 Ezra 6. This text states that the world is six parts land and one part water (the reverse is closer to the mark). By this logic, there's not much water on earth, making maritime travel from Spain to India feasible.

When early Europeans realized that there was a vast landmass between Europe and Asia inhabited by Indigenous peoples, some turned to another passage of 4 Ezra. 4 Ezra 13:39–47 states that the northern tribes of Israel, dispersed by Assyria in the eighth century BCE (2 Kings 17), settled in an unknown region called Arzareth (which derives from a Hebrew phrase, *aretz ahereth* ["another land"]). The new discoveries, it was thought, shed light on the location of Arzareth and its significance. One late sixteenth-century scholar, Gilbert Génebrard, argued that the "discovery" of the New World confirms that Arzareth is in northeast Asia (as printed on a 1570 map made by Abraham Ortelius) and that the lost tribes traveled from there to Greenland, from which they settled the rest of the American landmass. This is surprisingly close to the thesis, generally held today, that humans migrated to the Americas via the Bering Straits in Alaska. But Génebrard deployed his Arzareth-Greenland theory to contend that the native Americans are Jews, the long-lost descendants of Israel. This idea, discredited long ago, suggests that White Europeans made sense of the ethnic Other they didn't know (Native Americans) in terms of an ethnic Other they did (Jews).

In the same era, Protestants in Europe expressed widely divergent views about 4 Ezra. Luther, echoing Jerome's earlier disdain for the book, asserted that it contains "vain fancies," and refused to include it in the Apocrypha section of his Wittenberg Bible (it is in the King James Apocrypha). Luther was troubled by its vivid accounts of eschatological upheaval. He derided the book of

Revelation as open to "stupid" interpretation and complained that it is like 4 Ezra (which it is). He disliked the more radical Protestant groups, such as the Anabaptists, in part because of how they read Revelation—and 4 Ezra. Many of these sectarian movements held the books in high esteem as eschatological prophecy, with both comprising a road map for understanding their own day as the end-times. Luther also, as mentioned in the previous chapter, derisively compared 4 Ezra to the fables of Aesop.

Regarding 2 Esdras, the Council of Trent (1545–1563) is in odd agreement with Luther. This council published an authoritative list of the books that comprise the Catholic Old Testament. It does not include 2 Esdras. The book was, however, retained on the margins of Catholic scripture. The Sixto-Clementine Vulgate, which was published in 1592, included an appendix after the New Testament that comprises 1 and 2 Esdras and the Prayer of Manasseh. Catholic Bibles no longer include this appendix (see also the previous chapter).

Conclusion

In a sense, when 4 Ezra ends, not much has changed. God never answers the core question Ezra raises at the outset—why did you not remove our evil hearts? His critique that the evil heart prevents Israel from following the covenant remains unresolved. As Uriel asserts, salvation is *supposed* to be difficult, attainable by the few, not the many.

But in another way, everything has changed. The temple is gone. But the Torah, because of Ezra, has returned. He re-establishes the covenant between God and Israel. This provides a path to salvation—it is difficult but possible. The Torah is asserted as a foundational element of Jewish identity, as is mourning the loss of the temple. This resonates powerfully with rabbinic Judaism. Ezra also renews the covenant in the end of days. The eschatology of 4 Ezra is more in keeping with Christianity. 4 Ezra was produced within the same cultural matrix of first-century Palestinian Judaism, out of which rabbinic Judaism and Christianity emerge. The composition is, not surprisingly, similar to but different from both traditions. 4 Ezra illustrates one way Jews at the time confronted the trauma of losing the temple—by reimagining Jewish traditions in a way that affirms covenant fidelity and eschatological hope in a bleak world.

Guide for Further Reading

Hogan, Karina Martin. *Theologies in Conflict in 4 Ezra: Wisdom Debate and Apocalyptic Solution.* Leiden: Brill, 2008.
Longenecker, Bruce. *2 Esdras.* Sheffield: Sheffield Academic Press, 1995.
Najman, Hindy. *Losing the Temple and Recovering the Future: An Analysis of 4 Ezra.* Cambridge: Cambridge University Press, 2014.
Stone, Michael E. *Fourth Ezra: A Commentary on the Book of Fourth Ezra.* Minneapolis: Fortress Press, 1990.

4

All's Well That Ends Well

The Book of Tobit

Many readers of scripture today understand the Bible as affirming that God rewards the righteous. While some biblical books complicate this perspective, such as Job or Ecclesiastes, one story that teaches this idea in an entertaining way was removed from the Old Testament—the book of Tobit.

Tobit is unknown to many today because in the Protestant tradition it was relegated to the Apocrypha. It has been, however, and remains in the Old Testament in Catholic and Orthodox forms of Christianity. It has been a popular book for centuries. Parts of it are still today recited at Catholic weddings. Scenes from the book were a popular subject of famous Renaissance artists, such as Rembrandt. Though not in the Jewish Bible, Tobit was written as a Jewish text and has long been popular among Jewish readers. The famous Jewish novelist Saul Bellow, describing the book as "touching and funny," included it his anthology *Great Jewish Short Stories* (1963).

Bellow was right. Tobit is entertaining and at times funny. It's a story with burning fish guts, a demon, an angel in disguise, and bird poop. It is also a story designed to instruct. Tobit is a patriarch who exemplifies a mode of piety that stresses prayer, almsgiving (charity), and family. Though righteous, he suffers. He becomes blind for an odd reason—bird poop falls in his eyes. But in the end, he regains his sight. A key message of the book is providence: God rewards righteousness in his own way, which is often difficult for humans, as Tobit's blindness signifies, to see.

The Apocrypha: A Guide. Matthew Goff, Oxford University Press. © Oxford University Press 2024.
DOI: 10.1093/9780190060770.003.0004

The Book of Tobit: Historical, Textual, and Scriptural Issues

The book of Tobit takes place during the eighth and seventh centuries BCE, when the Assyrian kingdom, centered in what is today northern Syria and Iraq, dominated the ancient Near East. In 722 BCE the Assyrians destroyed the ten-tribe confederation known as northern kingdom of Israel (hence the "ten lost tribes"). Tobit tells the story of one of the Israelites who was forcibly relocated to Assyria.

While set in a much earlier period, scholars generally date Tobit to the third or early second century, or roughly 225–175 BCE. Like other Jewish texts from this period, Tobit takes great interest in a pious ancestor from the distant past. Tobit follows the law of Moses. This is a major reason why scholars understand the eighth and seventh centuries BCE as the book's narrative setting, rather than its time of composition. The Torah emerges as a central and authoritative source of Jewish identity in the third and second centuries BCE. The scriptural citations in Tobit also indicate a later dating. Tobit 2, for example, cites Amos. This prophet, his book suggests, was in the northern kingdom in the mid-eighth century BCE, before the Assyrians destroyed it—*before* Tobit was exiled! Also, the book makes chronological errors regarding Assyrian kings that suggest it was written later. Tobit 1, for example, states that King Shalmaneser (r. 727–722 BCE) was succeeded by Sennacherib (r. 705–681 BCE), but he was followed by Sargon (r. 721–705 BCE).

All the major early manuscripts of the Septuagint—Alexandrinus, Vaticanus, Sinaiticus—include Tobit. Many early Christian authors presume the book's scriptural authority. Clement, a second-century bishop of Alexandria, quotes Tobit 4:15 as from "scripture." Augustine (fourth century) cites Tobit extensively and records in one of his sermons that Christians read the book at the shrine of Theogenes, a North African martyr (a Christian killed because of his faith). Some early Christian authors, such as Origen (second–third centuries) in his *Letter to Africanus*, and Jerome (fourth century) in his preface to Tobit, state that it is not a book of the Hebrew Bible revered by Jews (see also the discussion of this letter in the next chapter). Some Christian exegetes considered it a problem that Tobit was not in Hebrew. Jerome states that Tobit was, while not in Hebrew, in the "language of the Chaldeans"—Aramaic. Given that Jerome's guiding star is *hebraica veritas*, which valorizes Hebrew as the proper language of Old Testament texts, it's odd that Tobit is in the Vulgate at all. He dedicated his translation of Tobit to the bishops Chromatius and Heliodorus, who were patrons of his scholarship. Perhaps he included the book because they wanted him to. He claims to have completed his translation of Tobit in a single day, working with a Jewish person who knew Aramaic and Hebrew. It seems Jerome was less interested in Tobit than Chromatius and Heliodorus were.

While there is no manuscript evidence to support Jerome's claim that the book of Tobit existed in Aramaic in his day, this could have been the case. Remnants of five ancient Tobit scrolls were discovered among the Dead Sea Scrolls. Officially published in 1995, they were produced in the first centuries BCE and CE. Only one of them is in Hebrew (4Q200). The other four are in Aramaic (4Q196–199). Two additional Aramaic Tobit fragments came to light in the early 2000s, but it has been established that they are forgeries. The Qumran texts cover approximately a fifth of the book. The Qumran Aramaic Tobit texts appear to be somewhat different than whatever Aramaic text of Tobit Jerome allegedly used. Tobit is, for example, entirely in the third person in the Vulgate, but the Qumran Tobit texts, like the Greek, are in the first person in chapters 1–3. The ancient Tobit scrolls indicate that even though the book was never scripture in rabbinic Judaism, some Jews before the turn of the common era regarded it as a legitimate part of their ancestral heritage.

Of the three major Septuagint manuscripts mentioned above, Vaticanus and Alexandrinus were long known, whereas the Sinai

Codex first came to light in the mid-nineteenth century. The German biblical scholar Constantin von Tischendorf acquired it under dubious circumstances from St. Catherine's Monastery, in the Sinai peninsula of Egypt. The version of Tobit in the Sinai Codex, it was soon realized, is substantially different from that of Alexandrinus and Vaticanus. The Sinai version (sometimes called the S text) is longer, with over 1,700 additional words (some examples are below), even though it leaves out 4:6–19b and 13:6b–10. The shorter form of Tobit in Alexandrinus and Vaticanus is called GI (Greek I) and the longer recension of the book in S, GII (Greek II). *A New English Translation of the Septuagint* (2007) places the two versions side by side for easy comparison. The Qumran Tobit texts accord with GII more than GI. This suggests that the longer GII version of Tobit is older than the shorter GI version. The form of Tobit that circulated as scripture for centuries within Christianity, it appears, is an abridged version of the book. Because of the antiquity of the GII format, recent editions of the Bible often use it as the base text for Tobit, such as the NRSV, whereas older versions, such as the King James, which was published over 200 years before the Sinai Codex was discovered, follow GI.

There are also several medieval manuscripts of Tobit in Hebrew (5) and one in Aramaic. They are translations of the book from Greek or Latin. A couple of these manuscripts were produced by Christian Hebraists, Christian scholars who knew Hebrew and promoted christological interpretations of Jewish texts. Sebastian Münster (1488–1552), for example, compiled a Hebrew text of Tobit, published in Constantinople in 1516. Other medieval Tobit manuscripts indicate that the book was popular in some Jewish circles, despite not being in their Bible. The Hebrew Gaster manuscript (named after the scholar who published it in 1897) states that it is to be read on the second day of Shavuot. This is the Festival of Weeks (Pentecost), which has long been a major Jewish holiday. It commemorates God giving the Torah to Israel. This Jewish liturgical link between Shavuot and the book is based on its content. In Tobit 2, Tobit's family observes Shavuot with a large meal—one of the earliest accounts of a Jewish family commemorating this festal day. There are also early modern translations of Tobit into Yiddish. Saul Bellow was not the first Jewish reader to conclude that Tobit is a "Great Jewish Short Story."

The Book of Tobit: Two Stories Come Together

The book features two separate plot lines that become intertwined. The first centers on Tobit. He lives among the exiles in Nineveh, the capital of the Assyrian empire. He is an ethical and upright person. Like Job, he does not deserve to suffer, but he does, in part by becoming blind. He becomes unhappy and prays to God to die. The second plot thread centers on a woman named Sarah. She is a relative of Tobit who lives in Ecbatana, a city in Media (western Iran). She is also unhappy. Sarah has been engaged seven times, but each time a demon named Asmodeus killed her fiancé. She, like Tobit, prays to die.

Tobit urges his son Tobias to travel to Media to retrieve a large amount of money, ten talents of silver (a talent being roughly sixty pounds or slightly more), that is being held in trust for him in Rages, a town in Media. But Tobias doesn't know the way. With almost comic immediacy, a person named Azariah shows up; he knows the route very well, is a kinsman, and is willing to be his guide. Azariah is actually the archangel Raphael, an important angel in ancient Judaism, but they don't know that yet. During their travels east, accompanied by a dog (according to Tob 6:2 in GII, not GI), a strange thing happens—when camping for the night by the Tigris River, a large fish jumps out of the water and attacks Tobias. The fish attack illustrates that God restores the righteous in strange ways. The fish's heart and liver, Azariah explains, can repel demons when burned. Its gall (bile) can cure blindness. The fish guts constitute the solution to Sarah and Tobit's problems. The fish attack, combined with angelic instruction, is a form of divine assistance. This is perhaps why Raphael and the fish have been a popular subject of artists, both in Europe and further east, in the Mughal court of India (Figure 4.1). This Muslim court, which flourished before India became a British colony, took a genuine interest in Jesuit missionaries and the Bible they brought with them to India, especially Tobit.

Azariah, who knows quite a lot about fish guts, also plays matchmaker. Now the two plotlines come together. When traveling in Media, Azariah suggests that they lodge for the night at the home of one of their kinsmen, Raguel. Azariah tells Tobias that Raguel has a beautiful daughter, Sarah, and that he has the right to marry her. The story presumes knowledge of levirate marriage, a practice mandated in the Torah. According to this custom, if a husband dies without producing children, his brother is obligated to marry the widow, to ensure that she will bear children within the family line; if he can't marry her, the man with the next closest kinship tie to the dead man must. Tobias is next in line because Asmodeus killed all of Sarah's prior suitors.

Tobias and Sarah are quickly betrothed. Raguel presumes that Asmodeus will murder Tobias as he did the other men. He even has a grave dug for Tobias; a concern for the dead runs in the family, as discussed below. But Azariah, who seems to know everything, shows Tobias how to defeat Asmodeus. On the night Tobias and Sarah are to consummate their marriage, Azariah has Tobias burn a kind of incense that most newlyweds would not want beside their conjugal bed. He burns the fish's liver and heart on incense ashes. The smoking guts repel the demon, presumably because of their nasty stench. It is a fumigation exorcism. In the medieval Aramaic Tobit and the medieval Hebrew Münster text, Tobias burns the fish guts in a pan *under* Sarah's clothes, which, I have no doubt, would

Figure 4.1 The angel Raphael (Azariah) from the book of Tobit. By Husayn Naqqash (Mughal court painter), circa 1590.
© RMN-Grand Palais/Art Resource, NY.

make her wedding night unforgettable. According to the composition, the couple does three things on their wedding night—burn fish guts, pray, and sleep. In the Vulgate, in an addition stressing chastity perhaps written by Jerome, the couple waits three days before they consummate their marriage. In any case, Tobias returns to Nineveh with Azariah, his new wife, and the ten talents of silver. Tobias applies the fish gall to the eyes of his father Tobit and his sight is restored. They live happily ever after. His work done, Raphael reveals to the family his true nature and returns to heaven. He exhorts Tobit to write down what happened. The book ends with its own origin story.

Structure, Comedy, and Narrative Artistry

Whether from a single author who is lost to history or later scribes who revised it (it is likely both), Tobit is a well-designed story. The story was written in a way that presents the problems of Tobit and Sarah as thematically similar. Before they pray to die, they each have a tense verbal exchange with someone in their household—one of Sarah's female slaves, angry about being beaten, tells Sarah that she is herself to blame for the deaths of her fiancés; Tobit gets into an argument with his wife over a goat. Job likewise had a dispute with his wife before he wished that he had never been born. The prayers of Tobit and Sarah, uttered in different locales (Nineveh, Ecbatana), reach heaven at the same time. This explains why God offers one solution (sending Raphael) to resolve both problems. The story exhibits a kind of narrative artistry, an intent to give the story an organized, recognizable structure. Appreciating the book's design is not simply a literary issue. It's a theological one. It begins as a story narrated by Tobit, in the first person. But with Sarah's plotline it shifts to an omniscient narrator. Now the book tells a story Tobit is himself not aware of. Each character is aware of their own story and draws their own conclusions based on what they see. Independently, Sarah and Tobit discern their own problems and want to die. But neither sees the whole picture, which includes the odd way, by means of a deceptive angel and fish guts, that God helps them both. Not unlike the Joseph novella in Genesis 37–50, the structure of Tobit conveys that God orchestrates events and will reward the righteous, but in ways that they cannot necessarily perceive. As I have seen in my own teaching, students when learning about the book are struck by the fact that Tobit is blinded by bird poop. They, after a quick Google search, will point out that getting bird excrement in your eyes actually can make you go blind (ocular histoplasmosis). While this may be a genuine ailment, Tobit's blindness signifies a larger point—he cannot see the complex chain of events God has set in motion that will result in the restoration of his sight.

Because of Tobit's happy ending, the book can be helpfully characterized as a comedy. Here I do not mean simply that readers often find parts of it funny. Comedy is the name of a literary genre, denoting dramatic works written and performed in ancient Greece. Famous authors of such comedies include Aristophanes and Menander. Typically in such comedies, any problems the characters face are in the end resolved. All's well that ends well, as Shakespeare puts it. Comedies often end with a marriage, not unlike Tobit. Luther understood Tobit as a comedy in this sense and even went so far as to suggest that the genre of ancient Greek comedy derives from Tobit.

Tobit: A Good Man in a Cruel World

Tobit, from the tribe of Naphtali, describes himself as a righteous, Torah-observant Israelite. Before he was exiled, he would travel from northern Israel to Jerusalem to worship. The book presumes the polemical stance in the Hebrew Bible toward the northern kingdom. As recounted in 1–2 Kings, the united twelve-tribe monarchy broke up into two kingdoms, north and south. The northern kingdom did not recognize Jerusalem as its religious or political center, as it was the capital of the southern kingdom. Tobit is the exception to the rule that the northerners did not worship God correctly.

The righteousness modeled by Tobit stresses charity to the poor, or almsgiving. The Torah advocates kindness towards the needy. But for Tobit, charity has more value than that. In chapter 4 he teaches that "almsgiving delivers from death." Ben Sira 29 offers similar instruction: "Store up almsgiving in your treasury and it will rescue you from every disaster." Tobit was rescued from disaster because of his almsgiving. Charity to the poor, Tobit teaches, is a kind of investment in one's own standing with God. He didn't pray for his eyesight back, but for death. Tobit, however, was so righteous that God decided to give him a long, fulfilling life instead.

Another major aspect of Tobit's ethics is burying the dead. The Torah states that the body of an executed person must be buried before nightfall. But Tobit's commitment to the dignified disposition of fellow Israelites goes beyond any specific injunction of the Torah. It keeps him depressingly busy. There seems to be no shortage of dead Israelites. The Assyrians would kill Israelites and discard their corpses behind the city walls. One gets the impression that life in Nineveh was dangerous for the exiles.

Tobit initially prospered in exile. He became wealthy and had a senior position in the Assyrian court. He was the main purchaser for King Shalmaneser. Like Daniel and Esther, Tobit illustrates that a Jewish person can ascend to power in a Gentile court. But as a minority people, the Jews in Nineveh are exposed to the vagaries of power. Advances achieved in one era can be erased in the next. Tobit buries the dead at great risk to himself. When it becomes known that he is burying dead Israelites, the king wants him killed. Tobit loses everything and goes into hiding. It is a Joban moment. His righteousness is repaid with loss. Tobit is, however, restored by his nephew Ahiqar (more about him later). Tobit's commitment to burial also leads to his blindness. At his family's Shavuot dinner, he leaps up from the table when he learns that the body of an Israelite who was strangled is lying in the market. After burying him at night he sleeps outside by the wall of a courtyard. On it are perched several sparrows with amazing aim. If Tobit had not decided to bury

that one victim, he would not have been at that place at that time—
and would not have gone blind.

Kinship, Endogamy, and the Book of Genesis

The importance of kinship is another major teaching of the book.
The composition abounds in family language. Some scribes presumably thought it had too much. Some of the composition's family
language was over time abridged. In GI Tob 1:22, for example, Tobit
identifies Ahiqar with one term, "my nephew." But in the older GII
the verse uses two terms, "my nephew and from my kinsfolk." The
still older Aramaic version of the line from Qumran (4Q196) uses
three: Ahiqar is "the son of my brother, of my father's house and of
my family." Tobit, thinking Azariah is a fellow kinsman, often calls
him "brother." All Israelites are in a sense from the same family.
They all face the same risks, as a persecuted minority in exile. This
context gives new relevance to their ethnic identity, which the book
conveys with language of kinship.

The book's blending of ethnicity and kinship explains another of
Tobit's death-bed lessons: his sons are not to marry foreign wives.
The book unapologetically advocates for endogamy; that is, one
should marry someone within their kinship group. This intolerant
position accords with the book of Genesis. Abraham and Isaac both
urge their sons not to marry among the Canaanites. Tobit draws
on Genesis traditions in several ways. It is one of the earliest Jewish
texts to invoke Adam and Eve as a model for cisgender marriage.
How Tobias meets his future wife Sarah clearly draws on the story
in Genesis 24. After Abraham urges his son Isaac to leave Canaan
to find a wife among their kin in Haran (near Nineveh, in northern
Mesopotamia), Isaac's unnamed servant plays a prominent role
in how he finds and marries a kinswoman, Rebekah, as Azariah
helps Tobias find Sarah (also the name of Abraham's wife). Genesis
24 links the servant to a guardian angel who ensures success on

their travels; in Tobit these two roles are combined in the figure of Azariah. Comparison with Genesis also illustrates how family is thematized as a harmonious social structure. While Tobit clearly engages Genesis traditions, one major theme from that book is strikingly absent—strife within a family, famously on display between Jacob and Esau.

Ahiqar, Tobit's Wise Nephew: Tobit as an Aramaic Short Story from the Hellenistic Age

The book of Tobit was probably written in Aramaic. This is suggested by the fact that there are more Qumran manuscripts of the text in Aramaic (4) than in Hebrew (1), as mentioned above. Other factors support this conclusion as well. Tobit 1:2–3:6, also as mentioned above, is in the first person, as if it were written by Tobit. Other Jewish Aramaic texts likewise preserve narratives in the first person, purportedly written by important ancestors from the distant past such as Daniel or Enoch.

It adds verisimilitude to depict Tobit, as an Assyrian Israelite in the late eighth–early seventh centuries BCE, writing in Aramaic. It was a major language in the Assyrian kingdom at that time. Genesis presents this region as the traditional domain of the early ancestors of Israel. It situates Laban and his family in Haran (northern Mesopotamia) and presents Aramaic as their language (Gen 31:47). In the Hellenistic era, Aramaic could be regarded as the language an early ancestor like Tobit would have used.

One relatively minor character, Ahiqar, sheds light onto the ancient literary Aramaic milieu in which the composition of the book of Tobit should be understood. He is Tobit's nephew. When he becomes king, Esarhaddon (r. 681–669 BCE) appoints him to a higher post in the Assyrian court than Tobit had. Ahiqar becomes, as the Qumran Aramaic form of Tobit 1:22 confirms, the Rabshakeh, or "chief cupbearer." This is a senior position in the

Assyrian court (for a striking depiction of an Assyrian Rabshakeh, see 2 Kings 18). Ahiqar becomes, like Joseph in Genesis, second only to the king.

Ahiqar, like Tobit, is a victim of the unjust exercise of monarchic power. The full story is not in the book, but it is clear that Ahiqar's own nephew, Nadab, is to blame. Tobit 14 states that Nadab deceived his uncle and tried without success to have him killed, and that Nadab fell into the trap he set for Ahiqar. The book of Tobit likely only alludes to this story because it presumes its readers were familiar with it. In 1907 a large cache of Aramaic documents was discovered at an island named Elephantine in southern Egypt (near what is today the border between Egypt and Sudan), at the site of an ancient military colony manned by Judeans and other peoples. These texts include correspondence, contracts, and business documents that provide an impression of community life at that ancient outpost.

The Elephantine corpus includes a lengthy text, in Aramaic, about Ahiqar. It is in the first person, like Tobit. In that text Ahiqar is an important figure in the court of King Esarhaddon, as in Tobit 1. He raises his nephew, named Nadin, as his own son and arranges to have him succeed him in court. But Nadin schemes against his benevolent uncle and arranges to have him killed. The plot is unsuccessful. One of the men, Nabusumiskun, sent to kill Ahiqar had been previously rescued by him from being falsely accused of murder. Nabusumiskun, remembering this kindness, does not kill Ahiqar but instead hides him, as one of his slaves. Tobit 14 was likely written with knowledge of a version of the story recounted in the Elephantine text about Ahiqar and his nephew. Also in this Elephantine text, after the narrative about Ahiqar there is a collection of over a hundred sayings and proverbs attributed to him.

The Elephantine Ahiqar text is written on a palimpsest, on top of an erased business document about import and export duties that includes a legible date—by our calendar, 475 BCE. The Elephantine Ahiqar text is older than the book of Tobit. It supports the position that Tobit drew on an older story about Ahiqar. Moreover, Ahiqar, while attested in the Bible only in Tobit, was known throughout the ancient world as a legendary sage. Various versions of the Ahiqar narrative attested at Elephantine, along with collections of sayings, spread throughout the ancient world and survive in a wide array of languages, including Arabic, Church Slavonic, Armenian, Romanian, and even Sogdian (a central Asian language).

Because of Ahiqar's fame, people in various cultures claimed him as one of their own. This is evident from a text from Hellenistic Mesopotamia written in Akkadian known as the *Uruk List of Kings and Sages*, dated to 165 BCE (thus roughly contemporary with Tobit). The text pairs sages with the kings in whose reign they lived. For King Esarhaddon, this text says "Aba-Enlil-dari was the sage, whom the Arameans call Ahiqar." Tobit 1 and the Elephantine text also link Ahiqar to this Assyrian king. According to the *Uruk List*, there was a local Mesopotamian sage by the name of Aba-Enlil-dari, whom the Arameans knew by a different name—Ahiqar. "Aramean" in the text may denote a distinct ethnic group, a North Syrian people whose language was Aramaic, but it may simply mean that Ahiqar is associated with Aramaic, which at the time was spoken by many peoples. Aramaic was by the Hellenistic period widespread across the ancient Near East because it was an important administrative language not only for the Assyrian Empire, but also then the Babylonian and Persian empires, a range from the eighth to the fourth centuries BCE.

There is also a Greek example of the appropriation of Ahiqar legends. It is incorporated into the life story of Aesop, a famous man of wisdom in the Greek world to whom many sayings and fables involving animals were attributed (still often read today as children's literature); ample animal fables are also ascribed to Ahiqar in the Elephantine text. The *Life of Aesop*, an ancient text that survives in various later versions, incorporates part of the Ahiqar legend known from the Elephantine text. Aesop becomes the trusted advisor of the king of Babylon, named Lycurgus. Aesop adopts a child named Helios as his son. He educates him and arranges for him to succeed him in court. Helios, however, writes a false letter which alleges that Aesop is a traitor. Lycurgus orders that he be killed; the captain tasked with the job does not carry it out because Aesop is a good man, not unlike the story in the Elephantine Ahiqar text.

The *Uruk List* and the *Life of Aesop* provide Greek and Mesopotamian evidence that in antiquity people from disparate cultures knew the Ahiqar legend and appropriated it to valorize local sages (Aba-Enlil-dari and Aesop, respectively). The book of Tobit engages in the same cultural politics. It, like these other texts, appropriates and "nativizes" the figure of Ahiqar. In the Elephantine text, it is not at all clear that Ahiqar is Jewish. At the very least this text attests a kind of Judaism that is at odds with that of Hebrew Bible. Several times the Ahiqar sayings, for example, invoke Shamash, a Mesopotamian sun god. But in Tobit, Ahiqar is unambiguously an Israelite. He literally becomes a member of the family. He is now the son of Tobit's brother, a lineage nowhere in the Elephantine text. Tobit is *older* than Ahiqar. Ahiqar's wisdom, righteousness, and success become a consequence of Tobit's moral leadership of his family. Appropriation of Ahiqar may also explain why the book depicts Tobit uttering a sequence of proverbs (ch. 4). The incorporation of Ahiqar into Tobit's family shows that this composition did not only draw on native Jewish literary traditions, such as Genesis. The book of Tobit was also informed by a broader, international Aramaic literary culture in which legends about Ahiqar were prominent. Since Aramaic was widely known in the Hellenistic period, knowledge of the Ahiqar legend could and did circulate in this language throughout the ancient world. Other Qumran Aramaic texts contemporary with Tobit also suggest this language was a medium used by Jewish scribes to encounter and appropriate lore from other cultures. The Qumran *Book of Giants*, for example, a narrative about giants who lived before the flood (Gen 6:1–4), names one of them Gilgamesh—the name of the famous hero of Mesopotamian epic.

Understanding Tobit as written in Aramaic also suggests that Jewish scribes translated it from Aramaic into Hebrew (recall that one Tobit text from Qumran is in Hebrew). As Ahiqar, a legendary sage known throughout many cultures, was transformed into an early ancestor of Israel, so the book of Tobit itself became Jewish in another way, by becoming a story told in Hebrew.

Asmodeus, Jerusalem, and Tobit's Persian Milieu

Sarah, it will be recalled, is afflicted by Asmodeus in the Persian city of Ecbatana. Asmodeus is a well-known demon in Persia. His name derives from two words in Avestan, an ancient Persian language—*aeshma* and *daēuua*, producing together "demon of wrath." In Persian literature he is a major demon, often called simply Aeshma ("Wrath"). The *Yasnas*, an important text of Zoroastrianism (the traditional, pre-Islamic religion of Iran), describes demons and wicked humans as allied with Aeshma. The behavior of Asmodeus in Tobit is also consistent with the malicious conduct ascribed to demons in Mesopotamia. They often seek to undermine harmony within a family—by killing a newborn, for example, or seducing the husband. Asmodeus, by preventing Sarah from marrying, is a negative counterpart to the positive portrayals of marriage and family in Tobit.

At the end of the book, on his deathbed Tobit becomes a sort of prophet. He urges Tobias and his family to leave Nineveh because he "predicts" an event proclaimed by the prophet Nahum—that Nineveh will be destroyed because of its wickedness (the Babylonians razed the city in 612 BCE). Tobit also predicts that the temple will be destroyed and then rebuilt. The exiles will return to Jerusalem and enjoy a blissful existence. Gentiles, Tobit claims, will abandon their idols and worship God. The construction of the Second Temple in 516 BCE becomes part of an eschatological, utopian future. The eschatological conversion of the Gentiles espoused by Tobit is a common trope in post-exilic prophetic texts (e.g., Isa 60).

Tobit's inclusivist message regarding Gentiles is at odds with the book's consistent stress on endogamy. His blessing and deathbed testament (chs. 13–14) have been understood as secondary additions to the book. It is also possible that Tobit, formerly blind, acquires an enhanced form of vision, a kind of prophetic sight, by seeing the angel Raphael in his true form.

The book ends on a decidedly Jerusalemite note. The book, set in exile, is framed by the city of Jerusalem. At the beginning, when in northern Israel, Tobit would travel there to worship; at the end of the book, it's the eventual home of the pious exiles. Tobit, however, urges his family to move not to Jerusalem but to Persia. Tobias and his family relocate to Ecbatana, his wife's former home in Media. Tobias has a long and prosperous life there.

The book of Tobit is likely a product of the ancient Jewish community of Persia, or at least the eastern Diaspora, not unlike Daniel 1–6 or Esther. The book does, however, have geographical errors, suggesting that at least some people involved in its scribal transmission were not familiar with Media. Ecbatana is roughly 200 miles from Rages, but Tobit 5 states it is a two-day journey on foot; this is likely why some versions of the verse change its locations.

Tobit is nevertheless helpfully understood against the backdrop of Persian culture. The book utilizes native Persian demonological traditions (Asmodeus/Aeshma). The Assyrian court's hostile reaction toward Tobit burying the dead may presume Persian cultural values. Zoroastrianism prohibits the internment of the dead in the earth; corpses are thought to pollute it. The proper disposal of the dead, according to the Zoroastrian text *Vendidād*, is to expose the corpse to carrion-eating birds. Even the dog as Tobias's travel companion can be understood against the background of Persian culture. The Hebrew Bible takes a highly negative stance toward dogs, treating them as violent and unclean animals. Some medieval Jewish versions of Tobit omit the dog entirely. In ancient Persia, by contrast, dogs were highly regarded. The *Vendidād* stipulates, for example, punishments for harming various kinds of dogs. According to the *Bundahishn*, another Zoroastrian text, dogs were created to oppose demons (as were chickens!). So understood, the dog in Tobit would not be a family pet but another form of divine assistance. The composition of Tobit in Aramaic is also consistent with an eastern milieu.

The book of Tobit is moreover important in the history of Jews in Persia. Jews lived there as a minority people for centuries. It was held among Persian Jews that the book of Tobit recounts the community's origins. In recent years the first manuscript of Tobit in Judeo-Persian (a Persian language in Hebrew script) has come to light, demonstrating that Tobit was read by Persian Jews. The book of Tobit was likely written in Persia, and definitely read and transmitted there.

Conclusion

The story of Tobit, which has its origins as a Hellenistic Aramaic short story, became a book of the Christian Bible about one family that engages issues which are important for all families—marriage and burial. The book tells the story of this family to illustrate to its readers the value of righteousness. Tobit experiences genuine hardship and when he prays to die, God responds by sending an angel who ensures that Tobit instead lives a long, satisfying life with his sight restored. This tale was particularly relevant in the Diaspora context in which the book was apparently composed. Jews, as a minority people in a Gentile world, experienced discrimination and persecution. In this context, the idea that God rescues Tobit from adversity because of his righteousness takes on new significance, as does the book's teaching that how God helps the pious is not always evident to them. The composition encourages piety and Torah observance as a response to hardship. It is unfortunate that many readers of scripture are not familiar with the book of Tobit.

Guide for Further Reading

Bledsoe, Seth A. "Ahiqar and Other Legendary Sages." Pages 289–309 in *The Wiley Blackwell Companion to Wisdom Literature*. Edited by Samuel L. Adams and Matthew Goff. West Sussex: Wiley Blackwell, 2020.

Fitzmyer, Joseph A. *Tobit*. Berlin: de Gruyter, 2003.

Jacobs, Naomi. *Delicious Prose: Reading the Tale of Tobit with Food and Drink*. Leiden: Brill, 2018.

5

Judith, the Queen of Hearts

Judith is a rare example of scriptural book in which a woman takes center stage. While there are other prominent women in the Bible, such as Esther or Ruth, Judith is in a league all her own. She is seductive and deadly. When the powerful Assyrian army threatens Israel, Judith tempts its general Holofernes with sexual allure, and when they are alone together in his tent, she chops off his head. Judith, at least in the West, has attracted perhaps more attention than any other figure examined in this volume. One of the oldest surviving written poems in English is a retelling of Judith (in the eleventh-century Nowell Codex, which also includes the epic *Beowulf*) and one of the first full-length Hollywood movies tells the story of Judith—*Judith of Bethulia* (1914). She has been revered or disparaged as a hero, a revolutionary, a queen, a seductress, a *femme fatale*, and a feminist icon. The diversity of ways she has been imagined correlates with her ambiguous depiction in the book of Judith, as a woman who adheres to and transgresses patriarchal social norms. The figure of Judith serves as a kind of lens with which to gauge ways in which people over the centuries have expressed their support for, anxiety over, and hostility toward women with power.

The Book of Judith: Language and Scriptural Status

The oldest evidence for the book of Judith is in Greek. Judith is attested in the three major Septuagint manuscripts from the

The Apocrypha: A Guide. Matthew Goff, Oxford University Press. © Oxford University Press 2024.
DOI: 10.1093/9780190060770.003.0005

fourth and fifth centuries that comprise our oldest versions of the Old Testament: Alexandrinus, Sinaiticus, and Vaticanus. While some scholars argue the Greek is a translation of a lost Hebrew or Aramaic text, many contend that Judith was composed originally in Greek, written in a way that mimics the style of the Septuagint.

While the issue cannot be decided conclusively, understanding Judith as written in Greek would explain a key fact—why the book is not in the Hebrew Bible and thus not in the Jewish canon of scripture. The Dead Sea Scrolls include no ancient manuscripts of Judith. That we have no evidence for Judith in ancient Hebrew accords with a claim made by Origen (second–third centuries CE). In his *Letter to Africanus* he states that Jews told him they do not use Judith or Tobit and that those books are not among their "Hebrew apocrypha." Elsewhere he uses the term "apocrypha" to signify writings which, he claims, Jews retained while hiding them from people. The word is often deployed in late antiquity in a disparaging sense, by authors who want to distinguish "apocryphal" writings from scripture (see Chapter 1). Origen in this letter suggests that rabbis preserved some non-biblical Hebrew writings. This is possible, even though they discouraged Jews from reading such books (here also see Chapter 1), since rabbinic literature demonstrates knowledge of Hebrew texts not in the Jewish Bible, such as Ben Sira. But according to Origen, Judith, like Tobit, is not among such Jewish apocryphal works. Jerome claims to know of an Aramaic version of Judith (also discussed below), but this assertion cannot be corroborated.

There are several Judith texts in Hebrew, such as the *Megillat Yehudit* (the *Scroll of Judith*). They are much later than Origen or the Dead Sea Scrolls. These compositions are medieval, often loosely translated from the Latin Vulgate. Judith was in a sense "re-Judaized." The Hebrew Judith tales often associate her story of saving Israel from Holofernes's invasion with Hanukkah, which commemorates the victory of the Maccabees over the Seleucid king Antiochus (discussed in Chapters 12–13). Several of these texts add a story similar to Judith about a sister of Judas Maccabee named Hannah (there is no such woman in 1–2 Maccabees). Her brothers save her from being married to a powerful Gentile by cutting off his head, a Judithean trope. Also reflecting the assimilation of Judith into a Jewish milieu, the book was translated into Yiddish in the sixteenth century.

While early Protestants placed the book in the Apocrypha, Judith remains in the Old Testament in both the Catholic and Orthodox traditions. In *1 Clement*, the earliest reference to Judith, she is praised by Clement, one of the earliest bishops of Rome (late first century CE), as a brave and pious woman. Some early Christians revered the book. There were, however, differing opinions about the scriptural status of Judith. In his preface to Judith in the Vulgate, Jerome describes the book's authority as contested, even though, he says, it is included among the "Hagiographa" of the Jews. This term has long denoted the third section of the Jewish Bible, the "(Sacred) Writings." Perhaps Jerome's use of the term indicates that this canonical sense of the phrase was not yet firmly in place. Elsewhere Jerome counts Judith among the apocrypha, which he distinguishes from canonical scripture (see Chapter 1). Jerome likely claims that Judith is a non-canonical text preserved by Jews. This is at odds with Origen's assertion that Judith is not among the "Hebrew apocrypha." Their conflicting testimony may reflect differing views in late antiquity regarding the non-biblical books Jews preserved. That Judith is not attested in Jewish sources until the medieval period accords more with Origen's claims about Judith than Jerome's.

Given Jerome's commitment to translating Old Testament texts from Hebrew into Latin, it is odd that he translated the book at all. In his preface to Judith, he asserts that he has access to an Aramaic version of the work, as mentioned above. There is, however, no evidence to corroborate this claim. The Vulgate version of Judith is nevertheless quite different from that of the Septuagint. Many of the differences accord more readily with Jerome's own interests (discussed below), rather than a putative lost Aramaic Judith text.

There is a smattering of rabbinic evidence for Judith in Aramaic. The rabbi Nahmanides (thirteenth century) cites in his commentary on the Torah a small portion of Judith 1 in Aramaic. He asserts that the passage comes from the *Scroll of Susanna* (*Megillat Shushan*). The inclusion of Judith in a work associated with Susanna (see Chapter 10) suggests Nahmanides is not citing Jerome's Aramaic Judith, but rather a version of the *Book of Women*. In Syriac Christianity, a traditional mode of Christianity in the Middle East, several biblical books in which women were prominent circulated as an anthology distinct from the Bible, called the *Book of Women*. It would often include Ruth, Esther, Susanna, Judith, and the *Acts of Paul and Thecla*, an early Christian text about a female martyr, Thecla. Nahmanides was also familiar with the Wisdom of Solomon, in a form mediated in the Syriac tradition (see further Chapter 7). His citation of *Megillat Shushan* is likely another example of this rabbi drawing on biblical books as found in the Syriac Christian tradition. This title suggests that Nahmanides is citing a *Book of Women* that begins with the story of Susanna. Syriac is a Christian form of Aramaic, which would explain why the rabbi cites Judith in Aramaic.

The Story of Judith: The Weak Defeat the Strong

The book has sixteen chapters and falls into two roughly equal parts. The first half (chs. 1–7) focuses on the powerful Assyrian army and its leaders. Nebuchadnezzar, who is the king of Assyria, conquers much of the ancient Near East. He appoints his top general Holofernes to conquer regions west of Assyria, including Israel. His forces are brutal and overpowering. When areas surrender, Holofernes destroys the local shrines and makes people worship Nebuchadnezzar.

The looming Assyrian threat terrifies Judah. Leaders in Jerusalem order two towns in the highlands of northern Israel, Bethulia and

Betomestaim, to block strategic narrow passes in the mountains through which Holofernes and his army would have to travel to reach Jerusalem. Holofernes summons Canaanite leaders to learn more about the region. Achior, leader of the Ammonites, tells him about Israel. He espouses a view also expressed in Deuteronomy— that when the Israelites follow the covenant, their God is with them. So unless they sin, they cannot be defeated. Achior's description of Israel angers the general, who considers him overly sympathetic to his enemies. He hands him over to Bethulia, the first Israelite city he plans to destroy. This city appears nowhere else in the Bible and there is no evidence it was ever an actual town. Bethulia is, however, central in the book of Judith. Holofernes encamps his vast army outside the city and seizes control of the springs that supply its water. The town's leaders are mortified and agree to surrender in five days.

Enter Judith. She is the main figure of the book's second half (chs. 8–16). She is brave, pious, rich, and gorgeous. Judith is also a widow. Widows were often destitute in ancient Israel, since the extent to which women unattached to men could support themselves financially was limited. But Judith received a large inheritance when her husband Manasseh died. She rebukes the leaders of Bethulia and makes them abandon their plans to surrender. Leave everything to me, she says. And they do.

After praying to God, she adorns herself with fine clothes, ointment, and jewelry. She goes over to the Assyrian camp with her (unnamed) female slave. Judith falsely claims that she wants to defect to their side. She requests to meet Holofernes, claiming that she can give him key intelligence about how to defeat Israel. The book shows no qualms with Judith lying to help her people. She prays to God that her "deceitful words" may hurt her enemies.

Judith spends several days in the Assyrian camp. They allow her to go to a valley regularly, where she prays each night. When Holofernes's slave Bagoas invites Judith to drink wine with his "lord" Holofernes in his private tent, it being clear that he intends to seduce her, she replies, "Who am I to refuse my lord? Whatever pleases him I will do at once." Judith's statement is a clever double-entendre that plays on the word "lord." Her response lets Bagoas think she is receptive to Holofernes's wishes, but she in fact affirms her loyalty to the Lord, the God of Israel. Alone with Judith in his tent, the general drinks too much wine and passes out. Judith beheads him with his own sword. She leaves the camp with her slave, who has the head hidden in a food bag. The soldiers, accustomed to her leaving the camp to pray, let them go. They return to Bethulia and display Holofernes's head. The Israelites attack and defeat the Assyrians, who panic when they realize their general is dead. Because of Judith, Bethulia and thus all Israel achieve victory against an enemy which vastly outnumbers them.

Is Judith a Feminist Book? Judith as an Exceptional Woman in Patriarchal Israel

Judith has been hailed as a feminist icon. Centuries ago, Christine de Pizan in her *The Book of the City of Ladies* (1405) extolled Judith as a scriptural model for women attaining political power. Judith is indeed a leader among men. She is decisive and fearless when a powerful man threatens her people, unlike the men who run Bethulia. She forces them to agree to her plan (without telling them what it is), rather than the other way around. As a wealthy, unmarried woman without children, she enjoys independence and autonomy. Her life is not defined by placating or deferring to men.

If women find the book of Judith to be an empowering resource, that's great. But it was in all likelihood written by men immersed in a patriarchal culture. The book presumes a basic axiom of patriarchal societies—that women are subordinate to men. When she displays Holofernes's head in Bethulia, Judith exclaims: "the

Lord has struck him down by the hand of a woman" (ch. 13). She attributes Israel's deliverance from Assyria not to herself but to God—that he did so through a "mere" woman illustrates this point. Assuming patriarchal views from the period, a woman defeating a powerful man is improbable, so her victory must testify to God's power. Through Judith, God demonstrates that he, not Holofernes or Nebuchadnezzar, is the ultimate alpha male.

While in Bethulia, Judith exerts power in the public sphere, but when she is in the Assyrian camp, she utilizes a type of power available to women in a patriarchal society—that they manipulate powerful men behind the scenes with deceit and sexual allure to get what they want. Judith's victory song at the end of the book asserts that she used her beauty against Holofernes. She presents herself to him wearing beautiful attire and jewels, successfully enticing him to desire her sexually, leading him to lose self-control, which is his undoing. Judith takes advantage of the male presumption that women do not constitute real threats. An Israelite man would not have been allowed to be alone with Holofernes in his tent, much less enter the Assyrian camp.

Feminism can be defined by the conviction that all people, regardless of gender, are equal and should have access to the same opportunities. Judith never advocates for such an ideal. She is an exceptional woman with wealth and power. She does not face the difficulties many women endured in antiquity or in later periods of history. Judith subverts prevailing gender norms during a political crisis. Once the Assyrian threat has passed, she never challenges the male leaders of Bethulia and returns to a life of private devotion. Judith's bravery ensures that Israel's male leadership is not disrupted. While gravely concerned about Assyrian oppression of Israel, Judith never brings up the subordination of Israelite women to Israelite men. Consistent with the book's interest in Judith rather than women in general, she is literally the only woman in the story who is named.

Gender Hierarchies and Power Dynamics: Judith as (Male) Israel, (Female) Israel as God's Wife

In a patriarchal culture, the tenet that men are strong and women are weak is normative. This perspective can give gender a hierarchizing potency. The application of male or female gender codes to people is a way to make assertions about power. Associating people with traits regarded within a culture as male is a way to convey that they are strong, and with traits understood as female that they are weak, irrespective of their biological gender. In terms of interpreting the book of Judith in its ancient context, at issue is not gender fluidity in the sense that men and women can "perform" their gender however they wish. It's more an issue of gender ambiguity via "code-switching," with stereotypical traits of women applied to men, and vice versa, as a way to articulate how people relate to each other within a social hierarchy.

Holofernes, and by extension Nebuchadnezzar, in relation to God is weak. The book conveys this point by de-masculinizing him and associating him at times with feminine tropes. Being overpowered by a woman, against the backdrop of the patriarchal culture that produced the book, is a demeaning way to die. Holofernes is emasculated. His decapitation is a kind of castration. The general's desire to force himself upon Judith sexually highlights his virility, which constitutes a key aspect of his masculinity. In antiquity, a common view was that a strong man could control his body and its urges. While sexual violence is endemic in military conflicts, discipline and self-control during war were espoused in antiquity as important male virtues. Male celibacy as an ideal during warfare is expressed in the David-Bathsheba story, for example, when the soldier Uriah refuses to sleep with his wife. That Holofernes succumbs to his sexual desires and drinks too much wine during a military campaign demonstrates his lack of self-restraint and thus that he is weak. He is in a sense feminized.

The book exhibits a rich ambiguity with regard to Judith and gender. On the one hand, as a woman she serves as a "weak" vessel through which God demonstrates his dominion. On the other, while Holofernes can be considered feminine, Judith's gender codes are at times masculine. Unlike Holofernes, she never loses self-control. Her mode of killing has a masculine dimension. Killing the general with a sword is a phallic mode of murder. He wanted to penetrate her. But she penetrated him.

Judith's gender ambiguity, as a woman coded as masculine, is important for understanding why a woman stands at the center of the story. She is reasonably understood as representing Israel. A woman symbolizes a male-dominated society. To understand the sexual dynamics at work, it is helpful to examine Judith's town, Bethulia.

While Judith was likely written in Greek, the city's name suggests it was written with some knowledge of Hebrew. Bethulia resonates with the Hebrew word for a female virgin, *betulah*. The city is the "virgin" which Holofernes wants to violate through military force. The town's placement at a narrow pathway in the mountains, which Holofernes must enter to conquer Jerusalem, emphasizes Bethulia's vulnerability and its thematization as a site of sexual penetration. Sex can demonstrate in a visceral way who has power over whom. The person being penetrated, regardless of their gender, could be viewed as submissive to and weaker than the penetrator, and thus, in relation to that person, female. Sex can thus function as a potent metaphor in military conflicts. One example of this point, from a different cultural context, are the *glandes Perusinae*. These are lead slingshot bullets used in combat in 41/40 BCE. Octavian (Augustus), who became the first Roman emperor, besieged the Italian city of Perugia, where forces hostile to him were assembled. They inscribed vulgar messages on sling-stones which they hurled at Octavian's army, such as "I seek Octavian's asshole," or "Loose Octavius, sit on this." These bullets are arrowhead shaped and were understood as phallic. The Latin word *glans* (pl. *glandes*) can denote both sling-stones and the head of the penis. By lobbing these stones during a battle, one side framed its violence against the other in sexual terms, as a kind of rape propaganda, to assert dominance over their opponents. They wanted the enemy to regard them as the (male) penetrator and themselves as the (female) penetrated.

The virginal name of Bethulia allows Holofernes's planned devastation of the city to be understood in analogously sexualized terms. Its name conveys that the town is the feminine victim of masculine aggression, perpetrated by the Assyrian army. But whereas with the *glandes Perusinae* soldiers depict their enemies in derisively feminine ways, Bethulia names *itself* as the vulnerable female, the virgin. The book of Judith emphasizes Israel's weakness in relation to the Assyrian threat to underscore that victory is only possible with the help of God. There is a gendered dimension to Israel's depiction of itself as weak. By achieving victory through a woman, God reverses the sexual dynamics. The weak (female) defeats the strong (male).

Judith's gender ambiguity, as a woman depicted in masculine terms, underscores a larger point—that she represents Israel. Her name literally means "Jewish woman" (or "Jewess"). Israel was a patriarchal society, so it may seem odd for it to be represented by a woman. The Hebrew Bible describes the relationship between God and Israel as a covenant. Membership in the covenant is defined in male terms, through circumcision of the phallus. The covenant is a legal bond that formalizes Israel's acknowledgment that God is superior, and that Israel will obey him. In return, God extends his protection to Israel.

The Bible expresses the hierarchal relationship between God and Israel in terms of gender. Biblical texts describe the covenant with the metaphor of a marriage. God is the husband and Israel the wife. The prophets Hosea and Ezekiel describe Israel's violation of the covenant by imagining the nation as an unfaithful wife and God as a cuckolded husband. At times the prophets convey this point with disturbing, explicit imagery (if you don't believe me, read

Ezekiel 16 and 23). As a social institution in a patriarchal culture, marriage was an arrangement between two unequal parties and thus aptly signifies the covenant between God and Israel. Casting male-dominated Israel as the female in the covenant relationship articulates its inferior status with respect to God.

By symbolizing Israel with a woman, the book of Judith is consistent with the scriptural tradition of representing the nation as God's wife. But while the prophets portray Israel as a disobedient wife to explain how God will punish her (often by sending invading enemies), the book of Judith makes the opposite point, which Achior stressed to Holofernes—that when Israel is loyal to God (i.e., a "good wife"), he will protect her from even the most powerful enemy.

Judith, Judges, and Scriptural Traditions

Along with the covenant, the book of Judith utilizes other scriptural traditions. In her prayer for success against Holofernes, Judith invokes the rape of Dinah (Genesis 34), urging God to replicate in the present crisis Simon's vengeance against the men of Shechem. That she cuts off Holofernes's head with his sword recalls David, who likewise decapitates Goliath with his own weapon. Similarity between the violent acts of David and Judith has been recognized. Michelangelo, for example, paired these two scenes on the ceiling of the Sistine Chapel.

That Judith rises to power to save Israel during a crisis accords with the book of Judges. This book presents the judges as brutal men who save Israel from powerful Canaanite enemies. They are not kings but are regarded as leaders because of their military prowess. Like Judith, the judges often combine violence and deceit, as in the case of Ehud. This judge gets close to the Moabite king Eglon, under the pretense of relaying a special message from God to him, and thrusts a blade deep into his stomach, killing him. Judges also tells the story of Jael. She kills a Canaanite general named Sisera in a way that resembles Judith's murder of Holofernes: when Sisera is asleep in her tent, Jael hammers a tent-peg into his skull. It is likely that this story from Judges helped shape the Judith tale. The medieval Hebrew Judith tales also connect her to the judges tradition. In the *Megillat Yehudit*, for example, Judith does not retire from public life at the end of the story but becomes a judge.

Nebuchadnezzar, King of Assyria: The Construction of the Past in the Book of Judith

If the book of Judith utilizes scriptural traditions, a key problem arises. Why, when compared to biblical books, does it get so much wrong? As anyone who has taken Introduction to the Old Testament knows, Nebuchadnezzar was a king of Babylon (r. 605–562 BCE). But in Judith he is king of the Assyrian Empire. The book begins in the twelfth year of his reign, which would be 593 BCE. The Babylonians, however, destroyed the Assyrian kingdom in 609 BCE. Early in the sixth century BCE, Nebuchadnezzar devastated Jerusalem and deported many of its leading citizens into exile in Babylonia. But in Judith the Israelites have already returned from exile.

Many scholars have argued that such errors are intentional. They are in line with Martin Luther, who argued that the book's author deliberately added mistakes to convey that it is not a work of history but fiction. However, historical datapoints like the ones above, which professors like me make students memorize, were not necessarily regarded as bedrock, inviolable information in antiquity. While distinct empires, the Assyrian and Babylonian kingdoms are both Mesopotamian. Some ancient texts conflate the two. The *Uruk King List* from Hellenistic Babylonia, mentioned in the preceding chapter, presents Assyrian and Babylonian kings as part of a single sequence of kings, as if they were leaders of the same polity. Nebuchadnezzar as king of the Assyrians should not simply be identified as a historical error (which it is). Readers should ask what the book's construal of the past accomplishes.

In the biblical tradition, Babylon is associated with loss and destruction—devastation that, as Jeremiah proclaims, Israel deserved because it strayed from God. With Assyria the situation is different. In 2 Kings their massive army, when encamped nearby to destroy Jerusalem, is miraculously annihilated by God. Judith's theme of divine deliverance from a powerful enemy, in terms of the scriptural tradition, is much more compatible with Assyria than Babylonia. Envisioning the famous king Nebuchadnezzar as Assyrian makes him better suited to this key theme of Judith. As plaintively expressed in Baruch (see Chapter 9), while being sent into exile is punishment of Israel for its sins, the end of the exile demonstrates the renewal of Israel's commitment to God. In Judith, Israel is pious rather than disobedient with respect to God. It fits the book's purposes to imagine the story as taking place after the exile, not before or during.

The Maccabean crisis also likely shaped Judith's presentation of historical events. The villain in that story is Antiochus IV Epiphanes, ruler of the Seleucid, or Syrian, Empire. That Nebuchadnezzar in Judith is an Assyrian king may reflect a historical memory of Antiochus. A general of Antiochus who leads campaigns against Israel is named Nicanor. In 1 and 2 Maccabees, Nicanor is beheaded, evoking Judith's decapitation of Holofernes. The Maccabean victory against Antiochus is also compatible with a major theme in Judith, that when Israel is loyal, God will save them from even a powerful Gentile enemy.

The book of Judith was likely written after the Maccabean crisis took place in the 160s BCE. Understanding Judith as post-Maccabean would explain the ease with which it reworks events regarding Assyria and Babylonia which took place centuries earlier. The book is likely a product of the Hasmonean period (142–63 BCE), when a Jewish monarchy ruled Israel, whose descendants successfully led the Maccabean revolt. The Judithean themes of victory and deliverance accord with the triumphant nationalism of the period. Also, in the book the leadership of Israel includes a "council of elders" (sometimes translated as "senate"; *gerousia*) that holds session in Jerusalem. This reflects political innovations introduced by the Seleucid king Antiochus III around 200 BCE. Understanding Judith as written in Greek suggests it was written in the Diaspora, but the possibility that it was composed in Palestine cannot be ruled out.

Judith's Strange Journey: From Paragon of Chastity to Dominatrix

Over the centuries Judith, as a resolute woman who saves Israel, and who entices and murders a man, has had her admirers and detractors. The figure of Judith has often been used by people to articulate their views on a range of gender issues, such as women with power in patriarchal contexts or the complex array of male reactions to the female body, which include desire, anxiety, and revulsion.

In terms of the early reception of Judith, the latter mélange of issues is spectacularly on display with regard to Jerome. As discussed above, he translated Judith into Latin. He admits in its preface that he produced more of a loose paraphrase of the book than a strict translation. Jerome translated it, he asserts, not "word for word" but "sense for sense." Comparison of the book of Judith in the Latin Vulgate and the Greek Septuagint suggests he did just that. Like many Christians in his day, Jerome valued asceticism, a form of spiritual devotion that rejects base physical concerns. He was a fierce advocate of celibacy. In his preface to Judith, he praises her as a paragon of chastity, an example both women and men should follow. His translation of Judith expresses the same point. For example, in the Vulgate, not the Septuagint, Judith 15 states that God rewarded Judith with the strength to kill Holofernes because "you have acted courageously (literally, 'like a man'); and your heart has been strengthened, because you have loved chastity, and after your husband you have not known another." Judith's decision not to remarry is for Jerome the key to understanding the story. God gave her the strength to kill Holofernes as a reward for her celibacy. Jerome's transformation of Judith into a celibate hero had profound consequences since the Vulgate held sway for centuries as the Bible of Catholicism. With his translation of Judith he was able to endow his own hostile views toward sexuality with biblical authority.

Jerome also promoted anti-sex views in allegorical interpretations of the book. In his *Letter to Furia* he writes that Judith's defeat of Holofernes teaches that "chastity beheads lust." Judith's murder of the general, so understood, demonstrates that natural feelings of sexual desire can and should be overcome. A venerable Christian tradition developed of pairing Judith with Mary, the virgin mother of Jesus, also revered as a female symbol of chastity. The two women are connected, for example, in the fourth-century poem *Psychomachia* by Prudentius.

In early modern Europe, Judith became one of the most popular characters in the Bible. Many operas and plays dramatized her story. Mozart and Vivaldi both composed Judith oratorios. There was a virtual cottage industry of Judith art. Well-known artists, such as Lucas Cranach (1472–1553) and Caravaggio (1573–1610), produced famous portraits of Judith. Modern-era artists such as Gustav Klimt (1862–1918) and Jean Cocteau (1889–1963) also made Judith art. The portrayals of Judith by the Renaissance artist Artemisia Gentileschi (1597–ca. 1651) are particularly interesting since she was a woman (most painters at the time being men) and a rape victim, by another artist. Gentileschi's *Judith Slaying Holofernes* (1620–1621), which depicts Judith as unflinching and resolute when killing the man who sought to have sex with her, has been understood as a way Gentileschi engaged her own sexual trauma (Figure 5.1).

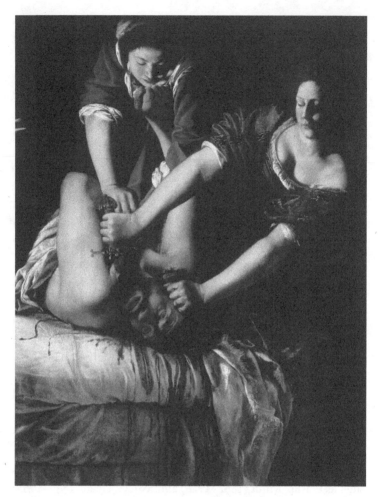

Figure 5.1 Artemisia Gentileschi, *Judith Slaying Holofernes* (1620–1621). Holofernes here struggles against Judith; in the book of Judith she kills him while he is passed out. Also, unlike in the text, here Judith's female slave helps pin Holofernes down.

Other women were interested in the image of Judith for different sexual reasons. In the Renaissance, courtesans (prostitutes for an elite male clientele) would hang portraits of her in the boudoir. It was good for business to associate themselves with Judith, understood as a woman of wealth, sex appeal, and beauty. For more aspirational reasons, lower-class bordellos likewise installed Judith art.

Judith was also marshaled to support the acquisition of political power by women. Earlier I brought up de Pizan's medieval proto-feminist tract, *The City of Ladies*. In the sixteenth century an important issue for many European political observers was that the monarchic system, despite being male dominated, was putting women in positions of supreme power, as queens. People could and did associate these women with Judith, a woman with divinely sanctioned power, to help legitimize their rule, which to many men seemed, while technically legitimate, problematic. Queen Elizabeth I of England (r. 1558–1603) was praised as a Protestant Judith. The poet Richard Barnfield in his collection of verse *Cynthia* (1595) praised the queen as "a second Judith in Jerusalem." Her cousin, the Catholic Mary I (Queen of Scots, r. 1542–1567) was also understood as a kind of Judith. John Knox in his *First Blast of the Trumpet against the Monstrous Regiment of Women* (1558) argues that Judith symbolism does not support rule by women. Male dominion is an inherent part of the natural order. While God is capable of allowing exceptions to this rule, he continues, the Bible illustrates that instances of female rule such as Deborah or Judith are restricted to the distant past. For him, Judith can be even further dismissed because it is in the Apocrypha.

Many other early modern Europeans, both Catholic and Protestant, highlighted another aspect of Judith's potency as a symbol: as someone who murders a powerful leader with divine assistance, she could be invoked to justify violence against the political status quo. Jeanne de Navarre (1528–1572), the leader of the Protestant Huguenot movement that fought against the Catholic monarchy in France, commissioned a poem by Guillaume Du Bartas, as a propagandistic component of this national struggle. His *La Judit* (1574) cultivated the image of the Huguenot queen as a Judith, leading a righteous struggle against tyranny. The tradition of connecting female monarchic power to the image of Judith, along with her association with glamour and danger, perhaps explains why the Queen of Hearts depicted on playing cards was once none other than Judith (Figure 5.2). This iconography, which developed in France, is the precursor to the Queen of Hearts in today's deck.

In the nineteenth century, views about Judith changed, and not for the better. The reasons for this are complex. Industrialization intensified a dichotomy between the public and private spheres, systemizing in a new way the restriction of women to the home. The modern women's rights movement also began in this era. In various cultural arenas, men reimagined Judith in ways that neutered

Figure 5.2 Judith as the Queen of Hearts, and David as the King of Spades. Leading cards from a game with a portrait of Limousin, Angoulême, J. Latasche, between 1770 and 1789: 2/12 playing cards, woodcut colored with stencil; 8.2 × 5.5 cm.
Don Paul Marteau, 1967. BnF, Estampes, Kh-383 (3, 87)-box fol.

her symbolic potency. The puppet show Punch and Judy, which was popular in England and other European countries by the eighteenth century, unapologetically taught audiences that the husband remains the king of the castle. The husband's name, Punch, is a bit on the nose. His wife is shrill and demanding. She is, to use the language of the period, a shrew. In shows from the period, he beats her repeatedly with a large stick, his "slapstick" (the origin of the comic phrase), along with many other characters, often killing them, including his wife. She, starting in the early nineteenth century, became known as Judy (earlier she was Joan). This shift evokes the figure of Judith, often regarded in popular culture as symbol of power, reimagined in a way which puts the woman in her place. Judith becomes a victim of male violence, a reversal of the story's core plot, framed as entertainment. Since Punch has a dog named Toby, the Punch and Judy shows may also, along with Judith, refer to Tobit; Tobias travels with a dog in that book (see the previous chapter).

In a more refined venue, the influential 1840 play *Judith* by the German playwright Friedrich Hebbel expresses male anxiety about Judith by rewriting the story. In his play Judith is not a widow but married, although still a virgin—until she is raped by Holofernes. This change transforms Judith's central act of violence. Her killing of Holofernes is no longer a divinely sanctioned act of heroism in defense of her people. It becomes the hysterical reaction of a woman to sexual trauma.

Judith's power was also relocated from the public sphere to the private realm of male sexual fantasy. Leopold Sacher-Masoch's erotic novel *Venus in Furs* (1870) fetishizes Judith's violence. This book, an important text of sado-masochism (a term that derives from the author's name, Masoch), is a male fantasy of being sexually dominated by women. The author's imagination was shaped by an erotically charged interpretation of the book of Judith. *Venus* ends with a citation of the Vulgate form of Judith 16:7: "But the Almighty Lord has struck him and has delivered him into the hands of a woman." The novel's main character, Severin, explicitly identifies with Holofernes and construes his decapitation as a paradigm for being sexually dominated, which he craves. Judith's violence is no longer a heroic act but a deviant source of male erotic pleasure. Jerome would spin in his grave if he knew how Sacher-Masoch read his translation of Judith!

Conclusion

The prominence in the book of Judith of a woman who is brave, beautiful, and seductive made Judith imagery popular throughout the centuries. Judith represents Israel, even though it is male dominated. This gender paradox illustrates a key point—that Israel, in terms of its covenant relationship with God, is the weaker of the two parties and must submit to him. Israel is also weak with respect to the Assyrians. That a woman can defeat the Assyrian general, and Israel win against the Assyrians, demonstrates that when Israel is loyal to God, no one can defeat his people, no matter their strength. The book creatively uses gender tropes to convey that with God the weak can overpower the strong.

Guide for Further Reading

Gera, Deborah. *Judith*. Berlin: de Gruyter, 2013.
Milne, Pamela. "What Shall We Do with Judith? A Feminist Reassessment of a Biblical 'Heroine.'" *Semeia* 62 (1993): 37–58.
Stocker, Margarita. *Judith: Sexual Warrior: Women and Power in Western Culture*. New Haven, CT: Yale University Press, 1998.
Wills, Lawrence. *Judith: A Commentary on the Book of Judith*. Minneapolis: Fortress Press, 2019.

6

Variations of a Beloved Tale

The Books of Esther

The book of Esther has long been popular among Jewish readers of the Bible. It is one of the Megillot ("scrolls"), a group of five biblical books each read on a Jewish holiday (along with Song of Songs, Ruth, Lamentations, and Ecclesiastes). Esther is read during Purim, which is held according to the Hebrew calendar on the 14th of the month of Adar, and in some cases on the 15th (February–March). It is a joyous occasion involving feasting, inebriation, and gift giving. Purim celebrates the story of Esther—a powerful man, Haman, attempts to exterminate Jews throughout the ancient Persian Empire, but his heinous plot is thwarted by the Jew Mordecai and his cousin Esther, a beautiful woman who becomes the queen.

The book is not as well known among Christians. It is never cited in the New Testament. Purim is not a Christian holiday. There is unfortunately a Christian tradition of dismissing Esther as an excessively Jewish book. Martin Luther, in a treatise with the cringe-inducing title *On the Jews and Their Lies* (1543), wrote, "Oh, how much they [the Jews] love the book of Esther which so well fits their bloodthirsty, vengeful, murderous greed and hope."

The book of Esther is important not simply in relation to Purim. Jewish and Christian Bibles preserve substantially different versions of the composition. Appreciating its textual diversity sheds light onto the scribal milieu of late Second Temple Judaism in which texts in the Bible and many other works were produced and transmitted. The textual diversity of Esther illustrates that in

The Apocrypha: A Guide. Matthew Goff, Oxford University Press. © Oxford University Press 2024.
DOI: 10.1093/9780190060770.003.0006

that era, texts were not simply copied but could also be reworked and transformed.

The Books of Esther

The Hebrew form of the book of Esther preserved in Judaism (the Masoretic text) is much shorter than the version in the Greek Septuagint (LXX). The text of Esther in the Catholic and Orthodox Old Testament, which derives from the Septuagint, is over 70 percent longer than its form in the Jewish Bible. It is essentially a different book of Esther. It has over 100 verses not in the Hebrew. These verses, often called the Additions to Esther, comprise six sections. Because scholars are very creative people, we classify them as Additions A through F:

Addition A   (11:2–12:6). Mordecai's Dream. The beginning of the story.

Addition B   (13:1–7). A Royal Edict against the Jews. After Esther 3:13.

Addition C   (13:8–14:19). Prayers by Mordecai and Esther. After Esther 4:17.

Addition D   (15:1–16). Esther in the Throne Room. After C.

Addition E   (16:1–24). A Royal Edict Countering the Anti-Jewish One (B). After Esther 8:12.

Addition F   (10:4–11:1). Interpretation of Mordecai's Dream. The end of the book (the versification of these passages is explained below).

There is another Greek version of Esther which is not in the scriptural canon of any confessional community today. It is called the Alpha Text (AT). The AT is approximately 40 percent longer than the Hebrew Esther, so substantially shorter than LXX Esther. Translations of the LXX and Alpha versions are available side by side in NETS (*The New English Translation of the Septuagint*), making it easy to compare the two different versions. There are no fragments of Esther among the Dead Sea Scrolls that could shed light on the ancient development of the text; scholars used to think that one text (4Q550) was an early version of the book ("Proto-Esther"). There is another ancient rendition of Esther in Greek written by the Jewish historian Josephus (first century CE). His version includes all the Additions except A and F (perhaps to avoid their opposition of Jews and Gentiles, a topic discussed below). There is a medieval translation of Josephus into Hebrew (*Yosippon*) which includes several of the Additions. It contains a form of Addition A even though that text is not in Josephus, suggesting Jewish engagement with the Christian Bible in the Middle Ages.

While the Additions to Esther are preserved in Greek, they were not necessarily written in that language. Scholars hold that all the Additions except B and E were likely written in Hebrew or Aramaic and later translated into Greek. This would imply that Jews were reworking the book in Hebrew in antiquity. Compatible with this possibility, the story is expanded in Jewish tradition in ways that resonate with the Additions preserved in Greek. A targum of Esther (*Targum Sheni*)—a targum is an often loose translation of Hebrew scriptures into Aramaic—in its account of Mordecai encouraging Esther to go before the king and save her people from Haman's edict (Esther 4) adds extensive speech, not unlike Addition C. According to the targum, Mordecai contextualizes Esther's opportunity to defeat Haman by reminding her of numerous episodes of deliverance and victory in the Hebrew Bible, such as God's command to erase any remembrance of the Amalekites (Deut 25), to whose lineage the rabbis connected Haman, and Jael's killing of the Canaanite general Sisera (Judges 4). Also, it should not be presumed that all six Additions were incorporated into the story at the same time. The long version of Esther is more likely the result of multiple revisions of the book made over time.

Scribes retained in the centuries after the beginning of the common era a greater range of Esther's Second Temple–era textual diversity than is often the case with biblical books. The composition's relatively open textual status in antiquity is perhaps related to the fact that it was not universally recognized as an important or even a scriptural text. Many early Church authors do not cite the book. The bishop Athanasius (fourth century) distinguishes Esther, along with books such as Tobit and the Wisdom of Solomon, from the "canonized" books of the Old Testament (see Chapter 1). Some early Christian canon lists, such as the one by Gregory of Nazianzus (fourth century), omit Esther. Eventual Christian acceptance of the book involved associating Esther with Mary and interpreting Haman as an anti-type of Christ. In this way he oddly became understood as like Christ, as his mirror opposite. The Sistine Chapel, for example, depicts Haman being crucified, even though in the book he is hung on gallows.

Even among rabbis there were disputes about the composition's canonicity. According to the Babylonian Talmud (tractate *Megillot*), some early rabbis asserted that the book "does not defile the hands," an idiom that means it is not sacred scripture. This accords with the testimony of an early Christian bishop, Melito of Sardis (second century). He claims to have traveled to the east to acquire accurate knowledge about the books of the Old Testament. This likely means he traveled to learn from Jews about their scripture. Melito lists their twenty-two books—and there is no mention of Esther. There was perhaps hesitancy among Jews regarding Esther because the book did not seem particularly biblical, with major topics such as Israel or the covenant absent from the text (a major topic discussed below). One leading trend in rabbinic interpretation of Esther is to counter such views by arguing that the book's details are consistent with the rest of the Hebrew Bible.

The Bible in the Eastern Orthodox tradition, based directly on the Septuagint, includes the longer version of Esther. In this context, the Additions are simply part of the story; they are not additions. The situation is different with the Vulgate Bible that has been foundational in Catholicism. While there is substantial variety among the Latin manuscripts of Esther, Jerome in his translation made some unusual decisions which proved influential. He had a dismissive attitude toward the book's lengthy sections in the Septuagint that have no analogue in the Hebrew Bible. He removed them from the main story, which he translated from the Hebrew, and put them at the end of the book. Thus in the Vulgate, Esther accords with the Hebrew up to Esther 10:3, its last verse in the Jewish Bible. The Additions then follow, comprising Esther 10:4–16:24 as a long hodge-podge of an appendix. Jerome placed the Additions in the order F, A, B, C, D, E; this oddly places the interpretation of Mordecai's dream (F) before the dream itself (A). Jerome's removal of these Additions from the main story reinforced the view that they are not important. Referring to them as Additions is a legacy of Jerome's editorial work. In Catholic Bibles one can now find the Additions returned to their locations in the story as found in the Septuagint, sometimes printed in italics.

Protestant Reformers took Jerome's idea of relocating the Additions to the end of the book one step further. They removed them from the Old Testament entirely. The Old Testament of the original King James Bible (1611), for example, has a book of Esther, based on the Hebrew, while its Apocrypha section includes "the Rest of Esther," referring to the Additions attested in the Septuagint. "The Rest of Esther" does not form a coherent story on its own. The form of Esther in the Protestant Old Testament matches that of the Jewish Bible, whereas the book in the Catholic and Eastern Orthodox traditions is longer.

Esther's unusual textual situation is illustrated by its presentation in NOAB (the *New Oxford Annotated Bible*). This edition includes in its Apocrypha section not simply the Additions but rather the entire Septuagint version of Esther; the Hebrew-based version of the book is in its Old Testament. The book of Esther is in *two* different sections of the Bible. NOAB's format allows for easy comparison of the two different versions of the composition. While it includes the Additions where they appear in the Septuagint, NOAB retains the versification established when Jerome relegated them to the end of the book. Thus Esther 11:2–12:6 comes before chapter 1 and Esther 13:2–7 is within chapter 3 (Additions A and B, respectively). Because Jerome placed F first among the Additions and A second, which in the LXX frame the book, the first verse of the book is Esther 11:2 and its final verse, bizarrely, is 11:1. NOAB accurately conveys Esther's unusual career as a biblical book.

Palace Intrigue, Deliverance, and Vengeance: The Hebrew Book of Esther

The book of Esther, in its Hebrew form, is a strange little story. At its core the book affirms Jewish identity. Jews are presented as a coherent group by means of their victory over Haman's efforts to kill them, their association with Esther and Mordecai, and their obligation to observe Purim. Core features of Judaism, however, are nowhere to be found. The word "God" never appears in the book. There is no sense that Israel is or should be the home of the Jewish people. The book never mentions the Torah or the covenant. God is reasonably understood in the book as operating behind the scenes, orchestrating events indirectly, as in the Joseph novella (Gen 37–50). Both Esther and the Joseph story are tales from the Diaspora that relate how Jews, despite pitfalls and adversity, rise to success in the court of Gentile kings (so too Daniel 1–6 and Tobit).

Esther is set amidst the opulence and splendor of the court of the Persian Empire during the reign of King Ahasuerus. The Persian Achaemenid dynasty ruled much of the ancient Near East from approximately 550 to 330 BCE. Ahasuerus is the Hebrew name for King Xerxes I (486–465 BCE). The book of Esther is thus often dated to the fourth century BCE, although it may have been written somewhat later, most likely in Persia or at least the eastern Diaspora.

Figure 6.1 Xerxes I, king of the ancient Persian Empire (485–465 BCE), depicted in the movie *300* (Snyder, 2007) as a false god-king. In ancient Jewish tradition, unlike this movie, he is not vilified. The Persian king whom the biblical heroine Esther marries (Ahasuerus) is often identified as Xerxes I.

When Xerxes was king, the Persian Empire was at the height of its power. The Persians were expanding into the Mediterranean region. They controlled Egypt and fought against Greece, as recounted by ancient historians such as Herodotus. The jingoistic film *300* (2007) drew on such accounts to depict Xerxes as a powerful villain, against whose armies the famously outnumbered Greeks fought at the battle of Thermopylae (480 BCE) (Figure 6.1). The oldest surviving Jewish visual depiction of Ahasuerus, from the Dura Europos synagogue in Syria, is much more positive— and based on the book of Esther (Figure 6.2). The biblical books of Ezra and Nehemiah likewise depict Jews as loyal servants of the powerful Persian Empire. The story of Esther also has a long-standing importance in a Persian milieu. There is a venerable tradition among Persian Jews that Esther and Mordecai are buried in the Iranian city of Hamadan (where one can visit the tomb in which they are purportedly buried). The book very well may have its origins as a Jewish Persian folktale.

While the book of Esther presents the Persian kingdom as powerful and important, it depicts the king himself as oddly passive.

Figure 6.2 The Purim panel of the Dura Europos Synagogue (Syria, third century CE). Left: Haman leads Mordecai on a horse (Esth 6:7–11). Right: King Ahasuerus with Queen Esther.

Haman convinces him to marshal state power against the Jews, and then Esther persuades him to reverse course. Nevertheless, in the book Jews' association with the Persian royal court and its power, in striking contrast to the film *300*, is a source of pride.

The story starts with the king displaying his lavish wealth in the royal citadel in the Persian city of Susa, a fortress where the book of Nehemiah also begins. Xerxes holds a banquet that lasts no less than 180 days. At another banquet Xerxes, when drunk, commands his queen, Vashti, to parade before his guests to show them her beauty. She refuses. This enrages the king, and his advisors fear that her action will encourage women throughout the empire not to obey their husbands. The court rescinds Vashti's royal status. An empire-wide beauty pageant is held to find the most beautiful virgin to replace her. It is a kind of misogynistic fairy tale. A Cinderella figure, Esther wins the competition and is elevated from obscurity to become the new queen. She was raised in Susa by Mordecai, who works at the citadel. Esther keeps her ethnic identity secret.

Another plot thread involves the conflict between Mordecai and Haman. Mordecai foils a plot by two guards to kill the king. He is not, however, given any recognition or honor. Enter Haman. The king promotes him instead. Other officials are required to bow down before him. Mordecai refuses. His obstinance can be easily understood as motivated by resentment. Haman, without a clear rationale, was elevated by the king, whereas Mordecai, who deserved to be honored, was not. Mordecai's conduct enrages Haman. Ones he learns that Mordecai is Jewish, he wants to exterminate all Jews in the Persian Empire. He has the king promulgate a decree throughout the kingdom that on one day, the 13th of Adar, all Jews, men, women, and children, are to be killed and their goods plundered. The deployment of state power to kill Jews is also a major theme in 3 Maccabees (see Chapter 15).

Esther, after consultation with Mordecai, goes before the king in court. This is an act of bravery. Approaching the king uninvited is treated as a breach of protocol for which one can be killed. Xerxes, however, is pleased to see her; she asks the king that he and Haman join her at a banquet (there's a lot of banqueting in this book). The king agrees. The invitation delights Haman, which he takes as a sign of royal favor. But he cannot fully enjoy himself since he is consumed by his hatred of Mordecai. He has almost comically large gallows made, 50 cubits high (roughly 75 feet), on which to hang him. Haman wants the king to agree to Mordecai's execution before the banquet—so he can fully enjoy the honor.

But the tables turn. That same night the king cannot sleep, so he has the royal annals read to him (which suggests they make dry reading). In this way the king learns that Mordecai was never rewarded for uncovering a plot against him. At that early hour Haman just happens to enter the court. He is eager to secure the king's approval of Mordecai's execution. The king summons him to ask, "What shall be done for the man whom the king wishes to honor?" There is a wonderful ambiguity in this question. Xerxes is speaking about Mordecai. But Haman, in his arrogance, presumes the king has him in mind. Haman thus recommends a lavish display of honor—that such a person be dressed in royal robes and led by a top official on one of the king's horses through the city. In a wonderful reversal, the king commands Haman to carry out exactly that for Mordecai. He must lead Mordecai on a royal horse, a scene illustrated at Dura Europos (Figure 6.2). Mordecai's honor is Haman's humiliation.

Things only get worse for Haman. At the banquet, Esther tells the king that a wicked man has plotted the demise of her people—and that the instigator is their dinner guest. Haman was eagerly looking forward to the banquet. But it becomes his final meal. The king has him hung on the very gallows he intended for Mordecai. The one who plotted murder is himself murdered. Mordecai is elevated in the court and given Haman's now vacant senior position, and his house as well. The book, while beginning with male fear of a female insurrection, ends, like the book of Judith, with a woman foiling the plans of a man to attack the Jews. Queen Esther has a second royal edict written that counters the anti-Jewish one promoted by Haman. Reflecting the view that the word of the king cannot be revoked, this new edict does not rescind the first. Rather, it grants the Jews the right to defend themselves on the prescribed day (the 13th of Adar) and even kill anyone who attempts to harm them.

So everyone lives happily ever after. Well, not exactly. The stunning reversal of the Jews' fate does not go unnoticed in the empire. Through Mordecai and Esther, the sublime power of the Persian court is extended to the Jewish people as a whole. People are afraid of the Jews, and some Gentiles even profess to be Jews. When the 13th of Adar arrives, they are not the victims but the oppressors. It is a brutal "purge day." The Jews kill their enemies—no less than 75,000 people, and rest on Adar 14. In the citadel of Susa the Jews kill an additional 300 people on the 14th and rest on the 15th. This variation in Esther 9 explains the modern tradition that walled cities—above all the Old City in Jerusalem—celebrate Purim on Adar 15, as in Susa (Shushan Purim), whereas most Jews observe it on Adar 14. In the book, Mordecai calls for their victories to be commemorated by Jews in perpetuity with two days of feasting and celebration, on Adar 14 and 15. The two days correspond to the Purim, or "lots"; a "lot" here denotes a divine apportionment of fate by God; the two lots also relate to the two edicts, and thus represent the core element of the story—Haman's plot against the Jews and their deliverance from it.

While hailed as a tale in which the Jews are saved from the murderous plot of Haman, Esther is also about vengeance, the killing of one's enemies. The brutality and violence embedded within the book were tragically weaponized in 1994, when an American Israeli right-wing extremist, Baruch Goldstein, after reading Esther on Purim at his synagogue, went to a mosque and opened fire. He killed 29 people, including children, as they prayed, and wounded 125 others. The ending of the book of Esther makes many of us uncomfortable—but unfortunately not all of us.

A Pious Reconfiguration: The Septuagint Version of the Book of Esther

The longer LXX version of Esther, while telling the same basic story as the Hebrew, is surprisingly different. The Persian king is no longer Xerxes but his son Artaxerxes (465–425 BCE), who appears elsewhere in the Bible as a powerful king to whom Ezra and Nehemiah are loyal. Whereas modern scholars understand the name Ahasuerus as denoting Xerxes, it was common for Jewish scholars in antiquity to interpret the name as signifying Artaxerxes, a tradition also attested in later Jewish midrash (e.g., *Esther Rabbah*).

The historical development of the text of Esther and how to understand the relationship between the LXX, Masoretic, and Alpha versions of the book are matters of scholarly debate. But Septuagint Esther adapts a form of the tale that is similar to the Hebrew form of the book. Esther 9:16, for example, was revised to state that the Jews did not kill 75,000 people but rather 15,000. The statement in verse 5 of this chapter in the Hebrew that "the Jews struck down all their enemies with the sword, slaughtering and destroying them" is not in Septuagint Esther. Some scribes were likely squeamish about the book's "purge day" and revised the text.

Expansion of older texts is a common scribal technique evident in the longer version of Esther. In the Hebrew, for example, the two edicts central to the tale are summarized. Additions B and E, by contrast, quote the text of the edicts. Providing copies of official documents gives Septuagint Esther an annalistic character, not unlike the book of Ezra, which purports to quote correspondence with the Persian court. Haman's edict condemns the Jews as seditious and disloyal to the state, as does Ptolemy's decree against the Jews in 3 Maccabees 3. The second edict counter-asserts that it is rather Haman who is the traitor. Addition E, in a clear example of a scribe updating a text, asserts that Haman is a Macedonian. He thus becomes a kind of "Manchurian candidate," a high official, secretly undermining the Persian Empire from within, preparing the way for its eventual collapse at the hand of Alexander the Great and his Macedonian army in 330 BCE.

The expansionistic character of Septuagint Esther is also evident in Addition D. This text lengthens and intensifies the key scene of Esther approaching the king at court. Replacing Esther 5:1–2 in the Hebrew, Addition D dramatizes how scared Esther was to walk before the king arrayed in his full splendor. He is angry at her, presumably because she approaches him without being summoned. In the Hebrew she wins his favor as soon as he sees her. In the Greek she faints when she observes his angry visage. Esther's fainting before the king has been famously depicted in Western art, by painters such as Tintoretto, Jean-François de Troy, and Francesco Fontebasso. In the Septuagint her collapse functions as a form of fear and humility that triggers a response from God. When she faints, the deity changes the king's dour mood. Thus he agrees to her proposal about the banquet with Haman, setting in motion the chain of events that leads to the deliverance of the Jews.

The successes achieved by Esther and Mordecai are ultimately attributed to God. This highlights arguably the most important difference between the Greek and Hebrew versions of Esther: whereas the latter never mentions God directly, the former refers to him constantly.

Key expansions in Septuagint Esther make the role of God more explicit and emphasize the piety of Esther and Mordecai. According to Addition C, unlike the Hebrew, once they decide that she will approach the king, Mordecai and Esther pray to God. They ask God for deliverance from this crisis. The text provides the words of their prayers. While Mordecai can be understood in the Hebrew as not bowing down to Haman because he feels more deserving of royal honor than Haman (as mentioned above), Addition C offers a more theological interpretation—that Mordecai only genuflects before God, not a human being. LXX Esther 6 stresses that God prevents the king from falling asleep. His insomnia becomes an example of how the deity indirectly controls events. It is because the king is awake at night that he reads the royal annals, and thus realizes that Mordecai had never been honored, setting the stage for the reversal of Haman's fate. The Greek version, unlike the Hebrew, also emphasizes that when Esther hides her ethnic identity, she nevertheless maintains her piety. LXX Esther 2 adds "she was to fear God and keep his laws, just as she had done when she was with him (Mordecai). So Esther did not change her mode of life" at court.

In the longer Greek version, Jews are defined as a group not only through their close relationship with God but also by their ancestral laws, whereas neither is an explicit theme in the Hebrew. The text of the second edict affirms that Jews "are governed by the most righteous laws and are children of the living God, most high, most mighty." Addition C suggests that Esther follows the dietary laws of the Torah (discussed below). According to LXX Esther 8, when Gentiles profess to be Jews because they feared them after the elevation of Mordecai, many of them become circumcised, a crucial marker of Jewish identity grounded in the Torah. This detail, which is not in the Hebrew, makes it harder to interpret these Gentiles as simply trying to pass as Jewish to avoid retribution—it becomes instead a kind of conversion.

A New Take on the Two Lots of Purim: Jews and Gentiles

Jewish tales about Gentiles becoming Jews because they were afraid of them constitute a kind of fantasy. It is understandable that Jews would imagine such stories against the backdrop of discrimination they faced in the Diaspora. While this was surely an issue when the book of Esther was initially written, the longer version of Esther intensifies the view that Jews and Gentiles constitute two opposed ways of life. A stark distinction between Jews and Gentiles is also prominent in several other Hellenistic-era texts examined in this book (e.g., 1 Maccabees; *Jubilees*). In the Hebrew, as mentioned above, the two lots of Purim signify respectively Haman's plot against the Jews and their deliverance from it. Addition F suggests, by contrast, that one lot signifies the Gentiles and the other the Jews. In her prayer Esther proudly declares that she has never slept with an uncircumcised (non-Jewish) man and refuses to eat at the king's feasts. LXX Esther implies that the queen follows Jewish dietary law. This strains a key plot point, that Esther keeps her ethnicity hidden at court. In Daniel 1, when Daniel keeps kosher, it causes problems in the Babylonian court. But Esther never encounters such issues. This revision reflects the view, which became more prominent in the Hellenistic period, that Jewish identity is bound to the Torah. This example illustrates that by making changes to clarify one issue (that Esther followed the Torah), scribes inadvertently introduced new inconsistencies into the story.

Addition F portrays an opposition between Jews and Gentiles as an inherent part of God's plan. Septuagint Esther begins with an account of a dream of Mordecai (Addition A). In the genre apocalypse, which flourished in the Judaism of the Hellenistic age, dreams constitute a form of revelation, conveying knowledge through cryptic symbols about the divinely established scenario that orchestrates the flow of events. This is evident, for example, in Daniel and *1 Enoch*. Dreams function similarly in LXX Esther. Mordecai dreams of two powerful dragons, eager to fight each other. The people of a "righteous nation" are terrified and cry out to God. A small spring becomes a great river, which is associated with light and the rising sun.

Apocalyptic visions are often accompanied by divinely revealed interpretations of them (e.g., Daniel 7; 2 Esdras 12). So too in Septuagint Esther. Mordecai at the end of the book offers an interpretation of his strange dream (Addition F). The righteous nation is the people Israel. The river denotes Esther. In the Alpha Text the spring is Esther and the river instead signifies the Gentiles. In the LXX (and Alpha) the two dragons are Haman and Mordecai. The animosity between Mordecai and Haman so understood follows a plan ordained by God before they ever met. The interpretation of Mordecai's dream serves as a context for the assertion that the two lots denote Jews and Gentiles. The lots are not in the dream itself. By associating the lots with the dream, Addition F correlates the two lots with the two opposed dragons; in this way, LXX Esther conveys that the lots of Purim constitute two different, incompatible ways of being human established by God. Greek Esther begins with Mordecai's dream, and its interpretation ends the story (Additions A and F). Together they frame the narrative, conveying that the entire set of events recounted in the book occurs according to the will of God.

A Colophon Promotes Purim

The ending of the longer version of Esther is unique among biblical texts. It has a colophon, which is a brief statement at the end of the text that gives the name of the scribe who produced it. It also often states when and where they did so. The colophon of LXX Esther reads:

> In the fourth year of the reign of Ptolemy and Cleopatra, Dositheus, who said that he was a priest and a Levite, and his son Ptolemy brought to Egypt the preceding Letter about Purim, which they said was authentic and had been translated by Lysimachus son of Ptolemy, one of the residents of Jerusalem.

This could be a rare instance of a biblical book breaking the fourth wall, a "tag" that provides the name of the scribe responsible for translating the text and states when he did this textual labor. Another would be the prologue of Ben Sira (see Chapter 8). What exact textual form of Esther would have been translated by Lysimachus of course remains unknown. The colophon at the end of Septuagint Esther, however, is not necessarily a neutral depository of scribal information. The edicts in Additions B and E testify to a scribal willingness to add texts to the book of Esther.

The colophon was perhaps written to suggest that the composition which it concludes, with its emphatic endorsement of Purim, comes from the Jerusalem temple—an Israelite focus that is nowhere else evident in the book. The composition was, according to the colophon, translated into Greek in Jerusalem and then a priest named Dositheus brought it to Egypt. The colophon also stresses that Dositheus emphasized his priestly status once he arrived there and that he and his son asserted that their document is from Jerusalem. It is odd that Dositheus purports to be a priest *and* a Levite. In the Jewish literature from the period these are generally two different sacerdotal groups, with the Levites hierarchically lower than the priests. Such problems may explain why most manuscripts of the Alpha Text omit the colophon. Whether historically accurate or not, the colophon situates the Greek translation of Esther in the early first century BCE. Its reference to the "fourth year" of Ptolemy and Cleopatra is generally identified as 78–77 BCE, in which case they are Ptolemy XII and Cleopatra V. The "preceding Letter about Purim" mentioned in the colophon is reasonably understood as a reference to the book of Esther itself. This may be an early attestation of a view in rabbinic tradition (e.g., *Targum Sheni*) that the term "letter" in Esther 9 denotes the book of Esther. But in Esther itself this perspective is clearer in the Greek than in the Hebrew. In the latter, Mordecai writes "letters" which he sends to Jews throughout the empire, enjoining them to observe Purim. Esther 9:24–25 briefly reiterates the plot of Esther, suggesting the letters Mordecai sends out tell the basic story of the book. In chapter 8 of the Alpha Text, unlike the other versions, Mordecai sends out letters with a royal seal which affirm that Haman was behind the plot against the Jews and is now dead. According to Esther 9:29 (Hebrew), Queen Esther along with Mordecai writes "this second letter about Purim." There is a Jewish interpretation that Purim was first established only in the city of Susa and that "this second letter" establishes it for the entire world. It is a debated point among scholars how to interpret this "second letter," but it adds Esther's royal authority to Mordecai's prior written efforts to promote Purim.

In LXX Esther 9 it becomes more explicit that at issue is an early form of book of Esther—attributed to Mordecai. In LXX Esther 9:20 he writes not "letters" but a "book" to Jews throughout the empire. Verses 23–25 establish that his "book" recounts the core plot of the Esther story. Events that are mentioned in these verses involve Mordecai, not Esther, which is consistent with the fact that they are in a book of Mordecai. There is no longer a reference to a "second letter"; rather, in LXX Esther 9:29–32 Mordecai and Esther write down their experiences. In this manner they promote "the letter about Purim," which in context likely signifies Mordecai's book (that is, a form of the book of Esther). LXX Esther shows more awareness of its own textuality than the Hebrew. This accords with the fact that it is a revision of an older form of the book.

The colophon presents the promotion of Purim as the core rationale for the translation and dissemination of the book. In particular, it encourages the observance of Purim by Jews in Egypt. 3 Maccabees emphasizes that its story of divine deliverance from state oppression in Egypt is likewise commemorated with a festival there. LXX Esther's colophon also accords with 2 Maccabees, which begins with two letters addressed to the Jewish community of Egypt, encouraging them to observe festal days, including Hanukkah.

2 Maccabees also suggests that some form of Purim was practiced by the second century BCE. At the end of that book, after Judas Maccabee defeats the Seleucid general Nicanor, a despised enemy of the Jews, he displays his severed head in Jerusalem and declares that the day of his defeat be commemorated on the 13th of Adar, which is "the day before Mordecai's day" (2 Macc 15:36). While a debated point, "Mordecai's day" is likely a reference to an early form of Purim. Naming this event after him accords with the emphasis in LXX Esther 9 on Mordecai over Esther and the colophon's interest in promoting Purim. 2 Maccabees 15:36 suggests the day of Mordecai would be Adar 14; this accords with the days associated with Purim in Esther. 2 Maccabees likely adapts an early form of Purim and its commemoration of the defeat of Haman as a model for its own efforts to establish a day to memorialize the defeat of Nicanor.

A Day of Nicanor, though unknown today, was a Jewish festal day that was observed in antiquity (this is discussed in Chapter 13). The Dead Sea Scrolls show no awareness of Purim, suggesting that when the sect they describe flourished (early first century BCE)— the same time period of LXX Esther's colophon and its promotion of Purim—it was not yet a universally held festival among Jews.

Conclusion

The case of Esther illustrates that different versions of the Bible can attest different versions of the same book. The Greek forms of the book of Esther, in the Septuagint and the Alpha Text, provide insight into how Jews understood the story in the Hellenistic age. It makes the agency of God more explicit, intensifies the piety of Mordecai and Esther, and more robustly connects Jewish identity to the Torah, among many other alterations, both great and small. The scribes who transmitted the book should be regarded not simply as copyists but as authors in their own right, who turned an old story into a new one.

Guide for Further Reading

Bickerman, Elias. *Four Strange Books of the Bible.* New York: Schocken Books, 1967 (pp. 171–240).

Koller, Aaron J. *Esther in Ancient Jewish Thought.* Cambridge: Cambridge University Press, 2016.

Levenson, Jon D. *Esther: A Commentary.* Louisville, KY: Westminster John Knox, 1997.

Stone, Meredith J. *Empire and Gender in LXX Esther.* Atlanta: Society of Biblical Literature, 2018.

7

The Noble Philosophy of Judaism

The Wisdom of Solomon

The Wisdom of Solomon encourages its readers to seek wisdom, be righteous, and be devoted to God. This message is uttered by King Solomon himself, to whom the work is attributed. He is the teacher, and the readers are his students. The king, whose legendary wisdom is praised in the Bible (1 Kings 3–4), attributes his success to his love and reception of wisdom (in Greek, *sophia*). The Wisdom of Solomon poetically describes wisdom as both a woman and a spirit which pulses throughout the cosmos and binds it together. This perspective is reliant upon the Jewish sapiential tradition, which personifies wisdom as a woman. The composition's depiction of wisdom as a spirit draws upon an intellectual tradition that is relatively unknown today: Hellenistic philosophy. A synthesis of Jewish and Greco-Roman learning is one of the distinctive features of the Wisdom of Solomon. The book was written in Alexandria (Egypt) and is a product of the Jewish Diaspora, that is, Jewish communities outside of Israel. They were a minority people in a Gentile world. Consequently, the composition valorizes Judaism in ways that would appeal to Gentile (non-Jewish) intellectuals. It frames the Jewish religion and its scriptural heritage not as the tradition of a particular people, but rather as a type of moral philosophy that is of benefit to all humankind, able to inculcate a love for wisdom and instill an accurate understanding of the world.

The Apocrypha: A Guide. Matthew Goff, Oxford University Press. © Oxford University Press 2024.
DOI: 10.1093/9780190060770.003.0007

Structure, Genre, and Provenance

The Wisdom of Solomon was written in Greek. The composition is conventionally divided into three sections: the Book of Eschatology (1:1–6:21), the Book of Wisdom (6:22–9:18), and the Book of History (10:1–19:22). The opening section of the Wisdom of Solomon asserts that one who possesses wisdom loves justice and righteousness, and that the souls of the righteous have immortal life. One should therefore strive to have wisdom and be righteous. While the intended readership of the composition is Jewish, its opening section is addressed to the "rulers of the earth," who are invited to seek wisdom. This broad focus draws on traditions evident in Proverbs 8, in which wisdom, personified as woman, asserts "by me kings reign and rulers decree what is just." The wisdom that a just king displays, denoting not only knowledge but also a commitment to ethics, is a model for how a person should live. In the second section, Solomon presents himself as an ideal king, offering an extensive description of wisdom and a poignant account of how he fell in love with her. His successes as a king, he emphasizes, should be attributed to his possession of wisdom. Chapters 11–19 offer an extensive reformulation of the Exodus story. Because of the composition's organization and cohesive structure, scholars generally hold that it was written as a unified text, and that it is not a combination of discrete sources.

In terms of genre, the Wisdom of Solomon is a wisdom, or sapiential, text. Wisdom literature is a modern genre classification for ancient Jewish writings that focus on pedagogy and instruction. The wisdom texts of the Hebrew Bible are Proverbs, Job, and Ecclesiastes. There is one Deuterocanonical composition considered sapiential aside from the Wisdom of Solomon, the book of Ben Sira (Ecclesiasticus; see Chapter 8). Several Dead Sea Scrolls are also considered wisdom texts, such as 4QInstruction. Sapiential texts are typically written by teachers to students. They encourage one to acquire wisdom, understood as the capacity to comprehend the world and lead a successful and fulfilling life, or they critique the ability of wisdom to do so, as in Job and Ecclesiastes. The Wisdom of Solomon's emphasis on the acquisition of wisdom accords with the sapiential tradition, as does the text's attribution to Solomon. Proverbs is likewise attributed to Solomon, and the Wisdom of Solomon draws extensively from traditions attested in Proverbs.

The composition also exhibits reliance upon Hellenistic didactic genres and forms of rhetoric. The work is often characterized as a *logos protreptikos*, a type of speech that encourages one to believe or do something that is just and reasonable. This genre was employed in ancient Greece to arouse people's interest in philosophy and reason. The "Book of Wisdom," with its lengthy praise of wisdom, resembles the encomium, a genre in which the subject of the work is praised. The "Book of History" can be compared to epideictic, a type of rhetoric that exhorts people to embrace a particular idea on the basis of historical examples.

The Wisdom of Solomon does not state where it was composed, but most scholars would say it was written in Alexandria, Egypt. This is a reasonable position since this city was famous in antiquity as a center of Hellenistic learning, and the Wisdom of Solomon was clearly written by someone who was educated in Hellenistic philosophy (more on this below). The composition's strong interest in the Exodus story also accords with an Egyptian setting.

Scholars generally understand the Wisdom of Solomon as written around the turn of the common era. The Greek vocabulary of the book accords with the first century CE. No text older than that cites or displays knowledge of this work. During the reign of the brutal Roman emperor Caligula (37–41 CE) there were extensive anti-Jewish riots and attacks against synagogues in Alexandria. The Wisdom of Solomon several times describes the righteous being killed before they attain old age. This may reflect this Roman-era crisis. Dating the work to the time of Caligula is a common scholarly position today and was earlier espoused by Luther. It is not necessary, however, to posit a single historical event as the context for the work. It is reasonable to understand the text as written in the middle of the first century CE or perhaps somewhat earlier (roughly 30 BCE–50 CE). This would put the Wisdom of Solomon in the same time (and place, Alexandria) as Philo, the important Jewish philosopher and exegete (ca. 20 BCE–50 CE). Philo's writings appear to come out of the same intellectual culture that produced the Wisdom of Solomon. Both richly combine Torah education with Greek philosophy, although Philo does so in a more complex and extensive manner than the Wisdom of Solomon.

The Wisdom of Solomon is a classic text of the Protestant Apocrypha and in the Old Testament in the Catholic and Orthodox traditions. In Catholicism the book is often simply referred to as Wisdom. The book is prominent in the liturgy of the Eastern Orthodox tradition.

While early canon lists and manuscripts often include the Wisdom of Solomon in the Old Testament, the Muratorian Canon, an important early Christian canon list, includes the composition as a book of the New Testament. This suggests that the text had a degree of scriptural authority at a time when the canon of Christian scripture was still in flux. Some early Christian authors, particularly those with a philosophical bent such as Origen and Augustine, were drawn to the Wisdom of Solomon, as it was one of the more explicitly philosophical texts of their scriptural tradition, and they cited it extensively.

There was some hesitation among Christian writers, long before Luther relegated the Wisdom of Solomon to the Apocrypha, regarding its scriptural status. Origen observes in his *First Principles* (third century) that not everyone regards the composition as authoritative. Jerome (fourth century), in his preface to the Solomonic books of the Vulgate Bible, asserts that the composition is "falsely ascribed" to King Solomon. Jerome also associates the work with the "apocrypha," which he distinguishes from canonical scripture (see further Chapter 1), and he asserts that the Wisdom of Solomon was never a book of scripture among the Jews.

Jerome was right. It is not a book of the Jewish Bible, and rabbinic Judaism displays no knowledge of the Wisdom of Solomon. One exception is Nahmanides. Writing in the thirteenth century, this rabbi had access to a form of the book in Aramaic that likely derived from its translation made by Syriac-speaking Christians in the Near East. Not unlike Jerome before him, he doubted the inspired status or Solomonic authorship of the Wisdom of Solomon.

God, the Cosmos, and Wisdom

While the Wisdom of Solomon's core teaching on wisdom is located in the middle of the composition (chs. 7–9), the importance of this theme is established at the outset. Key for understanding this motif is the cosmology of the work. The Wisdom of Solomon portrays God not simply as a powerful deity, but also as an overwhelming force for good in the cosmos. Chapter 1 emphatically associates God with life: "he created all things so that they might exist, the generative forces of the world are wholesome." So understood, the cosmos is not void or empty space, but rather is imbued with divine purpose, inherently predisposed toward life.

The composition conceptualizes wisdom as a spirit, a benevolent entity that fills the universe. She is "philanthropic," literally a lover of humanity, and oriented positively toward life and humankind. According to chapter 1, it is her existence that gives the cosmos its coherence and structure: "the spirit of the Lord has filled the world"; she is "that which holds together all things." Wisdom of Solomon 8 similarly asserts: "She reaches mightily from one end of the earth to the other, and she orders all things well." She does not enter the wicked. The cosmic ubiquity of wisdom explains God's omniscience. A modern analogy to wisdom, as a cosmic entity devoted to goodness and righteousness, is the "Force" in Star Wars—a power that connects all living things.

The Wisdom of Solomon's portrayal of wisdom is very similar to its depiction of God. Indeed, at times the composition muddles the distinction between the two. Amazingly, Wisdom of Solomon 7 claims that wisdom, not God, is "the fashioner of all things." This chapter also states that she is "a pure emanation of the glory of the Almighty" and "a reflection of eternal light, a spotless mirror of the working of God, and an image of his goodness." God and wisdom are difficult to distinguish because wisdom represents the immanent extension of the deity into the world. He also has a transcendent aspect that is beyond the physical realm. Using mythological language, Solomon urges God to send wisdom "forth from the holy heavens, and from the throne of your glory send her" to him. The Lord has a throne in heaven from which he dispatches his envoy, the spirit of wisdom, into the human world, much as he would an angel.

Also, whereas people today tend to think of something spiritual as non-physical, influenced by the modern Cartesian distinction between spirit and matter, the Wisdom of Solomon teaches that the spirit of wisdom is a fine, material substance. Wisdom of Solomon 7:22–24 uses no fewer than twenty-one adjectives to describe wisdom. She is a spirit, for example, that is "mobile" and "subtle," referring to her physical composition. In this composition, wisdom is an active and benevolent spirit that fills the universe and an emanation of a monotheistic, transcendent God into the world.

The Bricolage of Wisdom: Biblical Creation Theology and Stoic Natural Philosophy

The figure of wisdom in the Wisdom of Solomon is a product of bricolage, the weaving together of elements from different traditions into something new. The book combines Jewish traditions known from the Bible with motifs drawn from Hellenistic philosophy. One major strand of traditions upon which the book relies, as mentioned above, is the wisdom literature of ancient Israel. At the center of Proverbs, as in the Wisdom of Solomon, stands the figure of wisdom, personified as a woman. Proverbs 1 depicts wisdom crying out in the streets, asking people to heed her teaching, not unlike Solomon in the Wisdom of Solomon. In Proverbs 8 she provides firsthand testimony about God's formation of the world, claiming to be present when it happened.

A connection between wisdom and the cosmos is also important in the Wisdom of Solomon. But appeal to Proverbs 8 alone cannot explain this point. This is particularly the case with regard to the book's assertions that wisdom is a spirit that pervades the cosmos. Stoicism, a major school of Hellenistic philosophy, extensively influences the composition's depiction of the cosmos. The Stoic *Hymn to Zeus*, for example, teaches that the will of Zeus shapes the entire universe, that this god directs "the universal reason (*logos*) which runs through all things." In this philosophical tradition the *logos*, a major topic of ancient Greek philosophy, is conceptualized as a rational, divine principle that permeates the cosmos. Stoic cosmology envisions the *logos* as a breath or spirit (*pneuma*) that is the soul of the cosmos. Some Stoics understood this soul as a rarified, sentient fire that exists throughout the universe. Diogenes Laertius in his *Lives and Opinions of Eminent Philosophers* (third century CE) explains that "Nature in their view (the Stoics) is an artistically working fire, going on its way to create, which is equivalent to a fiery, creative, or fashioning spirit." The Wisdom of Solomon's view that wisdom is an intelligent spirit with a physical form relies upon Stoic cosmology, in terms of both its ideas and terminology. Stoic thinkers described the spirit of the cosmos as that which holds (*to synechon*) its material elements together. Wisdom of Solomon 1 likewise asserts that wisdom is what holds together (*to synechon*) all things. 4 Maccabees also draws extensively on Stoic traditions (see Chapter 16).

The Wisdom of Solomon combines Stoic cosmology with Jewish monotheism, teaching that the wisdom-infused cosmos is the product of the transcendent God of Israel. This is consistent with the Middle Platonism that flourished in Hellenistic intellectual circles around the time the Wisdom of Solomon was composed. This philosophical tradition merges Stoic cosmology with the classic emphasis in Platonic thought on a transcendent world beyond the realm of the senses.

Love Wisdom

With wisdom construed as a cosmic spirit, one might suspect that the Wisdom of Solomon leaves little room for any anthropomorphization, the conceptualization of wisdom as a human being. The opposite, however, is the case. As already mentioned, the sapiential tradition of personifying wisdom as a woman is central in the Wisdom of Solomon. Solomon discusses how he "sought her from my youth" and desired her as a bride. Proverbs 8 likewise depicts wisdom as a woman exhorting people to love her: "I love those who love me." The Wisdom of Solomon shows that the sapiential trope of loving wisdom is compatible with philosophy, which literally means "love of wisdom." Solomon in the Wisdom of Solomon loves wisdom and he urges that his (male) audience should too.

Solomon's relationship with wisdom in the Wisdom of Solomon also draws upon and expands traditions about the famous king evident in 1 Kings. In the Wisdom of Solomon, he recounts how he long ago prayed to receive wisdom (8:21–9:18), a motif depicted in 1 Kings 3. In the Wisdom of Solomon, he can be understood as uttering his famous prayer while still a boy, as a sign of his natural inclination toward wisdom (8:19–21), whereas in 1 Kings he prays for wisdom after he is married. Solomon's account of his love and commitment to wisdom as a bride is a very positive take on his marital practices. In 1 Kings 10 he marries 1,000 foreign women and worships their gods!

Death, Eschatology, and the
Immortality of the Soul

Having explicated the book's description of wisdom and the cosmos in the composition's second section ("the Book of Wisdom"), its first and third parts become easier to understand. The first ("the Book of Eschatology") stresses, as mentioned above, that God is an active force for good and a promoter of life. God, so envisioned, as chapter 1 states explicitly, did not create death. At issue is the death of the body (physical death) and perhaps also the death of the soul (spiritual death). Death was not part of God's original design for the cosmos. Wisdom of Solomon 2:23 claims that "God created man for incorruption and made him an image of his own eternity." The latter phrase offers a Platonizing understanding of the creation of Adam in Genesis 1:27. He is not made in the image of God. Adam *is* the image of God. This difference suggests that the divine image was not a model God utilized when fashioning him, but rather that Adam is a reflection of God's eternal nature. One of the Dead Sea Scrolls, a text entitled 4QInstruction, alludes to the figure of Adam and utilizes Genesis 1:27 to associate him with an elect type of humankind, which it terms the "spiritual people." This group, the text stresses, has a natural affinity with the angels, and as such has the prospect of eternal life. The Wisdom of Solomon likewise associates Adam and Genesis 1:27 with eternal life, but, unlike 4QInstruction, does so with the language of Hellenistic philosophy. The word that signifies the immortality of Adam in Wisdom of Solomon 2:23 is "incorruption." This is a technical term from another type of Hellenistic philosophy, Epicureanism. In that tradition the word "incorruption" denotes the attribute of the gods that distinguishes them from other physical entities, making it impossible for them to decay or fade away. This provides a materialist explanation for the immortality of the gods. The Wisdom of Solomon combines Jewish traditions regarding Genesis 1–3 and currents of

Greek philosophy to assert that God intended humankind to be eternal.

The Wisdom of Solomon thematizes death as a perversion of how God created the cosmos. According to chapter 1, the ungodly "summoned" death by their wicked deeds. They harass and kill the righteous. The presentation of death as a corruption of the natural order caused by the wicked is consistent with the view that they are out of sync with God's creation, which turns against them (a topic discussed below). Wisdom of Solomon 2 asserts that "through an adversary's envy death enters the world." This probably attests the view that the wicked through their actions bring death into the world. The Greek term for "adversary" (*diabolos*), however, can also be translated as the "devil." This could be an allusion to the serpent in Eden, and in that case the verse attributes the origins of human death to what transpired in the garden. But while Satan could be understood by the first century CE as a supernatural opponent of God (see Revelation 12), the conception of the cosmos as filled with a benevolent spirit leaves no room for such a grand enemy. Still, the explicit connection in Wisdom of Solomon 2 between language from Genesis 1–3 (the "image of God," discussed above) and the theme of death suggests the term "adversary" may hint at the figure of Satan, understood as the Edenic serpent. The composition may allude to the devil in a mythic or figurative sense, as a way to depict the wicked as allies of Satan who create death through their evil ways. The passage's emphasis is on human adversaries, not on Satan as a supernatural power.

In any case, death for the Wisdom of Solomon remains a theological problem. Given the book's understanding of God as a force for life who does not approve of death, immortality can be considered the "natural" condition of humankind. The reality of death complicates this scenario. The existence of death implies God's approval of it. Perhaps this is why the text awkwardly connects death to Satan rather than God.

The Wisdom of Solomon solves the problem of death, in the sense of the end of corporeal life, through appeal to the Platonic concept of the immortality of the soul. For the righteous, physical death only appears to be the end. Wisdom of Solomon 1:16–2:24 contains a narrative vignette in which the wicked falsely reason that physical death is the end of human existence. They conclude that all humans will eventually be forgotten, an opinion also found in the book of Ecclesiastes. It follows, they reason, that the wicked face no punishment after death. Thus, as Dostoevsky puts it in *The Brothers Karamazov*, everything is permitted. Their slogan could be, to use the language of Isaiah 22, "Eat and drink, for tomorrow we die." They engage in hedonistic pleasures, such as drinking wine and wearing perfume. Being wicked, they delight in hurting innocent people. They take a particular dislike to the righteous person, whom they accuse of boasting about his special relationship with God. They torture and kill him.

While the wicked think physical death is the end for all humans, this is not the case for the righteous. The soul, without the body, continues to exist with God. After physical death, the souls of the righteous enjoy the condition of immortality that God originally established for humankind. Bodily death, however, is the ultimate end of the wicked. They, not the righteous, are the ones who upon physical death will be gone forever.

The Wisdom of Solomon combines the Platonic idea of the immorality of the soul with conceptions of eternal life that developed in Jewish apocalypticism. This tradition, which flourished in the second and first centuries BCE, is characterized by vivid depictions of the afterlife. Wisdom of Solomon 3 describes the ultimate rewards of the righteous: "in the time of their visitation they will shine forth and will run like sparks through the stubble." The righteous are numbered among the "children (lit. "sons") of God" and "their lot is among the holy ones" (ch. 5). These assertions are compatible with the apocalyptic worldview described in the Dead Sea Scrolls. These writings were preserved by a Jewish sect active in the first century BCE which considered its members to have elect status. One of their writings, known as the *Community Rule*, claims that they are in "lot of the holy ones," referring to the angels. This statement construes the elect as like the angels, as we saw above with 4QInstruction. The elect thus have the prospect of eternal life after death, the ability to participate in a mode of existence enjoyed by angels. In Hebrew, "sons of God" is a common term for angels. The claim in the Wisdom of Solomon that the righteous will be among the "children of God" may reflect the view, prominent in Jewish apocalyptic texts, that the elect shall attain fellowship with the angels.

One important theme of Jewish apocalypticism is the final, or eschatological, judgment. This topic is also present in the Wisdom of Solomon. However, the book does not assert that a cataclysmic moment of universal judgment will take place. The soul of the righteous joins God at the physical death of the individual, not at the end of history. The Wisdom of Solomon has a personal rather than a universal eschatology. The composition's eschatological imagery gives vivid expression to the ultimate hope of the righteous, the dwelling of the immortal soul in heaven after the expiration of the body.

The Wisdom of Solomon also teaches that wisdom can provide a vast breadth of knowledge about the cosmos. According to 1 Kings, after Solomon prays, he acquires encyclopedic knowledge about flora and fauna. The Wisdom of Solomon also states that the legendary king learned such things when he acquired wisdom. But they are now minor parts of a much more profound revelation of knowledge which God disclosed to him: "it is he who gave me unerring knowledge of what exists, to know the structure of the world and the activity of the elements, the beginning and end and middle of times" (ch. 7). This resembles what one can learn according to 4QInstruction from studying the mystery that is to be (in Hebrew, *raz nihyeh*). This text emphasizes that through the contemplation of divinely revealed knowledge (the mystery that is to be) one can attain a comprehensive understanding of reality. 4QInstruction expresses this extensive epiphany, not unlike Wisdom of Solomon 7, by invoking a tripartite division of time—that one can learn what has been, what is, and what will be. The full publication of the Dead Sea Scrolls, completed at the beginning of the twenty-first century, indicates that the Wisdom of Solomon is consistent with older Jewish traditions about obtaining eternal life and acquiring totalizing knowledge about the cosmos, couched in the idiom of Greek philosophy.

Righteous Israel and Wicked Egypt: The Salvific Wisdom of the Torah

The final section of the Wisdom of Solomon, "the Book of History," provides a series of examples drawn from scripture to illustrate that the success of the righteous should be attributed to the guidance and protection of wisdom. Chapter 10 contains seven examples of righteous men who were saved by wisdom. They appear in the sequence in which they appear in Genesis and Exodus (Adam, Noah, Abraham, Lot, Jacob, Joseph, and Moses). The composition's overarching thesis regarding the salvific power of wisdom is clear in Solomon's description of Adam—wisdom "delivered him from his transgression and gave him the strength to rule all things." The text claims that God forgave Adam. This may sound odd to readers of scripture familiar with the doctrine of original sin. The theological argument that wisdom saves the righteous is, however, important in the Wisdom of Solomon. It functions as an exegetical principle. It becomes a thread that connects various biblical tales. It is wisdom that successfully guided Noah's ark during the flood. Lot's escape from the city of Sodom before its destruction is attributed to wisdom. When Joseph was sold into slavery and imprisoned, wisdom accompanied him; his rise to prominence in the Egyptian court is likewise ascribed to wisdom. Significantly, in none of these vignettes are the names of the patriarchs used. In each case, wisdom saves "a righteous man." This underscores the universalizing ideal that anyone who is righteous can be delivered by wisdom.

Wisdom of Solomon 11-19 contains an extended exposition of the Exodus story. Again, the basic point is that wisdom is a guiding force for the righteous. The survival of Israel in the desert after the exodus from Egypt is attributed to her. The pillar of cloud that guided Israel is identified as wisdom.

Wisdom of Solomon 11-19 comprises a set of seven antitheses (11:1-14; 16:1-4; 16:5-14; 16:15-29; 17:1-18:4; 18:5-25; 19:1-9) that are accompanied by a long section which derides the idolatry of the Egyptians and Canaanites (11:15-15:19). The terms "Israel," "Egypt," and "Canaan" are not found in the Wisdom of Solomon. Rather, as in the "Book of Eschatology," the core distinction is between the righteous and the wicked. The righteous, however, can be clearly recognized as the Israelites and the wicked as the Egyptians and the Canaanites. The first antithesis, for example, relies on a contrast involving water—those who follow wisdom were given water from a rock when they were thirsty, whereas their enemies suffered from thirst because their river became defiled with blood. Nature provides water for the righteous but denies it to the wicked. This contrasts the story of the Israelites asking God for water (Numbers 20) with the first of the ten plagues, the turning of the Nile to blood. In stark contrast to the Wisdom of Solomon, in Numbers 20 Israel's request for water in the desert is presented as a problem, an indication that they lack trust in God. The Wisdom of Solomon's exegesis of pentateuchal stories is shaped by the theological principle that the righteous are in harmony with the cosmos and the wicked are not. The perspective is evident in other antitheses. The Egyptians, for example, endure a plague of hail and lightning storms, while God rains down manna to Israel. The Red Sea parts to allow the salvation of Israel, but its water drowns the Egyptians. The Wisdom of Solomon invokes the plagues of Exodus not primarily as a consequence of the pharaoh's refusal to let the

Israelite slaves go, but rather to illustrate how the natural world rejects the wicked.

The theme that the wicked are out of harmony with the cosmos helps explain why the "Book of History" includes bitter and lengthy polemic against idolatry. While biblical texts often lampoon the worship of idols as a foolish and worthless endeavor, the Wisdom of Solomon makes an argument against idolatry that is much more extreme. According to chapter 14, it is "the beginning and cause and end of every evil." Idol worshippers are murderers and sexual deviants who participate in frenzied, bizarre rituals at which they slaughter children. Idolaters, by refusing to revere God, do not have wisdom and thus do not understand the goodness of his creation. They are, the composition teaches, not simply foolish or misguided but wicked and horrible people.

Part of the composition's intense hatred for idolatry stems from disdain for Egyptian religion, an opinion also found in Philo's writings and other Hellenistic Jewish texts. The Exodus plagues, for example, are at times thematized as punishing the Egyptians not for enslaving Israel, but rather because of their religion. The animals sent in the plagues (frogs, locusts) correspond, the Wisdom of Solomon suggests, to the animals they revere. Expressing such anti-Egyptian sentiment was a way for the Hellenized, educated Jews who produced the composition to show their affinity with Greek (Gentile) intellectuals, who also denounced traditional Egyptian religion.

The Transformation of Jewish Wisdom in the Diaspora

The final, Exodus-based section of the Wisdom of Solomon raises a core issue for understanding the book as a whole—its tension between universalism and particularism. On the one hand, wisdom is "philanthropic" and the elements of the cosmos, filled with this spirit, are beneficial to all life. The core message of the composition, for all to embrace wisdom and love righteousness, utilizes Israel's national traditions in a way that strips them of their particularity. Not even King Solomon is mentioned by name. On the other hand, the book's universalist message clearly has a specific readership in mind—a Jewish audience in Alexandria, who would have discerned the composition's allusions to Solomon and other scriptural figures.

The Wisdom of Solomon encourages Jews to seek wisdom and be loyal to the God of Israel. The book may have been produced and circulated by Jews who were persecuted and suffered other difficulties at the hands of a Gentile majority in Egypt during the first half of the first century CE. Elements of Judaism that emphasize ethnic and cultural differences with Gentiles, such as circumcision, the Sabbath, or dietary laws, never come up in the Wisdom of Solomon. The composition reformulates Jewish traditions in a way that is compatible with a Diaspora setting, in particular among Greek intellectuals trained in philosophy and rhetoric. The cosmos studied by Greek philosophers, the book teaches, was created by the God of Israel. Jews should be devoted to God and his envoy wisdom because their religion is a noble philosophy that promotes righteousness and justice. The Wisdom of Solomon valorizes Judaism in a way that Greek intellectuals could appreciate.

Guide for Further Reading

Collins, John J. *Jewish Wisdom in the Hellenistic Age.* Louisville, KY: Westminster John Knox, 1997 (chs. 10–11).
Grabbe, Lester L. *Wisdom of Solomon.* Sheffield, UK: Sheffield Academic Press, 1997.
Winston, David. *The Wisdom of Solomon.* Garden City, NY: Doubleday, 1979.

8

Find a Great Teacher like Me

The Book of Sirach (Ben Sira)

The book of Ben Sira is also known as Sirach or Ecclesiasticus. Sometimes scholars use the term "Sirach" for the book and "Ben Sira" to denote the sage to whom the book is attributed. It is a large composition. It has fifty-one chapters and a prologue. Like the Wisdom of Solomon discussed in the previous chapter, the book of Ben Sira is generally understood by scholars as a wisdom text. This designation highlights the composition's relentless stress on teachers and learning, and its reliance on older sapiential material, most notably the book of Proverbs. Sirach provides instruction on a range of topics relating to ordinary life, such as finances and relationships with friends and parents. The composition also engages more speculative concerns, such as the individual's responsibility for their own sins and the nature of death. Much of the book comprises clusters of sayings on a particular topic, giving it an anthological character. Major textual units of Sirach include the praise of wisdom (ch. 24), the praise of the fathers (chs. 44–49), and hymnic poetry on the beauty of the natural order (39:12–35; 42:15–43:33).

Ben Sira is a classic book of the Protestant Apocrypha and it is in the Old Testament in the Catholic and Orthodox traditions. Like other books Luther relegated to the Apocrypha, in antiquity there were differing views regarding the status of Sirach as Christian scripture. While major early Septuagint manuscripts include the book of Ben Sira (e.g., Vaticanus), and many early Christian authors cite the book, it is not included in some canon

The Apocrypha: A Guide. Matthew Goff, Oxford University Press. © Oxford University Press 2024.
DOI: 10.1093/9780190060770.003.0008

lists, such as those by Cyril of Jerusalem and Gregory of Nazianzus. Jerome distinguishes Sirach from the canonical books of the Old Testament. As discussed in Chapter 1, Jerome was dismissive of Old Testament books that were not extant in Hebrew. In the case of Sirach, he took this view, even though he claims to have known a Hebrew form of the book. This reflects his deference to the canon preserved in Judaism, which does not include the composition. The Hebrew of Ben Sira, long lost, would come to play an important role in understanding the text.

Hebrew Discoveries

The Greek form of Sirach includes a prologue. The author of this opening text claims that he translated a work of instruction written by "my grandfather Jesus," from Hebrew to Greek. Jesus, as the end of chapter 50 makes clear, is the first name of Ben Sira, to whom the rest of the book is attributed. The grandson observes that the Greek translation differs "not a little" from his grandfather's Hebrew text. For centuries one had to take the prologist's word on this point. It was the Greek version of the book, not the Hebrew, that survived in Christendom as part of the Septuagint.

The Jewish reception of the book of Ben Sira is surprisingly extensive. Numerous rabbinic texts cite it in Hebrew, often positively. In the Mishnah, Rabbi Akiva (late first–early second century CE) discourages people from reading the "outside books," a designation for texts sharply distinguished from scripture. In the Babylonian Talmud (tractate *Sanhedrin*), Rav Yosef (fourth century) asserts that these unwelcome books include Ben Sira. Rulings that discourage Jews from reading Ben Sira assume they have some sort of access to it, presumably in Hebrew. This, like the rabbinic citations of the book, suggests that Ben Sira was transmitted in Jewish circles despite not being in the Jewish canon. But no Hebrew manuscripts of the book of Ben Sira were extant. It was lost knowledge.

The situation changed at the end of the nineteenth century. In 1896 two Scottish sisters, Agnes Lewis and Margaret Gibson, acquired manuscripts in Cairo. It was a time when many European academics were procuring ancient manuscripts in the Middle East, often via quasi-legal channels. The sisters brought a sample to Solomon Schechter, a rabbi and professor at Cambridge University in England, who successfully identified it as a Hebrew text of Ben Sira.

The manuscripts were from the genizah of the Ben Ezra Synagogue in Fustat (Old Cairo) in Egypt. A genizah is a storeroom in a synagogue where texts which have been degraded through heavy use are kept. A massive number of documents, well over 300,000, were in the Cairo genizah. They provide a rich impression of Jewish life in Islamic Egypt, principally between the tenth and thirteenth centuries. Substantial portions of six Hebrew manuscripts of Ben Sira from the Cairo Genizah have so far been identified. Approximately two-thirds of the book are now available in Hebrew. New Genizah fragments of Ben Sira have come to light as recently as 2011. The Cairo Genizah texts also include fragments of texts that rework passages of Ben Sira so that the Hebrew rhymes. It is possible that more Ben Sira texts remain to be discovered from among the numerous texts of this corpus, which is not fully published.

Schechter and many subsequent scholars were interested in these Hebrew manuscripts because they were thought to contain the "original" text of Ben Sira. But they are medieval documents, produced centuries after the time of Ben Sira. While the Hebrew manuscripts clearly do preserve much older forms of the text, they also show how the text of Ben Sira changed and developed throughout the centuries in its Jewish transmission. For example, one of the Ben Sira Hebrew manuscripts includes a sixteen-line poem, "the Hymn of Divine Names," between, going by the Greek version, verses 12 and 13 of Sirach 50. The poem was unknown until the discovery of the Cairo Genizah. The hymn is now often included in modern Bibles. It is typically given the versification Sirach 50:12a–o. The poem is likely to have been added to the book of Ben Sira during its later Jewish transmission. The grandson was correct. The Hebrew differs "not a little" from the Greek.

Parts of the composition are also now available in ancient Hebrew manuscripts. In 1964 the Israeli archaeologist Yigael Yadin discovered at Masada a Hebrew scroll that contains a section of the book (Sir 39:27–44:17). Masada is a fortress on a mountaintop near the Dead Sea, built by King Herod, that was held by Jewish rebels during their unsuccessful revolt against Rome. This scroll was made in the first century CE, written before the year 73, when Masada fell, occupied by Jews as a rebel stronghold. The Dead Sea Scrolls include a small fragment of Ben Sira 6 from Cave 2 and a large scroll of psalms from Cave 11 which contains a form of Sirach 51:13–30, a very interesting phenomenon discussed below.

Authors, Authorship, and Preserving the Words of Sages

The prologue is important for understanding the figure of Ben Sira, the putative author of the book of Sirach. The author of the prologue, as already stated, claims he translated a text written by his grandfather, named Jesus. Ben Sira 50:27 gives the grandfather's full name as Jesus ben Eleazar ben Sirach (ben = Heb. "son of"). The variant "Ben Sira" comes from the Hebrew form of 50:27 (and 51:30), which gives a longer version of the sage's name.

The prologue also provides a sense of when Ben Sira lived. The grandson states that he "arrived in Egypt in the thirty-eighth year of the reign of King Euergetes." The Egyptian king at issue is Ptolemy VIII Euergetes II, who had two non-consecutive reigns, 170–164 and 146–117 BCE. This ruler's thirty-eighth year would likely be 132 BCE. The grandson probably completed the translation after this king died in 117 BCE. This historical context for the grandson, combined with the fact that the book of Ben Sira shows no knowledge of the Maccabean crisis (160s BCE), has traditionally led scholars to conclude that Ben Sira wrote his Hebrew instruction in the early second century BCE, probably in the 180s. Because of the book's emphasis on the temple and the upper class (discussed below), it was most likely composed in Jerusalem.

Ben Sira can be, and has been, understood as the earliest identifiable Jewish author—the first to sign his own name to his own book. But two factors should temper this claim. One, the complicated textual situation of the book, with very different versions in different languages (Hebrew, Greek, Latin, Syriac), makes it difficult to recover what the historical Ben Sira may have actually written.

Second, the conception of authorship in Ben Sira's day was not the same as our own. The book of Genesis never credits a specific author for writing the book, whereas modern novels prominently display this information on the cover. Most ancient Jewish texts are anonymous. Some texts are attributed to legendary figures from the past, such as Ezra or Enoch. In ancient Judaism, attributing a text to a particular personage was a way to endow it with authority, or to show that the composition belongs to a particular tradition. Authorship was often not regarded as a form of intellectual ownership, as it is today. These factors help explain why attributions of authorship in antiquity could vary. The version of Sirach 51:13–30 in the Cave 11 Psalms Scroll from Qumran is *not* attributed to Ben Sira. Rather, all the hymns in the scroll are ascribed to King David, in keeping with the venerable tradition that he was a gifted musician who wrote the Psalter. Sirach 51:13–30 was likely not written by the historical Ben Sira, but is rather a Hebrew poem that was appended to the instruction. The ascription of a Davidic psalm to Ben Sira suggests the sage was highly regarded in the circles that transmitted the instruction, as if he exemplified or could even rival in stature the legendary King David.

The association of texts like Sirach 51:13–30 with the figure of Ben Sira should probably be understood in terms of the ancient Jewish educational milieu in which the instruction attributed to him circulated. Ben Sira 51:13–30 stresses the acquisition of wisdom and the value of learning from a teacher. Sirach portrays Ben Sira as a great teacher who encouraged students to study under him. They became teachers, who in turn transmitted his teachings. The instruction attributed to Ben Sira was preserved by means of this pedagogical lineage. The form of the Hebrew instruction that the grandson translated is thus not necessarily the same text written by the grandfather. We cannot even be sure if the historical Ben Sira actually wrote a book. The grandson claims in the prologue he did, but this means that by 117 BCE he had a Hebrew book attributed to Ben Sira, his grandfather. Much of the content of the composition sounds like teachings a sage would have uttered when speaking to students. Socrates did not write down his teachings; rather, his student Plato did because he considered what his teacher said to be important and worth preserving. The origins of the book of Ben Sira as a written text could have been a creation akin to those of Plato, in a Hebrew scribal milieu. Such a process inevitably produces new iterations of the teachings that are ostensibly being preserved. As discussed in Chapter 1, the Dead Sea Scrolls suggest that when the book of Ben Sira was being transmitted, scribes could write forms of texts with a surprising degree of creativity and pluriformity. While Sirach may not be the product of a single author in the modern sense, it can be reasonably understood as the distillation of the mindset and values of an important group in ancient Jewish society: highly educated scribes who taught students and studied texts, represented by the figure of Ben Sira.

Wisdom Is a Woman, a Tree, a River, and the Torah

The arrangement of material in the book of Ben Sira is rather loose. Topics appear sporadically throughout the composition, without any indication that their placement is organized. The theme of friendship, for example, is taken up in chapters 6, 12, 13, 22, 27, and

37. Poems about wisdom, however, occur at important locations in the book, in chapters 1 and 24, the beginning and rough midpoint of the work, respectively. The text that concludes the instruction, Sirach 51:13–30, even though likely not written by Ben Sira himself, is also about wisdom. This arrangement emphasizes wisdom as an overarching theme of the instruction.

The book begins by asserting the divine nature of wisdom: "All wisdom is from the Lord." Piety and wisdom are closely allied in Sirach. The composition teaches that a man who possesses wisdom is necessarily devoted to God. The "fear of the Lord" is presented as an attitude of reverence one should adopt. Sirach teaches, not unlike the book of Proverbs, that those who possess wisdom will have fulfilling lives and not suffer from want. Wisdom, the book of Ben Sira teaches, is something that people can obtain and should strive for.

Wisdom is an abstract and difficult concept to grasp. Sirach draws upon the sapiential heritage of Israel to make it not only intelligible but desirable. Ben Sira 24, not unlike the Wisdom of Solomon, poetically refashions the portrait of wisdom personified as a woman in Proverbs 8. In Ben Sira 24, as in Proverbs 8, wisdom speaks, presenting herself as a teacher who beckons students to study under her guidance. Ben Sira 24, also like Proverbs 8, presents wisdom as active throughout the cosmos. The universe has structure and order because God created it with his wisdom. This view undergirds the book's lengthy poetic descriptions of the natural world, teaching that its beauty and grandeur testify to God's dominion. In chapter 24, wisdom claims she emerged from God's mouth, a metaphorical depiction of wisdom as divine speech: "I came forth from the mouth of the Most High and covered the earth like a mist." She covers vast distances, crossing over the "vault of heaven" and the "depths of the abyss."

But unlike Proverbs 8, Ben Sira 24 writes divine wisdom into the national history of Israel. God commanded wisdom to shift from her cosmic wanderings and reside permanently in Israel: "Make your dwelling in Jacob and in Israel receive your inheritance."

She took root and grew into a luxuriant tree in Jerusalem. At one level this is a figurative reference to the temple. The tree's fragrant aromas are akin to kinds of incense used in the temple. Imagined as a kind of talking tree, wisdom invites people to eat her fruits. The tree also signifies a teacher urging students to learn from her. It evokes the tree of the knowledge of good and evil from the Garden of Eden, with one crucial difference—here there is no prohibition against eating from it. One is encouraged, by the tree itself, to do so.

Ben Sira 24 invokes other types of Eden imagery as well. The chapter likens wisdom to rivers, including the four that Genesis 2 describes as flowing out from Eden (Pishon, Tigris, Euphrates, Gihon). The chapter poetically merges Eden and Jerusalem, utilizing scriptural tropes to portray Israel as possessing privileged and exceptional wisdom. An overarching goal of the book, to praise the wisdom of Israel, functions as a kind of exegetical principle that transforms the scriptural heritage that is being praised. Understanding this point explains why Ben Sira 24 never mentions a commandment not to eat from the tree (so too ch. 17). The book is not trying to explicate scripture and all its details, but rather to use motifs from scriptural stories to present wisdom as something extraordinary which students should strive to acquire.

The book's engagement with Jewish scripture is not limited to Genesis 1–3. Ben Sira 44–49, often called "the Praise of the Fathers," extols patriarchs from the Torah such as Abraham and Moses as models of virtue and piety. The Torah (the first five books of the Bible) is thematized as an important source of wisdom. It is a key manifestation of the wisdom of Israel. This view is explicit in Ben Sira 24 itself. After wisdom, in the form of a tree, encourages people to eat her fruits, the poem explains that "all this is the book of the covenant of the Most High God, the law that Moses commanded us as an inheritance for the congregations of Jacob" (24:23). While the nuances of this verse are much debated, it can be plausibly interpreted as the tree (wisdom) offering her fruit (the Torah) to Israel.

The book of Ben Sira is important for understanding the historical development of scripture. The instruction gives an impression of a sage in Jerusalem in the early second century BCE who used the Torah in his teaching. The composition suggests that by this time the Torah had some sort of authoritative status. This realization should be allied with evidence from the Dead Sea Scrolls, which are from the same general time period. Numerous texts from this corpus cite and interpret scriptural texts in myriad ways, affirming that they were important at the time. But they also illustrate, as mentioned above, that the textual form of scriptural writings was variable and somewhat fluid. Understanding the changeable nature of scripture in the period accords with Ben Sira 24 itself since it praises wisdom with ever-changing and expansive metaphors—it is a growing tree, overflowing rivers, and the Torah. While the Greek form of Sir 24:23 describes the "book of the covenant" as the "law" (*nomos*), the underlying Hebrew (unfortunately no Hebrew for this key chapter is extant) is surely the word *torah*. This term, while traditionally translated as "law," in Hebrew literally means "instruction." This fits very well with chapter 24 and the book of Ben Sira as a whole. Its emphasis is often not simply on a written text but on the voice of the teacher. This muddies any distinction in the composition between instruction (*torah*) given by the teacher figure and the scriptural traditions that he incorporated (the Torah) into his teaching. The composition marshals a conception of the Torah as a source of divine wisdom to convey that Ben Sira is a great sage, who can provide access to this exceptional wisdom.

Find a Great Teacher like Me: Sages, Students, and Social Setting

In Ben Sira 24, after wisdom is compared to water, Ben Sira, speaking in the first person (as wisdom does earlier in the poem), likens himself to water. He compares himself to a channel from a river that irrigates a garden: "I was like a canal from a river." This denotes not the garden of Eden, but rather a garden to which the waters of Eden flow. It is Ben Sira's own garden. This garden, in a sense, is where he teaches students and imparts wisdom to them. The teacher is imagined as both the gardener and the nourishing water he provides. The water imagery portrays the teacher as a conduit of divine wisdom. With great humility, the sage describes his own speech as divinely inspired, likening it to prophecy.

The book's emphasis on the authoritative and edifying words of a great teacher sheds light on the ancient Jewish pedagogical culture out of which the composition emerged. Learning and teachers are stressed throughout. People are taught that to reap the benefits of acquiring wisdom, one needs to do so under the tutelage of a teacher, as it says in chapter 6: "Stand in the company of the elders. Who is wise? Attach yourself to such a one. Be ready to listen to every godly discourse and let no wise proverbs escape you." This path of life is described as a harsh yoke that will turn into a splendid crown, denoting that lifelong devotion to study and self-discipline will result in a fulfilling life and the memorialization of one's name after death.

Even though Sirach 51:13–30 is likely a later addition to the book, it is fully in keeping with the composition's theme of desiring wisdom. The poem recounts in the first person a man's lifelong love affair with wisdom. Not unlike Solomon in the Wisdom of Solomon, the male speaker looks back to an earlier stage of his life when he fell in love with wisdom, personified as a woman: "While I was still young, before I went on my travels, I sought wisdom openly in my prayer." The Qumran form of the text depicts the relationship between the man and personified wisdom with erotically charged language: "my hand ope[ned her gates] and I perceived her unseen parts." The speaker in the corresponding verse in the Greek, by contrast, states that he spreads his hands out to heaven (51:19).

The image of the male student penetrating and discerning the nudity of wisdom conveys that acquiring wisdom denotes obtaining special and precious knowledge. In erotic language, the speaker conveys that he is a teacher with great wisdom. As in chapter 24, the speaker recounts this to entice students to learn from him. He invites them to reside in his "house of instruction." This phrase in later rabbinic Judaism denotes a room, often in a synagogue, in which the Bible is studied.

In keeping with the book's emphasis on teachers and learning, Sirach offers a highly idealized portrait of the scribe (38:24–39:11). The word "scribe" literally denotes someone who writes. In antiquity it can refer to bureaucrats and administrators, learned scholars who preserve and write texts, or individuals with more exalted positions, such as a king's trusted advisor. The book offers a picture of the scribe in keeping with the second meaning, but praises the office to such an extent that it often sounds like someone more important, such as an advisor to the king. The passage hails the scribe as a man of wisdom, a scholar who studies the Torah, and collects and studies proverbs. The profession of scribes is hailed as superior to more commonplace occupations, such as being a farmer or a smith.

There is clearly some hyperbole in the book's praise of the scribe in chapter 39. He travels widely and gives counsel to rulers. Rivaling the legendary Solomon, the scribe's wisdom is highly regarded throughout the world. It is hard to believe that every scribe in Jerusalem during the time of Ben Sira had acquired such an exalted international reputation. With such an elevated portrayal, the ancient Jewish scribes and teachers who helped transmit the instruction of Ben Sira accentuate the value and stature of their own profession. Ben Sira 38:24–39:11 imagines its idealized scribe working in an upper-class setting. The teachers represented by Ben Sira likely did work within an aristocratic milieu. Much of the instruction of the composition accords with this perspective.

Instruction for Elite Young Men

The book of Ben Sira raises the question how to understand education in ancient Judah. There were no schools in an institutionalized sense. Many people were poor and received hands-on training from their parents about skills necessary for survival, such as farming. They did not attend school as students do today. The sage Ben Sira, by contrast, was part of a formalized system of education. The kind of learning advocated by the book of Ben Sira offers a window into the pedagogical norms and customs of the upper class. Ben Sira, one can say, taught in the "ivory tower." The intellectual culture which Ben Sira represents is devoted to the training of elites who would obtain professions such as diplomats, government administrators, teachers (of elites), and other prestigious positions. This would suggest, given the patriarchal culture of the time, that the students taught by sages like Ben Sira were men, presumably elite, young men.

Numerous teachings in the book of Ben Sira presume an upper-class context. The composition gives advice on how to comport oneself when speaking before the wealthy and powerful. Chapters 31–32 contain an extensive lesson on table manners and etiquette when dining at a banquet, a staple component of Hellenistic aristocratic culture. At such meals, the book teaches, one should be moderate with regard to both food and wine, and cautious when speaking. The composition also presumes that its addressees could own slaves. The sage's advice on the subject is repugnant. Students were taught to make their slaves work hard and put heavy chains on the disobedient ones. The person who owns a single slave is to adopt a more lenient posture.

The book's teaching on money and finances assumes that the student-addressees are well-to-do. They are urged to give charity to the poor and lend money because it helps those in need, even though the loans may never be repaid. The possibility that they would themselves be in financial hardship never comes up.

Indebtedness was a widespread social problem in ancient Judean society. Unscrupulous creditors would give out loans with excessive interest and when the loans would not be repaid, they would seize the person's land or even family members as slaves. The book of Ben Sira teaches his affluent students to be ethical custodians of wealth. The composition acknowledges in chapter 13 the abuse the wealthy could inflict on the poor: "Wild asses in the wilderness are the prey of lions; likewise the poor are feeding grounds for the rich."

Also consistent with the upper-class setting of the book, the overall outlook of Sirach is rather conservative. There is no call for radical change. There is no broad critique of the world as unjust, or lament that Israel is under the dominion of wicked rulers (but see chapter 36, often considered secondary). The composition teaches that God's created order is essentially good, providing sustenance to the pious but destruction to the wicked. The deity created dangerous aspects of the world such as fire and hail to punish evildoers, a teaching that victims of such calamities would not find consoling. Individuals are responsible for their own sin, rather than God, who punishes wrongdoing. The book teaches that the person who works hard and acts ethically will lead a successful life. It contains no hint of the poignant theodicy or complaints about the world that are central in the biblical books Job and Ecclesiastes. This perspective fits well with the view that the intended addressees of the book by and large had comfortable, successful lives, at a time when few did.

The book of Ben Sira affirms and celebrates official domains of power, in particular the Jerusalem temple and its priests. The Dead Sea Scrolls establish that there was intense criticism of the temple at the time. A central tenet of the Jewish sect that produced the scrolls is that the priesthood is impure and corrupt. There is no such critique in Sirach. Quite the opposite is the case.

Sirach culminates in poetic praise of worship at the temple. The end of chapter 50 sounds like the end of the book, and material in chapter 51 likely constitutes later additions to the composition. The bulk of chapter 50 praises a high priest, the leading sacerdotal official of the temple in Jerusalem. The high priest in question is named Simon; this most likely refers to Simon II, high priest from 219 to 196 BCE. At the time, the high priest was not simply a temple official but also a politically powerful figure. Ben Sira 50 praises Simon for carrying out civic improvements to the city of Jerusalem, such as fortifying its walls and having a water cistern dug. Simon is depicted as a visually stunning, almost otherworldly figure in his priestly regalia:

> How glorious he was, surrounded by the people as he came out of the house of the curtain . . . like the sun shining on the temple of the Most High, like the rainbow gleaming in splendid clouds. . . . When he put on his glorious robe and clothed himself in perfect splendor, when he went up to the holy altar, he made the court of the sanctuary glorious.

He is compared to a tree, not unlike personified wisdom in chapter 24, who, as we have seen, is likewise associated with the temple. Chapter 50 depicts Simon leading a ceremony there. Priests blow their trumpets and the assembled crowds (probably in the courts of the temple, not the temple itself) fall to the ground to worship God. This is likely a depiction of how Yom Kippur, the Day of Atonement (still a major Jewish holiday), was conducted when the temple stood. The adoration of Simon in chapter 50 concludes the Praise of the Fathers in chapters 44–49, presenting the priest as the culmination of Israel's patriarchal heritage. It is as if the glories of an idealized past were rekindled and accessible through Simon. The book of Ben Sira could not be more laudatory of this priest.

Unfortunate Advice to Men about Women

One other major topic of instruction in Sirach is gender relations. While the sage Ben Sira displays genuine affection toward wisdom personified as a woman, when it comes to real women the composition often takes a very different attitude. The book's statements about women are jaw-dropping, even by biblical standards: "Better is the evil of a man than the goodness of a woman" (42:14). The composition has the dubious distinction of being the oldest known text to blame Eve for the origin of death: "From a woman sin had its beginning and because of her we all die" (25:24). Elsewhere the book takes a completely different attitude toward death, construing it as a basic part of the human condition established by God. Chapters 25–26 are filled with caustic teachings about women. Such views likely spurred on the willingness to blame death on Eve found in Sirach 25:24. The teacher stresses that there is nothing worse than marrying a bad or evil woman, asserting, for example: "I would rather live with a lion and dragon than live with an evil woman." It is disgraceful for a man to be supported by his wife, the book teaches, and a good wife is "silent" and "modest." The word for "modest" in the Hebrew is more literally translated as "shameful." The book teaches that a good wife is filled with shame. Her shame functions as a kind of self-discipline. She is easier for the husband to control because she polices herself.

The sage, unfortunately, has a lot to say about daughters too. They are a constant source of anxiety for the father. The feelings of the mother never come up. The father, according to chapter 42, should ensure that his daughter's room has no window, to prevent her from sneaking out or men seeing her without his supervision. The composition's major concern is that a daughter can embarrass her father. Young women, unlike Ben Sira's ideal wife who controls her behavior out of a sense of shame, are too immature to restrain their sexuality. Ben Sira 26:12 insultingly conveys this point. If the father does not watch over his "headstrong daughter," "she will sit in front of every tent peg and open her quiver to the arrow." Sons are not treated kindly either. Fathers should never laugh with their sons. They should beat them severely when they are young to ensure their obedience.

Should we imagine all the teacher-sages of ancient Jerusalem as misogynistic and dour as Ben Sira? It was a patriarchal world, but the composition displays a more offensive attitude toward women than other texts from the period. The book may reflect the particularly caustic views of the historical Ben Sira. Perhaps he was in an unhappy marriage and had daughters who resented his overbearing parenting style. In any case, such harmful views did not disqualify his teachings from being memorialized or his name being remembered in praise by other teachers and even his own family (his grandson). In ancient Judah, the book of Ben Sira suggests, wise old men could instill corrosive attitudes toward women in young elite men.

The Book of Ben Sira: Wisdom, Teachers, Students

The book of Ben Sira gives an impression of an upper-class society in which learning from sages and teachers was highly regarded. The composition does not simply represent the words of a single teacher, but rather is a distillation of a broader pedagogical culture in which students became teachers who memorialized and preserved iterations of what their teachers said. Sirach's utilization of scriptural traditions serves this larger goal. While some of the teachings of the book of Ben Sira are better left in the second century BCE, the composition is important evidence for understanding education in ancient Judaism.

Guide for Further Reading

Camp, Claudia V. *Ben Sira and the Men Who Handle Books: Gender and the Rise of Canon-Consciousness.* Sheffield, UK: Sheffield Phoenix Press, 2013.

Coggins, Richard J. *Sirach*. Sheffield, UK: Sheffield Academic Press, 1998.
Collins, John J. *Jewish Wisdom in the Hellenistic Age*. Louisville, KY: Westminster John Knox, 1997 (chs. 2–6).
Skehan, Patrick W., and Alexander A. Di Lella. *The Wisdom of Ben Sira: A New Translation with Notes*. New York: Doubleday, 1987.

9

Jeremian Scriptures in Exile

Baruch and the Letter of Jeremiah

Jeremiah, Baruch, and Their Writings

The book of Baruch imagines the exiles in Babylon recommitting themselves to God and the Torah. The Letter of Jeremiah is a polemic diatribe against the gods of Babylon. Despite their stark differences, these two books and their editorial history are intertwined, as are the figures of Baruch and Jeremiah.

According to the biblical book of Jeremiah, the prophet Jeremiah experienced firsthand the Babylonian destruction of Jerusalem and the deportation of many Judeans into exile in the early sixth century BCE. It also states that he had an associate, a scribe named Baruch ben Neriah. As his scribe, Baruch wrote texts for Jeremiah. The book of Jeremiah primarily depicts the prophet communicating via speech, not writing. In the few chapters of the book that recount Jeremiah's words being written down, Baruch is important. In Jeremiah 36, for example, the prophet dictates a message that Baruch copies onto a scroll, which he then reads aloud in the temple. Jeremiah cannot speak in the temple because the king banned him from entering it. Baruch's act of writing has a "single use" function; presumably if Jeremiah had been allowed in the temple, he would have gone there himself to speak, without any need for a scroll or Baruch. Chapter 29, by contrast, depicts Jeremiah's writing as having more enduring value. This chapter, which never mentions Baruch, purports to preserve a letter the

The Apocrypha: A Guide. Matthew Goff, Oxford University Press. © Oxford University Press 2024.
DOI: 10.1093/9780190060770.003.0009

prophet sent to the exiles in Babylon from Jerusalem, urging them to prepare to remain in Babylon for seventy years.

Whereas the Hebrew Bible primarily depicts prophets as figures who speak, chastising the people of Israel in the public square, writing emerges after the rupture of the exile as an important medium by which guidance from Jeremiah continues. In the Second Temple period, Jeremiah becomes revered as a prophet who wrote to the exiles, urging them to keep the Torah and avoid idols. It is a point of debate among scholars, but Jeremiah 29 could be a later addition to the book, an indication of a later, Second Temple–era conception of the prophet.

As a consequence of this later view about Jeremiah, new compositions were produced that were attributed to him, and also to his scribe Baruch (a literary convention scholars call pseudepigraphy). The book of Baruch and the Letter of Jeremiah are key examples of this phenomenon. Scholars do not hold that these two individuals wrote these books, but rather that they are later texts ascribed to them. They contain historical errors that suggest they were not written when Baruch and Jeremiah would have lived, the sixth century BCE (e.g., Belshazzar was the son of Nabonidus, not Nebuchadnezzar; Bar 1:11). Moreover, the phenomenon of pseudepigraphy was widespread in the late Second Temple period. Baruch and the Letter of Jeremiah are thought to have been written during or close to the second century BCE, but their precise date of composition cannot be established. Determining where they were written also cannot be determined with certainty. Their focus on exile, however, suggests they were composed in a Diaspora setting. The oldest textual evidence for Baruch and the Letter of Jeremiah is in Greek, but their text suggests that some or all of these works were translated from now lost Hebrew versions into Greek.

Additional texts are ascribed to Jeremiah. He is traditionally regarded as the author of the biblical book of Lamentations, which expresses pathos over the destruction of Jerusalem. One text from the Dead Sea Scrolls entitled the *Apocryphon of Jeremiah* preserves fragments of stories about Jeremiah from the second century BCE (thus roughly contemporary with Baruch and the Letter of Jeremiah).

The book of Baruch is sometimes called 1 Baruch to distinguish it from other ancient texts attributed to this scribe—*2 Baruch, 3 Baruch*, and *4 Baruch*. There is also an *Apocalypse of Baruch*, preserved among Jews in Ethiopia. In these later texts Baruch emerges as a recipient of divine revelation in his own right, rather than simply Jeremiah's secretary. These texts also engage the trope that Baruch is a scribe. *2 Baruch* concludes (chapters 78–87) with a lengthy letter Baruch writes to the Assyrian exiles (the lost northern kingdom of Israel). In *4 Baruch* he writes a letter to Jeremiah (delivered by an eagle!) who is in Babylon.

There is a long-standing tradition of blurring the lines between Jeremiah and Baruch, with regard to both these figures and the texts ascribed to them. This reflects the biblical trope that Baruch is Jeremiah's scribe. As such, Baruch writes the words of Jeremiah. Some early Christian writers, such as Athenagoras (second century CE), cite language from 1 Baruch and say it is from Jeremiah. Numerous lectionaries (excerpts of biblical texts that stipulate when they are to be recited in worship) do the same. Jerome in his preface to Jeremiah likewise explains that he "omitted" 1 Baruch— as if he were omitting it *from* the book of Jeremiah.

The perspective that both 1 Baruch and the Letter of Jeremiah are Jeremian writings is evident in early iterations of Christian scripture. They are both attested in the Vaticanus and Alexandrinus codices of the Septuagint. They place 1 Baruch between Jeremiah and Lamentations. Since these two latter texts are attributed to Jeremiah, it is implicit that 1 Baruch is as well. In these manuscripts the Letter of Jeremiah is after Lamentations, making it the endpiece of a cycle of Jeremian texts (Jeremiah, Lamentations, 1 Baruch, and the Letter).

Another sequence of Jeremian texts is attested in eastern Christianity, in versions of the Bible in Syriac (a Christian form of Aramaic). One major Syriac biblical manuscript (Codex Ambrosianus) includes *2 Baruch*. In the Syriac tradition, *2 Baruch* 78–87 is also often included in biblical manuscripts as a distinct text, separate from the rest of *2 Baruch*. It is commonly titled the "First Epistle of Baruch." Then follows the "Second Epistle of Baruch," a title that denotes what scholars call 1 Baruch, after which comes the Letter of Jeremiah. Jeremiah, Lamentations, and these letters can be marked in Syriac Bibles as a single series of Jeremian books by listing the prophet's name at the top of every manuscript page throughout this bloc of texts.

There is also a tradition of regarding the Letter of Jeremiah as the final chapter of the book of Baruch. This was common in Catholic Bibles in the Middle Ages and in early Protestant versions of the Apocrypha. The first edition of the King James Bible (1611), for example, lists "Baruch with the Epistle of Jeremiah" as a single text with six chapters; 1 Baruch has five chapters and the Letter only one.

1 Baruch and the Letter of Jeremiah are books of the Old Testament in the Eastern Orthodox and Catholic traditions. 1 Baruch began to be included in Latin Bibles in the Middle Ages, in keeping with its inclusion in the Septuagint, moving beyond Jerome's earlier decision not to translate it. He excluded it because it was not in the Hebrew Bible. As a book of the Catholic Old Testament that was not extant in Hebrew, Luther and other Protestant Reformers moved 1 Baruch to the Apocrypha. Luther was not a huge fan of the book. In his preface to it, he calls the composition "skimpy." He debated not including it in the Apocrypha, but decided to in part because of its polemic against idolatry— presuming, in keeping with Catholic norms, that the final chapter of 1 Baruch is the Letter of Jeremiah.

1 Baruch and the Letter of Jeremiah are not in the Jewish canon. The important early Christian author Origen (late second–early third centuries), however, in a text preserved by Eusebius, lists the books of the Hebrew scriptures as including "Jeremiah, with

Lamentations and the Letter," a likely reference to the Letter of Jeremiah. Epiphanius (fourth century) likewise affirms that when the Jews returned from exile they included in their scriptures "the letters of Jeremiah and Baruch." A Christian text, the *Apostolic Constitutions* (fourth century), claims that Jews would assemble on the 10th of Gorpiaeus (a month of the Macedonian calendar) to mourn the destruction of Jerusalem and read together Lamentations and Baruch. This Christian evidence may reflect a time before the Jewish canon as we know it was fully established. No Jewish text, however, corroborates their claims. Rabbinic literature gives no indication either book was ever part of the Jewish Bible. Also, the Dead Sea Scrolls include no ancient Hebrew versions of these two texts, although one small Greek papyrus fragment from Cave 7 of Qumran has been identified as from the Letter of Jeremiah. This scrap confirms that the Letter must be older than 100 BCE.

1 Baruch: Confession, Renewal, Restoration

The book of Baruch falls into four distinct sections:

- Historical introduction (1:1–14)
- Confession of sin (1:15–3:8)
- Poem praising the Torah as wisdom (3:9–4:4)
- Poem of consolation (4:5–5:9).

These units may have originated as separate texts. For example, while many biblical scholars hold that Baruch 1:1–3:8 was originally written in Hebrew, there is less consensus as to whether this is the case for the rest of the book. There are important differences across these units regarding terminology. The deity, for example, is repeatedly referred to as "Lord" in the confession of sin section, but this term is found neither in the Torah poem nor the poem of consolation, which refer to him instead, respectively, as "God" and "Everlasting."

If the poems of Baruch were composed individually, they were woven together to produce a coherent text. 1 Baruch as a whole delineates a clear theological progression—confession, renewal, restoration. The Jews in exile confess their sins and articulate their yearning to obey God (1:15–3:8). The way to follow God is to heed the Torah (3:9–4:4). The final poem imagines a restored relationship between God and Israel, symbolized by the exiles returning to Jerusalem (4:5–5:9).

The kind of prayer found in Baruch 1:15–3:8, in which the exiles confess their sins using the first person plural, is common in Second Temple literature (e.g., Daniel 9, the Prayer of Azariah, the Prayer of Manasseh). The traumatic experience of exile generated the production of confessional prayers. The prayer in Baruch explains why they are in exile. God had no choice but to punish Israel because "we have disobeyed him and have not heeded the voice of the Lord our God." Whereas 2 Esdras questions God's actions, 1 Baruch asserts that his punishment of Israel was just.

According to the prayer, Israel's disobedience is a fulfillment of the Torah. The end of the Torah (Deuteronomy) contains a series of often gruesome curses which are to befall Israel if it strays from the covenant. Deuteronomy 28, for example, contains a curse that was likely shaped by the Babylonian destruction of Judah— that God will send an enemy to destroy the land so utterly that people will have to eat members of their own families to survive. In 1 Baruch's prayer, the exiles affirm that this covenant curse came upon them. Some of them *did* eat their own children, according to Baruch 2. This chapter also quotes a form of another curse from Deuteronomy 28, which states that if Israel disobeys God, he will send them into exile. The deity also sent prophets to warn Israel, but the people ignored them (more on this below). The prayer in Baruch urges God to open his eyes and look upon Israel in exile, which is likened to a person "deeply grieved, who walks bowed and feeble, with failing eyes and famished soul." The prayer urges God to recognize the exiles' pathetic, sinful condition so that he might show mercy on them. This is critical for re-establishing the covenant between God and Israel.

Baruch 3:9–4:4 stresses that Israel must act as well. This poem reframes traditions attested in Proverbs and Job. In Proverbs the concept of wisdom is important and multivalent. It can denote the ability to understand the world and be successful in it. 1 Baruch presumes this conception of wisdom. In the mindset of the text, Israel is not doing well in the world and thus needs wisdom. Proverbs personifies wisdom as a woman who urges people to learn from her. The book of Job, by contrast, presents wisdom as inaccessible. Job 28 is a dark poem in which people scour the earth searching for wisdom, unable to find it. There is no wisdom on earth, according to this text.

1 Baruch, like Proverbs, presents wisdom as a feminine entity present on earth. But, in an ethnically exclusivist adaptation of Job 28, the composition teaches that she is unavailable not to all people, but most—the Gentiles. Israel, however, has access to wisdom through the Torah. Ben Sira 24 also associates the personified wisdom of Proverbs with the Torah. 1 Baruch connects this conception of wisdom to the Torah to convey that it is a gift which Jews should accept. The description in Baruch that wisdom was on earth ("she appeared on earth and lived with humankind"; Bar 3:36–37) took on new importance in Christianity. This passage was often cited by Christian exegetes, such as Quodvultdeus (a fifth-century bishop of Carthage) or the medieval theologian Thomas Aquinas who, equating "wisdom" with Christ, interpreted it as a reference to Jesus's incarnation, the physical manifestation of a heavenly being.

There is a tradition from the early Second Temple period that the decision by the Persian king Cyrus to end the Babylonian exile and allow the Jews to return home fulfills a prophecy by Jeremiah. This assertion is at the end of 2 Chronicles and the beginning of Ezra (both texts that can be dated to the fourth century

BCE), and also in 1 Esdras. There is a later Second Temple tradition that Jeremiah promoted Torah piety in exile. In the Qumran *Apocryphon of Jeremiah*, Jeremiah accompanies the exiles up to a river in Babylon (more on this below), whereas in the book of Jeremiah he escapes to Egypt. In this Qumran text, Jeremiah in Babylon urges the exiles to keep the covenant. The composition elsewhere locates the prophet in Egypt, suggesting that it is a collection of various Jeremian stories. In Egypt he urges the Israelites to keep the commandments of God. In another fragmentary text of this work, it appears that he exhorts the exiles in Babylon to keep the covenant by writing them a letter from Egypt. 2 Maccabees 2 depicts Jeremiah giving the Torah to the Jews while they are being deported to Babylon, urging them to not stray from it. In the late Second Temple period Jeremiah becomes a kind of Moses figure, giving the law anew to the Jews in exile. 1 Baruch, by associating its call for the exiles to follow the Torah with Jeremiah's scribe, should be understood against the backdrop of this Jeremian tradition, as should his letter to the exiles in the Letter of Jeremiah (more on both below).

The final poem of 1 Baruch (4:5–5:9) imagines the harmonious reunion of God and Israel, celebrated as the return of the exiles to Jerusalem. The poem's excitement regarding the return to Judah resonates with Second Isaiah (Isaiah 40–55), which likewise extols the end of the Babylonian exile. 1 Baruch personifies Jerusalem as a mother who speaks about the exiles as her estranged children. According to chapter 4, she was distraught but no longer grieves: "For I sent you out with sorrow and weeping but God will give you back to me with joy and gladness forever." Another speaker, perhaps the authorial voice of Baruch, urges Mother Jerusalem to look to the east and watch her children come home. They do not, however, arrive. Like the Torah, which ends with the people Israel on the edge of the promised land, 1 Baruch concludes with the reunification of God and Israel in Jerusalem as anticipated but unfulfilled.

Israel's New Beginning, On the
Wrong Side of the River

The theological progression described in the preceding section—
confession of sins, Torah renewal, restoration in Jerusalem—is a
process that begins in Baruch 1 by a river in Babylon. It starts when
a "book" (or better, a scroll) written by Baruch is read before the
exilic community by the River Sud, a name otherwise unknown.
The book in question is the text of Baruch itself, from 1:15 to its
end. The book of Baruch highlights its own textuality. Baruch 1:1–
14 makes clear that Baruch's book is an important document for
the exiles. Locating Baruch in Babylon is at odds with the book of
Jeremiah, which states that he went with Jeremiah to Egypt after
Jerusalem was destroyed (Jer 43). Some rabbinic texts, such as *Song
of Songs Rabbah*, state like 1 Baruch that Baruch went to Babylon.
In 1 Baruch the exilic location of Baruch accentuates that Babylon
is where Israel confesses and begins to return to God. Babylon also
serves as a site of religious renewal, a place where one sincerely
turns to God amidst difficult circumstances, in other texts, such as
the Prayer of Manasseh and the Danielic Prayer of Azariah. In 1
Baruch, Babylon signifies being out of the covenant relationship,
prompting the desire to restore it. Jerusalem represents the establishment of that renewal, an idealized relationship with Israel living
in harmony with God.

According to Baruch 1:2, Baruch wrote his book five years after
the Babylonians destroyed Jerusalem (581 BCE). 1 Baruch, written
in the second century BCE, shows an interest not simply in the exile
but its beginning stages. The exile is reimagined. In 1 Baruch, Israel
was offered a way to end the exile shortly after it began. In this composition, as mentioned above, the end of the exile is envisioned
but not yet attained. The text presents the exile as an ongoing experience. Several other texts from the late Second Temple period
are set during the Babylonian exile. Daniel 9, for example, which
was written against the backdrop of the Maccabean crisis (160s

BCE), depicts Daniel in the early days of the exile, reading about Jeremiah's seventy-year prophecy (for the Maccabean crisis as the context for Daniel 7–12, see Chapter 12).

The widespread interest in the exile during the late Second Temple period suggests it was understood as a metaphor for life in the Diaspora. The Diaspora, with its difficulties and forms of discrimination, could be imagined as a situation of ongoing, constant exile that did not end when the Persian king Cyrus allowed the Jews to return to the land of Israel. The exile so understood signifies a form of alienation from God that prods Israel to renew its relationship with him. The perspective that exile is a present experience is evident in Daniel 9. There the angel Gabriel tells Daniel that Jeremiah's prophecy signifies not seventy years but seventy *weeks* of years (not 70 but 70 × 7, or 490 years) and the present moment (the Maccabean crisis) is understood as close to the end of history. Daniel 9 presumes that Jeremiah's prophecy about the exile lasting seventy years did *not* come to pass and requires new interpretation to be understood as fulfilled. This conception of the exile also explains why at times 1 Baruch slips out of the historical context it provides for itself. As discussed below, critical for the composition is the public reading of Baruch's book in the Jerusalem temple—even though, according to Baruch 1:2, it was written five years after the temple was destroyed. In the exile of the Jewish imagination in later centuries, there is a temple in Jerusalem—far off and important.

Baruch presents his book as an authoritative text that reestablishes Israel's covenant relationship with God. When read aloud at the river, it provides the "voice" with which Israel expresses its desire to rekindle its commitment to God. Rivers in Babylon are important in the books of Ezekiel and Daniel, by which both men have encounters with angelic beings. The River Sud has a comparable significance in 1 Baruch, as a site where renewing a connection to God is possible. Perhaps also evoking Israel's crossing of the Red Sea in the Exodus tradition, the river demarcates a point of transition. Crossing it, or at least leaving from it, conveys Israel re-entering the covenant relationship. The river in 1 Baruch also draws on other traditions. In Ezra 8 the exiles assemble to fast and pray at a river in Babylon named Ahava and from there return to Jerusalem. Likewise in 1 Esdras 8, the exiles gather at a river (called Theras in some manuscripts) and depart for Jerusalem.

In 1 Baruch the name of the river where the exiles assemble is Sud, according to our oldest Greek manuscripts. But this is likely incorrect. The name of the river in the Syriac version of Baruch 1:4 is not Sud but Sur. In the *Apocryphon of Jeremiah* the exiles in Babylon read a letter from Jeremiah at a river named not Sud but Sur. In Hebrew the letters "d" and "r" (*daleth* and *resh*) look very similar (ד and ר). An older, now lost form of Baruch 1 likely existed in Hebrew that stated that the exiles read Baruch's book by the River Sur. When the text was translated to Greek, the letter "r" in Sur was misread as "d," producing Sud, a mistake that became normative in the Old Testament. The older name of the river accords with the Hebrew verb "to turn" (*sur*). This verb often denotes that Israel has turned away from God. God says, for example, in the Exodus story of the Golden Calf, "they have been quick to turn aside (*saru*) from the way that I commanded them." Signifying being off the right path, the term becomes associated with the exile, as in Second Isaiah. In Isaiah 49, Israel declares "I was bereaved and barren, in exile and wandering (*surah*)." The river Sur signifies in 1 Baruch both that they are in exile—on the wrong side of the river, one could say—and they want to restore their covenantal relationship with him. The name of the river conveys that they are turned away from God and want to turn back to him.

Upon hearing Baruch's book, the exiles weep and arrange to have it sent to Jerusalem, along with sacred vessels King Nebuchadnezzar had stolen when he destroyed the temple, and with money to fund many sacrifices there. The words of the book are to be read aloud in the temple. The book's journey to Jerusalem prefigures the return of the exilic community. The rest of the book, Baruch 1:15 to the end, can be reasonably imagined as read aloud in the temple, like the scroll Baruch reads in Jeremiah 36. The "voice" of the Babylonian exiles is in Jerusalem.

1 Baruch never explains how Baruch came to write his book. Another "loud silence" of the book regards Jeremiah. 1 Baruch, despite its connections to Jeremian traditions, never mentions this prophet. The confession of sin section in particular adapts language from an early version of Jeremiah. Jeremiah 7:34, for example, proclaims that God will make mirth and gladness cease in Judah and it then declares that the bones of the people of Jerusalem will lie on the ground unburied. Baruch 2:23 contains the same basic language as Jeremiah 7:34; it then asserts that the bones of the ancestors *were* thrown on the ground. Baruch presents the exile and the Babylonian destruction of Jerusalem as a fulfillment of proclamations uttered by Jeremiah. But it does so in a way that effaces the figure of Jeremiah. 1 Baruch 2 does not state that the language examined just above is from Jeremiah. Rather, it is from "the prophets." 1 Baruch presents Baruch as an independent figure, whereas in the book of Jeremiah he is a minor character, subservient to the prophet.

The absence of Jeremiah allows Baruch to be understood in a manner akin to Ezra in 2 Esdras. As discussed in Chapter 3, 2 Esdras presents Ezra as a new Moses who restores the Torah. Baruch in 1 Baruch, in a less explicit manner, is a kind of new Jeremiah, and perhaps a new Moses as well. As discussed above, Second Temple texts contemporary with 1 Baruch such as 2 Maccabees depict Jeremiah as a Mosaic figure, a prophet of Torah who urges Jews in Babylon to heed the commandments. In 1 Baruch, that's what Baruch does. In the book's renewal of piety in exile, Baruch is not simply another Jeremiah. Whereas Jeremiah yells at and chastises people, Baruch does not. Rather, 1 Baruch explains destruction that has already happened and how Israel can restore its severed relationship with God. The focus is not on hearing a prophet speak but listening to his written words, read aloud. As Jeremiah's scribe, it is apt to attribute this new mode of written prophecy to Baruch, whose book is a creative amalgam of Mosaic and Jeremian language.

A Jeremiad against Idols: The Letter of Jeremiah

A "jeremiad" is an archaic word that denotes a rant. The term is based on the lengthy, often angry, diatribes in the book of Jeremiah about the waywardness of Israel. The Letter of Jeremiah is a jeremiad. It is presented as a letter written by Jeremiah to the exiles. It has one overarching message, which it unrelentingly repeats—the gods of the Babylonians are nothing but idols. They are merely wooden statues, overlaid with gold and silver. They can be eaten up by termites or maggots. They can't wipe the dust off their own faces. There is a biblical tradition of disparaging the veneration of statues, evident in texts such as Second Isaiah and the Psalms. The Ten Commandments proclaim that God is not to be depicted in physical form. Like Second Isaiah and Bel and the Dragon, the Letter of Jeremiah's anti-idol invective focuses on Babylon. These texts transform prophets into harsh critics of Babylonian religion.

The history of the letter's interpretation, given its polemical content, is unfortunate. The book's disdain for Babylonian religion was easily applicable to other traditions. While utilization of the letter has not been extensive, Christian authors turned to the work to support their attacks against other religious traditions. Julius Firmicus Maternus (fourth century), for example, quotes from the letter extensively in his polemical treatise, *The Error of the Pagan Religions.* Centuries later, in the age of the Reformation, Protestants used the Letter of Jeremiah to argue against the Catholic devotion of saints. If you are looking for acceptance of religious diversity, you won't find it in the Letter of Jeremiah.

In the modern West, in which the Bible became a normative, authoritative text, the composition's polemic against idols is easy to understand as a reasonable, straightforward position. But in the ancient world it was common to venerate a statue or other physical representation of a deity. They were in temples, homes, and the public square. To rail against something so widespread as stupid and inane is quite radical. A modern analogy would be to rant against something equally common in our own day, such as electricity or the internet.

The Letter of Jeremiah, like 1 Baruch, emphasizes its own textuality. It presents itself as a "copy" of a letter written by Jeremiah. The letter's self-identification as a "copy" signals that Jeremiah originally wrote the document and it was then preserved by scribes, who thus provide a link between the reader and the prophet.

Since it is a letter, Jeremiah 29 may be a model for the Letter of Jeremiah. But it is at most a loose one. The Letter urges Jews to prepare to live in Babylon a long time, seven generations. This is likely an adaptation of the tradition in Jeremiah 29 that the exile will last seventy years. There is no polemic against the Babylonians or their gods in Jeremiah 29. There is, however, clear disdain for idols and Babylon elsewhere in the book (e.g., chs. 10, 51). The Letter of Jeremiah takes some of the anti-idol rhetoric in the book of Jeremiah and creates with it a new Jeremian text. The composition, for example, compares a statue of a god to a scarecrow in a cucumber patch. This derisive analogy is adapted from Jeremiah 10:5, now incorporated as a message to the exiles. Also, this verse is in the Hebrew (Masoretic) form of Jeremiah 10, not the Greek Septuagint, suggesting that the Letter of Jeremiah utilized a Hebrew form of the chapter (which in turn supports the position that the Letter was originally written in Hebrew).

The trope of taking language from Jeremiah 10 and reconfiguring it as a "copy" of a Jeremian letter intended for the exiles is also found in later Jewish tradition, in a targum. Targums are Aramaic translations of biblical texts from the early centuries after the common era. As translations, targums can be quite loose and often preserve older exegetical traditions. The targum of Jeremiah, in its iteration of Jeremiah 10:11 ("Thus you shall say to them: the gods who did not make the heavens and the earth shall perish from the earth"), presents this statement as from a "copy" of a letter Jeremiah wrote to the exiles in Babylon. In this new format, Jeremiah 10:11 more explicitly preserves guidance from the prophet, just like the Letter of Jeremiah, as to how Jews in exile should respond to the Babylonians when they urge them to worship their gods. This reconfiguration also offers a solution to an odd issue. The book of Jeremiah has over 1,300 verses in Hebrew, with one exception: 10:11. It is in Aramaic. Aramaic was an important language spoken in Babylonia. It would thus be fitting to speak to people there in Aramaic.

Whereas Jeremiah 29 is a letter the prophet sends to the exiles in Babylon, the Letter of Jeremiah is a document he gives them in Judah when they are about to go into exile. In 2 Maccabees 2, Jeremiah urges Jews heading into exile to keep the law, like 1 Baruch, and not follow the gods of Babylon, like the Letter of Jeremiah. 1 Baruch, as discussed above, is set during the early days of the exile. The Letter of Jeremiah similarly prepares the exiles to be wary of Babylonian gods before they see them. They in a sense carry Jeremiah's voice into exile (Baruch's book travels in the opposite direction).

The Letter of Jeremiah has a clear literary structure. It divides into ten stanzas:

1. vv. 8–16: Idols are helpless. They have tongues but can't speak.
2. vv. 17–23: Idols are useless. They are as useless as a broken dish.
3. vv. 24–29: Idols are lifeless. They have no breath. They don't even move when birds perch on them or cats sit on them.
4. vv. 30–40a: Idols are powerless. They cannot, for example, restore sight to the blind.
5. vv. 40b–44: It is foolish to worship idols.

6. vv. 45–52: Since they are made of human hands, they do not have a divine origin.
7. vv. 53–56: Idols are powerless (again). If there is a fire in a temple, the priests will escape but the idols will burn up.
8. vv. 57–65: Idols are helpless and useless (again). Spoons or doors have more value than idols.
9. vv. 66–69: Idols cannot do what God does.
10. vv. 70–73: Idols are likened to several undignified things—a scarecrow, a thornbush, and a discarded corpse.

Each unit concludes with an anti-idol statement. The fourth and fifth stanzas, for example, end with the question, "Why then must anyone think that they are gods or call them gods?"

Beyond the overarching anti-idolatry message of the Letter of Jeremiah, several issues run throughout the composition. One is that the false idols are overlaid with gold and silver. Statues of gods could be quite ornate; the Letter shows concern that their fine metals and aesthetic appeal could entice Jews. Indeed, the whole ethos of the composition implies that the exiles revering Babylonian deities was a legitimate possibility, which it seeks to discourage. Another common theme is that the priests of these gods are corrupt. Like Bel and the Dragon, the Letter of Jeremiah implies that their worship is a scam perpetuated by the priests because they benefit from it (see the next chapter). The composition does not like that women play a role in Babylonian worship. It dislikes that females who are menstruating or who have recently given birth can touch sacrifices devoted to gods (women in both situations, according to Leviticus, are impure). Also, the Letter of Jeremiah never envisages, unlike 1 Baruch, the end of the exile. It does conclude, however, by affirming that the non-gods of Babylon will eventually be destroyed. This assertion resonates with Bel and the Dragon, which depict the destruction of Babylonian gods. The name Bel, an epithet of the Babylonian deity Marduk, occurs in the Letter of Jeremiah, indicating the text contains some genuine knowledge of Babylonian religion, although not enough to prove that it was written in Babylon.

Conclusion

Baruch and the Letter of Jeremiah reformulate shared traditions to put forward contrasting models of Jewish piety during the Babylonian exile. 1 Baruch makes a positive statement—what Israel should do in the exile. The exiles are to confess their sins and restore their covenant relationship with God by following the Torah. The Letter of Jeremiah makes a negative statement—what Israel should not do in exile. The Jews should not regard the idols worshipped by the Babylonians as gods. Each text engages Second Temple traditions about Jeremiah, understood as a prophet who wrote to the Babylonian exiles and urged them to follow the Torah. The overriding interest that Baruch and the Letter of Jeremiah have in the exile suggests that life in the Diaspora could be understood as a form of ongoing exile, a present reality that encapsulates their experience as a minority people in a Gentile world, where Jews faced discrimination and pressure to be more like everybody else. Each in their own way, 1 Baruch and the Letter of Jeremiah urge the exiles to remain devoted to God and the Torah.

Guide for Further Reading

Adams, Sean A. *Baruch and the Epistle of Jeremiah*. Leiden: Brill, 2014.

Newman, Judith H. "Confessing in Exile: The Reception and Composition of Jeremiah in (Daniel and) Baruch." Pages 231–52 in *Jeremiah's Scriptures: Production, Reception, Interaction, and Transformation*. Edited by Hindy Najman and Konrad Schmid. Leiden: Brill, 2017.

Wright, J. Edward. *Baruch ben Neriah: From Biblical Scribe to Apocalyptic Seer*. Columbia: University of South Carolina Press, 2003.

10

Forgotten Flowers

The "Additions" to the Book of Daniel

In his 1534 translation of the Bible, Martin Luther placed in its Apocrypha section several texts which in Catholic and Orthodox Bibles were, and still are, chapters of the Old Testament book of Daniel. In his preface to these compositions, he compares them to flowers which he uprooted and replanted in a "little spice garden or flower bed." The "flowers" Luther and other Protestant Reformers removed from the book of Daniel are:

1. The Prayer of Azariah and the Song of the Three Jews
2. Susanna
3. Bel and the Dragon.

These stories are conventionally called "additions" to the book of Daniel. This perspective presumes that there was first the twelve-chapter format of the book, which is what many people have in their Bibles, and that these three stories were then added to it. The starting point, however, should not be the biblical book of Daniel, but rather the realization that there was an expansive wealth of ancient (pre-Christian) Jewish stories about Daniel which resulted in various compilations of stories about him. This prior Danielic diversity explains why different Bibles have different versions of the book.

The book of Daniel is longer in Catholic and Orthodox Bibles than in Judaism or the Protestant tradition. The three Danielic texts under discussion are not in the Hebrew Bible. They are not prominent in Jewish tradition, although material from these stories

The Apocrypha: A Guide. Matthew Goff, Oxford University Press. © Oxford University Press 2024.
DOI: 10.1093/9780190060770.003.0010

appears in a medieval Jewish text, the *Chronicles of Jerahmeel* (also called the *Book of Memories*). While absent in the Hebrew Bible, these texts are in the Septuagint, the ancient Greek translation of the Jewish scriptures (see Chapter 1). Like the book of Esther, Daniel is significantly longer in the Greek than the Hebrew.

Scholars hold that the language of the three Danielic compositions suggests that they were written in Aramaic or Hebrew and translated in antiquity into Greek. Unfortunately, no form of them in ancient Hebrew or Aramaic survives. They were not found among the Dead Sea Scrolls. The three stories were likely written before 100 BCE, the approximate date of the translation of Daniel into Greek. They are quite different from one another and offer no indication that they all stem from a single editorial effort to expand the book. It is more likely that various compilations of Danielic stories were in circulation in the second and first centuries BCE, in Greek, Hebrew, and Aramaic, and that iterations of this textual diversity are reflected in the later different versions of the biblical book of Daniel.

The three Danielic texts at issue comprise approximately 160 verses, a significant amount. Jerome in his Latin translation marked every one of these verses with an obelus (÷), the symbol later used in mathematics as the division sign. In this way he flagged that he questioned the authenticity of Daniel texts in the Septuagint without analogue in the Hebrew Bible, in keeping with his *hebraica veritas* (see Chapter 1). The Protestant Reformers adopted Jerome's attitude toward the non-Hebrew portions of Daniel by removing them from the Old Testament and putting them in the Apocrypha.

Ancient Danielic Diversity: Hebrew, Aramaic, Old Greek, Theodotion

Jews in antiquity told stories about a man of exceptional wisdom, piety, and righteousness named Daniel. The prophet Ezekiel, whose visions are dated to the sixth century BCE, offers early evidence for such legends: "You are wiser than Daniel, no secret is hidden from you" (ch. 28). Ezekiel was taken into exile in Babylon. Daniel is likewise situated in the eastern Diaspora. He is a remarkable member of the community of Jewish exiles in Babylon. In these tales, particularly Daniel 1–6, he reaches, not unlike Joseph and Esther, the highest echelons of the Gentile world and becomes a trusted sage in the court of kings.

Daniel 1–6 is an assemblage of tales about Daniel that stress his piety and his knowledge. They consistently portray him as the most capable member of the king's court. In chapter 2, for example, King Nebuchadnezzar forces the Babylonian wise men to interpret a dream he had, without telling them the dream. This is impossible for them. Daniel, by contrast, can do so because God reveals the knowledge to him, both the dream and its interpretation. Daniel and other Jews in court are devoted to God and their ancestral traditions. They are a religious minority in a Gentile world. Their religious commitments cause tensions and problems that are ultimately resolved. In Daniel 6, for example, Daniel is thrown into the lions' den because he prays to God, in violation of a royal law that people are to pray only to the king. When he sees that the lions do not kill Daniel, the Persian king Darius (r. 522–486 BCE) acknowledges that Daniel was saved by his God and sets him free.

While determining precise dates of composition is not possible, the stories of Daniel 1–6 are often dated to the Persian or Hellenistic periods. Most of them (chs. 2–6) are in Aramaic, an important language of the Babylonian and Persian empires. The tales were likely written in the eastern Diaspora. As a Jewish minority in a Gentile world, Jews could face humiliation and discrimination. While this produced social pressure for Jews to abandon their traditions, Daniel 1–6 promotes Daniel as an exemplary hero who succeeds not by forsaking his ancestral customs but by embracing them. The stories of Daniel 1–6, like the book of Esther, teach that the path for Jews to be successful in a Gentile world is to follow Jewish traditions.

Quite different from Daniel 1–6, chapters 7–12 offer visions filled with strange monsters and cryptic allusions to events from the Hellenistic era. Daniel no longer interprets the dreams of kings. Rather, he receives heavenly visions. He has, for example, a vision of four bizarre beasts in Daniel 7, including a leopard with wings, and chapters 10–12 recount a vision in which Daniel is shown a lengthy review of historical events from the fourth to the second centuries BCE, culminating in the Maccabean revolt, followed by eschatological judgment. Scholars generally date Daniel 7–12 to the time of the revolt, ca. 165 BCE, thus later than chapters 1–6. (The Maccabean crisis is discussed in Chapters 12–13 of this volume.) Chapter 7 is in Aramaic, while chapters 8–12 are in Hebrew. Chapters 7–12 indicate that during a catastrophe, Jews turned to the legendary figure of Daniel for answers. These chapters present him as an exceptional person to whom God revealed, centuries earlier, not only that the Maccabean crisis would occur, but also that it would culminate in the final judgment, at which the suffering righteous would receive their delayed recompense. The visions of Daniel 7–12 helped give Jews hope during a bleak situation.

While the Dead Sea Scrolls include remnants of scrolls that accord with the shorter form of Daniel that many readers are familiar with today, they also attest other Danielic writings that do not. They preserve fragments of two previously unknown Aramaic texts that have been entitled by modern scholars as "Pseudo-Daniel" compositions. This title is not helpful. It suggests that they are secondary or derivative of the book of Daniel. In fact, they demonstrate that at the time, people told a range of tales about Daniel before the book of Daniel took the form found in many Bibles today—and that this older wealth of Danielic tales is more extensive than the stories in the book of Daniel. The first (4Q243–244) appears to depict a conversation between Daniel and a Babylonian king that involves some sort of review of history, not unlike Daniel

10–12, which includes the primordial period. It mentions the flood and even the antediluvian sage Enoch (topics that do not come up in the book of Daniel). This composition likely had a vision that revealed knowledge about the full expanse of history, from creation to judgment, whereas Daniel 7–12 focuses on the final stages of history. The second fragmentary "Pseudo-Daniel" composition (4Q245) mentions Daniel and a book. A list of priests and kings follows which includes names from ancient Israel and the Hellenistic age, such as Solomon and Simon Maccabee; no such list appears in the book of Daniel. The names suggest that the book mentioned in the text contains revealed knowledge about epochs of history.

Another relevant Qumran text is the *Prayer of Nabonidus* (4Q242). Nabonidus was the last king of the Babylonian empire (r. 556–539 BCE). In the *Prayer of Nabonidus*, this king states in the first person that he was sick and in Teiman, an oasis in Arabia far removed from the Babylonian court; Babylonian historical records also connect Nabonidus with Teiman. According to this Qumran text, he was there for seven years until he prayed to God, aided by an unnamed Jewish exorcist. In Daniel 4, Nebuchadnezzar is removed from human society, living among animals for seven years until he acknowledges the power of God, a process assisted by Daniel. The *Prayer of Nabonidus* helps solidify the scholarly consensus that Daniel 4 reworks older traditions about King Nabonidus leaving Babylonian society and applies them to the most well-known Babylonian king in the history of ancient Israel, Nebuchadnezzar.

The Greek of Daniel attests a remarkable degree of diversity. The Septuagint, the reader will recall, became the Old Testament. But the situation is different with regard to Daniel. Jerome (fourth century) explains this in his preface to Daniel: "The Septuagint version of Daniel the prophet is not read by the Churches of our Lord and Savior. They use Theodotion's version but how this came to pass I cannot tell." Ancient Christians adopted a Greek text of Daniel attributed to Theodotion, who lived in the second century CE, after the books in the Septuagint were written.

The Old Greek of Daniel preserves an older and often forgotten version of the book which at times differs dramatically from the more widespread Greek version associated with Theodotion. Not many manuscripts of the Old Greek version have survived. It is an issue of scholarly debate, but the Old Greek may be a translation of a Hebrew/Aramaic text of Daniel that differs from that of the Jewish Bible. In any case, there is material in the Old Greek not found in either Theodotion or the Hebrew Bible. Only the Old Greek form of Daniel 6:3, for example, describes Daniel as clothed in royal purple in court, a sign of his elevated status. The Old Greek and Theodotion versions of Daniel 4–6 have a stunning range of differences when compared to each other, more so than the rest of the book. These chapters may have circulated in antiquity independently of a book of Daniel, which would explain why they have more textual variety.

In terms of appreciating the diversity of early forms of Daniel, one manuscript is of particular note. Papyrus 967, our oldest manuscript of Daniel in Greek (third century CE), attests the Old Greek text but has its own editorial innovations. This manuscript places chapters 7–8 before chapters 5–6. Daniel 7–8 is set during the reign of the Babylonian king Belshazzar. But he dies at the end of chapter 5. The scribal intervention evident in Papyrus 967 indicates that this chronological discrepancy was considered a problem to be solved. In late antiquity the book was increasingly understood less as a loose compilation of Danielic stories and more as a single, chronologically consistent book of Daniel. This manuscript indicates that the canonizing tendency of the era led not simply to textual standardization but also to creative scribal innovations.

Once the biblical book of Daniel became standardized, the production of new stories about the man and retellings of Danielic chapters did not stop. The late antique text known as the *Lives of the Prophets*, for example, offers a creative version of Daniel 4. It states that when Nebuchadnezzar was banished to dwell among the animals, the monster Behemoth would visit him and that the king was so forlorn over his own condition that he would cry until his eyes looked like "raw flesh."

Praying in a Furnace: The Prayer of Azariah and the Song of the Three Jews

The first of the three Danielic texts to be examined comprises two distinct hymns, the Prayer of Azariah (vv. 1–22) and the Song of the Three Jews (vv. 28–68), with a prose passage between them (going by the versification in NOAB). Daniel 3 focuses on three Jews who, like Daniel, are among a select group of young men from the exilic Jewish community chosen to serve in the court of King Nebuchadnezzar. Their Babylonian names are Shadrach, Meshach, and Abednego; their Hebrew names, respectively, are Hananiah, Mishael, and Azariah. Daniel never appears in Daniel 3. In the chapter, the king erects a large golden statue. It is reasonably understood as an image of the god Marduk (Bel), the chief god of the city of Babylon. A royal herald announces that everyone is to worship this statue. The king is informed that three Jews will not fall down before the idol. In an important engagement of Daniel 3 from the contemporary world, Dr. Martin Luther King Jr., in his famous "Letter from a Birmingham Jail," describes the three men's refusal to obey Nebuchadnezzar's decree as a precedent for his civil disobedience against legalized segregation in the United States.

In response to their disobedience, the king has the men thrown into a fiery furnace (3:23). In Jewish and Protestant Bibles, the following verse (v. 24; "Then King Nebuchadnezzar was astonished and rose up quickly") suggests that he is surprised that they do not die as soon as they are thrown in. He looks inside the furnace and sees a fourth person with them who "has the appearance of a god"

(v. 25). The king, realizing that the Jews have been saved by their God, has them removed from the furnace.

In the Greek, the men, once they have been thrown into the furnace, walk around inside it singing lengthy hymns. Narrative time in a sense freezes. They pray to God for deliverance from the flames, which he provides after they finish praying. The Prayer of Azariah and the Song of the Three Jews total 68 verses that, going by the versification in Jewish and Protestant Bibles, are *between* verses 3:23 and 24. In Catholic and Orthodox Bibles, Daniel 3 is simply longer and the hymns at issue are 3:24–90. While these hymns were likely written before 100 BCE, as mentioned above, a precise date of composition for them cannot be established. These two hymns likely originated during the third or second century BCE.

The Prayer of Azariah and the Song of the Three Jews together comprise the only one of the three "Additions" that is reasonably considered an addition, in the sense that they were attached secondarily to an older form of Daniel 3. The antiquity of the form of the chapter without the prayers is confirmed by two Daniel manuscripts from the Dead Sea Scrolls. The addition of prayers to existing stories is a pious mode of exegesis attested elsewhere, as in for example Esther and the Prayer of Manasseh (see Chapters 6 and 11). The inclusion of these prayers helps explain why God saved them: they asked for his help. The story so understood teaches that in a moment of crisis, the righteous turn to God for deliverance.

The Prayer of Azariah is a hymn of communal confession. The speaker, Azariah (the text uses his Hebrew name, not his Babylonian one, Abednego), consistently emphasizes that "we" have sinned, in the first-person plural. Azariah's words are easily understood as referring to the Jewish community in exile. Azariah proclaims that God was forced to hand "us over to our enemies" because the Jews had sinned against him. This sentiment accords with the perspective in Deuteronomy and the monarchic history of Samuel-Kings, namely that things go well for the Israelites when they obey God and they do not when they transgress his covenant.

The Prayer of Azariah is also consistent with roughly contemporary texts, such as Baruch and the Prayer of Manasseh, which thematize Babylon as a site of religious renewal, where Jews admit their sins and turn back to God.

Prayers that express a national confession of sin are common in Second Temple Judaism. Such a prayer, however, is an odd fit with Daniel 3. The men were thrown into the furnace not because of their sins but their piety—they refused to venerate Nebuchadnezzar's statue. This dissonance supports the perspective that these hymns originated separately from Daniel 3 and were later attached to it.

The Song of the Three Jews (sometimes called the Song of the Three Young Men), while likely having an origin separate from the Prayer of Azariah, functions as a set piece with it. In the Prayer of Azariah the three men ask for divine assistance; in the prose text between the hymns they receive it; and in the Song of the Three Jews they praise God for having saved them. The Song is highly repetitive, suggesting that it developed in a liturgical context. Most verses begin with the invocation "Bless the Lord," a plural imperative encouraging others to do so, and the second half of almost every verse reads "sing praise to him and highly exalt him forever." The refrain resembles those of Psalms 136 and 148. Also like Psalm 148, the Song urges aspects of the celestial and earthly realms to praise God, including the angels, sun, moon, stars, the mountains, and the birds. The hymn even urges fire to extol God, emphasizing divine control over the flames that threatened the three men.

Daniel 3, in its longer form with the hymns, has resonated with people throughout the centuries. Several of the Maccabean books invoke the tale, to stress that God rescues the righteous and hold up the three men as an ideal of piety to be emulated (1 Macc 2; 3 Macc 6; 4 Macc 13). This also indicates that the story was well-known by the first century BCE. Early Christians endured persecution, although the extent of the oppression is a matter of debate. The Danielic motif of praying when surrounded by flames resonated with them. Some of the earliest surviving Christian works of art, wall paintings in the catacombs of Rome (third century CE), depict the three men in the furnace with their hands raised in prayer. The Prayer of Azariah and the Song of the Three Jews have also long been important in Christian liturgy. Both hymns, like the Prayer of Manasseh, are in the Odes, a collection of biblical hymns in Codex Alexandrinus (see further the next chapter). Portions of the hymns of Daniel 3 are recited in the Catholic Mass during Lent and in the Liturgy of the Hours, a venerable Catholic practice of praying at set times throughout the day.

"A Daniel Come to Judgment": The Tale of Susanna

Unlike the Prayer of Azariah and the Song of the Three Jews, the tale of Susanna is not incorporated into a chapter of Daniel. It is a self-contained narrative. In the Old Greek and the Vulgate, Susanna is in Daniel 13 as a sort of appendix, after the dramatic and eschatological climax of Daniel 12. In Theodotion, however, Susanna is before Daniel 1, thus located at the beginning of the book (so too in Orthodox Bibles). This scribal change constitutes one way to transform a collection of disparate stories about Daniel into a single, chronologically consistent book of Daniel. Susanna takes place when Daniel is a young man, before he was tapped for royal service, and thus prior to the other stories in the book.

It is impossible to assign a specific date of composition to Susanna, but it is older than 100 BCE, when it was translated into Greek. It was probably written in the second or third century BCE. The entire narrative takes place within the Jewish community in Babylon. Unlike other stories in Daniel, in Susanna there is no wicked Gentile king and no focus on the royal court; Jewish-Gentile relations are not a theme.

Susanna is a beautiful married woman who obeys the Torah. As a pious woman, she resembles Judith but, unlike her, Susanna is not the hero of her story. Daniel is. Two judges, older men who are influential in the exilic community, conspire to have sex with her. One day they hide in her garden. While she is preparing to bathe there, they approach her and offer her a disturbing proposition: if she does not sleep with them, they will falsely testify in court that they saw her cheating on her husband with a young man. This is a serious allegation. As the corrupt judges know, the punishment in the Torah for adultery is death. She refuses their lurid proposal. The next day there is a trial. In the Old Greek she is stripped naked at the trial, in keeping with gruesome traditions regarding how women accused of adultery were shamed (see Ezekiel 16). Some scribes apparently found this image disturbing; in the later Theodotion version she is only unveiled at the trial. The assembly of judges and elders believe the bogus testimony of the two judges about Susanna being unfaithful and she is condemned to die. She cries out to God and he responds. This is a major theme of the tale—that God hears the prayer of the pious who suffer unjustly.

Enter Daniel. God answers Susanna's plea by rousing his spirit. Confident that false testimony was used against her, Daniel demands that the court be re-convened. He interrogates the two elders separately. He asks each one under what tree they saw Susanna and her lover together. The first states it was under a mastic tree and the second that it was under an oak. By discovering this contradiction in their testimony, the young Daniel exposes the lies of the elderly judges. They, not Susanna, are put to death. While modern readers can easily understand the men as guilty of attempted rape, they are convicted for giving false testimony. In the Bible this is a serious crime. It is prohibited in the Ten Commandments. Their punishment is in accordance with the Torah. As Deuteronomy 19 states, the witness who lies in court is to receive the punishment they sought to befall the other party—in this case, death. The ending of the story according to Theodotion emphasizes that Susanna's honor and reputation are restored, and that Daniel acquired the status of a great man in his community.

The tale of Susanna was important in early Christianity. Like the three men of Daniel 3, her image appears in the wall paintings of the Roman catacombs, with Susanna holding her hands aloft in prayer before her two accusers. The story's emphasis on powerful people abusing the innocent resonated with early Christians.

There were also early Christian debates about the story's authenticity. In a letter to Origen, written in the third century CE, Africanus observes that there are Greek puns in Susanna regarding the names of the two trees and the punishment associated with them that come up in Daniel's interrogation of the elders. Africanus concludes it was written in Greek, not Hebrew—and genuine Old Testament texts in his view were originally written in Hebrew. Origen defends the story of Susanna, pointing out that there are extensive differences between the Greek and Hebrew scriptures, and that Christian churches use and accept the Greek (a complex issue discussed in Chapter 1).

The story of Susanna is not prominent in Jewish tradition. One exception is the thirteenth-century rabbi Nahmanides, who demonstrates some knowledge of the book. As discussed in Chapter 5, he quotes material from the first chapter of the book of Judith and claims it is from a text called the *Megillat Shushan* (the *Scroll of Susanna*). Ethiopian Jews (sometimes called the Beta Israel or the Falasha) preserve a variant of the Susanna tale known as the *Gadla Sosana* (the *Life of Susanna*). In this version, Susanna is of royal ancestry and is accosted by three elders rather than two. The angel Michael rescues her, rather than Daniel.

In the modern West, Susanna has been a popular subject of art for centuries, including modern-era painters such as Picasso. Allured by a biblical narrative involving a nude woman, these painters, generally men, visualized the story in ways that convey its rich ambivalence. These paintings can arouse (male) viewers with the voyeuristic spectacle of a woman bathing, while simultaneously conveying that the judges commit a crime (Figure 10.1) Also attesting knowledge of the story of Susanna in the modern

Figure 10.1 *Susanna and the Elders*, by Alessandro Allori (1561). The (male) viewer is compelled to gaze upon Susanna's naked body along with the elders, as if he were complicit in their assault.

© RMN-Grand Palais/Art Resource, NY.

West, Shakespeare in the *Merchant of Venice* invokes the reputation of Daniel as an astute lawyer. The Jewish financier Shylock acknowledges respect for a lawyer by calling her "A Daniel come to judgment; yea, a Daniel!" The lawyer is Portia, a woman who argues a case in court while disguised as a man named Balthasar (likely a play on Daniel's double, Babylonian name, Belteshazzar) to save the merchant Antonio from harm—thus inverting the Susannean trope of a man saving a woman from punishment through his brilliance in court.

Don't Feed the Gods: Bel and the Dragon

Bel and the Dragon are not one story, but rather two similar ones. The first is about Bel ("Lord"), an epithet of the Babylonian deity Marduk (vv. 1–22), and the second is about a dragon worshipped in Babylon as a god (vv. 23–42). In Theodotion they comprise Daniel 13, and in the Vulgate Daniel 14, after Susanna. These stories highlight Daniel's commitment to expose the folly of Babylonian religion. They were written before 100 BCE and likely produced in the third or second centuries BCE. The stories' creative but inaccurate depiction of Babylonian religion (discussed below) suggests that while set in Babylon, they were not written there; they do not reflect direct familiarity with the gods of the city and their worship. In terms of its later reception, Bel and the Dragon have not made the same impact as the other Danielic tales examined in this chapter.

Bel and the Dragon are comparable to the extensive polemic against idolatry in the Hebrew Bible. Such biblical texts typically lampoon making a physical image of a god, such as a statue. Bel and the Dragon are less about the folly of idolatry in general and more focused on Babylonian religion, which these stories, like the Letter of Jeremiah, despise.

Whereas in Susanna, Daniel is a young man, in Bel and the Dragon he is a senior figure at court. He and the king speak as friends and virtual equals. In the Old Greek, the king is an unnamed Babylonian ruler. In Theodotion he is Cyrus the Persian (r. 559–530 BCE). The king worships Bel, which is befitting a Babylonian ruler, since Bel is the main god of Babylon. King Cyrus, like other ancient Persian kings, venerated Ahura Mazda, the Persian god of light. Specifying that the king is Cyrus constitutes a scribal change intended to make the chronology of the book of Daniel consistent, since Daniel 10–12 is set during the reign of Cyrus, and the stories of Bel and the Dragon follow these chapters. The Theodotion version also makes the story more consistent with the rest of Daniel by omitting the claim in the Old Greek that Daniel is a priest, an assertion nowhere else in the book. The Old Greek also begins by attributing Bel and the Dragon to Habakkuk: "From the prophecy of Habakkuk, son of Joshua, of the tribe of Levi." This prophet does appear in the narrative (discussed below). The later Theodotion version removes the ascription to Habakkuk. This revision likely reflects the emerging canonical conception of the book of Daniel as a single whole—as such, portions attributed to prophets aside from Daniel could seem out of place.

The story of Bel begins with a theological conversation between Daniel and the king. The king worships Bel, whereas Daniel reveres God. The king contends that Bel must be a real god because every day a large amount of food and wine is placed before his statue, and each day it disappears. According to the king, Bel is a "living" god because he eats and drinks. The two men agree to test the validity of this assertion. They ensure that on one day, once the food and drink are put out for Bel in his temple, its doors are to remain closed all night. The next day they enter the temple and discover that the provisions are gone. The seventy priests of Bel and their families had entered through a secret tunnel and consumed everything, as was their regular practice. Daniel, ever the clever man, had suspected some sort of foul play. Before they sealed the temple doors, Daniel, unbeknownst to the priests, had the floor covered in ash. Thus the footprints of the klepto-priests were evident. The story showcases, as does the Susanna tale, Daniel's intelligence. He proves to the king not only that his god does not eat or drink, but also that Bel is a lie perpetuated by priests so that they can steal the food offered to him. The king has the priests killed. Daniel destroys the idol of Bel and his temple, an act of violence that has no parallel elsewhere in the book of Daniel.

The next story, the Dragon, centers on a "great dragon" worshipped by the Babylonians. The animal could be understood differently since the Greek word for "dragon" can also be translated as "snake." In any case, in the story it is an actual animal. But no snake, much less a dragon, was an object of worship in ancient Babylon. The story can be profitably understood as a creative expression of Jewish cultural memories about life in Babylon, in which the iconography of Marduk was prominent. A key image related to this deity was the *mushhushshu*-dragon, sometimes called a snake-dragon. The Ishtar Gate, a monumental entrance in the city of Babylon built by Nebuchadnezzar, includes several depictions of this mythological creature. The *mushhushshu*-dragon became associated with Marduk since that god defeated him. The core images of false divinity in both Bel and the Dragon (a statue, a dragon) resonate with the iconography of Marduk.

In the Dragon story, Daniel and the king engage topics they discussed previously in Bel. The king asserts that the dragon is a "living god," an expression used in the earlier story, and that Daniel should therefore worship him. Daniel asks for permission to kill the beast without a weapon; the king, presumably thinking that this would be impossible, grants it. Daniel boils together resin, fat, and hair, and makes cakes with them. He feeds them to the dragon, which bursts open and dies. What a cook! As in Bel, by means of food Daniel exposes the nonexistence of the Babylonian god venerated by the king. A version of this violent act appears in Jewish midrash. In *Genesis Rabbah*, Daniel kills a dragon belonging to King Nebuchadnezzar by feeding him hay in which nails are hidden. Some later Jewish texts preserve a fuller account of this tale, suggesting that some Jews reworked a form of the story from the Christian Bible (see also Chapter 18).

Daniel's gustatory murder of the dragon-god enrages the Babylonians. They blame the king who, under pressure, hands Daniel over to the mob, which throws him into the lions' den. Daniel is also cast into the lions' den in Daniel 6. While the Dragon story may have been influenced by a form of Daniel 6, that the king throws his enemies in a lion pit may be an older motif which both texts utilize. In the Dragon tale, Daniel spends six days with the lions, whereas it is one night in Daniel 6. The longer amount of time in the Dragon story raises an issue that never comes up in Daniel 6—food. An angel picks up the prophet Habakkuk, while he happens to be holding bread and a bowl of stew, and carries him by the hair to Babylon, to deliver his victuals to Daniel. The sustaining meal Habakkuk gives Daniel contrasts the lethal cakes of fat and hair he feeds to the dragon.

Conclusion

The "forgotten flowers" of the book of Daniel—the Prayer of Azariah and the Song of the Three Jews, Susanna, and Bel and the Dragon—are entertaining to read. They include an angel in a furnace, a detective story with courtroom drama, and exploding dragons. They also express important and uplifting themes. The Prayer of Azariah and Susanna in different ways affirm that God will rescue the righteous who are suffering unjustly. The stories helped reinforce for Jews in the Diaspora that despite the difficulties they faced as a religious minority, they could succeed by remaining devoted to God and upholding their ancestral customs.

The stories also constitute crucial evidence for ancient scriptural diversity. They help us realize that there are different forms of the biblical book of Daniel. This pluralistic situation is a consequence of the Danielic diversity of ancient, pre-Christian Judaism—that

Jews told a range of stories about Daniel. Our evidence for such tales is richer and more extensive than the book of Daniel.

Guide for Further Reading

Collins, John J. *Daniel: A Commentary on the Book of Daniel.* Minneapolis: Fortress Press, 1993.

Holm, Tawny L. *Of Courtiers and Kings: The Biblical Daniel Narratives and Ancient Story Collections.* Winona Lake, IN: Eisenbrauns, 2013.

Wills, Lawrence M. *The Jewish Novel in the Ancient World.* Ithaca, NY, and London: Cornell University Press, 1995 (ch. 2; pp. 40–67).

11

The Rehabilitation of a Wicked King

The Prayer of Manasseh

The Prayer of Manasseh is a short psalm of fifteen verses. The prayer offers the plaintive voice of a sinner crying out to God for forgiveness. While relatively unknown today in the West, the Prayer of Manasseh is in the biblical canon of the Eastern Orthodox Church. It is in the Old Testament of neither Catholics nor Protestants. It has never been a book of the Jewish Bible.

To understand the Prayer of Manasseh, it is helpful to turn first to the two very different depictions of King Manasseh in the Hebrew Bible—one that is very negative (2 Kings 21), and one that is surprisingly positive (2 Chronicles 33).

2 Kings 21: Manasseh—A Wicked, No Good, Horrible King

The biblical books of Samuel and Kings recount the monarchic history of ancient Israel. The editorial perspective in these books, which scholars associate with the scribes who produced an early form of Deuteronomy, strives to show that success is a consequence of following God's commandments, and that bad things happen to those who do not. From this perspective, King Manasseh poses a problem. 2 Kings presents him as the worst king Judah ever had. He zealously promoted the worship of gods other than Yahweh. He set up altars for the god Baal and installed an idol of the goddess Asherah in the temple. According to 2 Kings 21:6, he made one

The Apocrypha: A Guide. Matthew Goff, Oxford University Press. © Oxford University Press 2024.
DOI: 10.1093/9780190060770.003.0011

of his sons "pass through fire," a form of child sacrifice. As if that wasn't enough, Manasseh had many other innocent people killed. Verse 16 claims he filled Jerusalem with their blood. King Manasseh had the longest reign of any king in the line of David: fifty-five years (697–642 BCE). A long reign, particularly by a Davidic king, can be easily taken as a sign of divine favor. He also dies peacefully, buried with his ancestors, whereas other wicked personages in the Bible die in gruesome ways (Jezebel, for example, is thrown out of a window and eaten by dogs). An ancient monument called the Esarhaddon Prism mentions Manasseh in a list of kings under the dominion of the Assyrian king Esarhaddon (r. 681–669 BCE). This suggests that there actually was a king of Judah named Manasseh, and that, if he did rule as long as 2 Kings 21 asserts, it was because he was a loyal vassal to the Assyrian Empire, in full submission to the kingdom that devastated much of Judah during the reign of his father Hezekiah. Kings of Judah are harshly criticized in the Bible for being a vassal to more powerful states. But for Manasseh it seems to have worked out.

2 Kings 21 takes the unusual step of blaming the Babylonian destruction of Jerusalem and the exile on Manasseh. According to verses 11–12, because of his evil deeds God says: "I am bringing upon Jerusalem and Judah such evil [in the sense of misfortune] that the ears of everyone who hears of it will tingle"; God also claims: "I will wipe Jerusalem as one wipes a dish, wiping it and turning it upside down." So King Manasseh's wickedness was punished. But Manasseh himself was not. His reign ended in 642 BCE, over fifty years *before* the destruction of Jerusalem (586 BCE). 2 Kings suggests that this unusual delay should be attributed to the piety of King Josiah (640–609 BCE). He ruled during much of the gap between Manasseh's reign and the Babylonian devastation of Judah. 2 Kings hails Josiah as a righteous king committed to the exclusive worship of God. Chapter 22 suggests that God waited until after Josiah's death to punish Judah, telling him: "your eyes shall not see all the disaster that I will bring on this place." Delaying divine

punishment to spare Josiah nevertheless leaves a fundamental issue unexplained—why Manasseh, despite his wickedness, was allowed to have such a long reign and die peacefully.

2 Chronicles 33: King Manasseh Changed His Ways—and He Prayed

2 Chronicles offers a solution to the problem posed by 2 Kings' account of King Manasseh. 1–2 Chronicles is a later reworking, often dated to the fourth century BCE, of the monarchic history in Samuel-Kings. Chronicles often whitewashes events recounted in these books, in order to portray the Davidic kingdom as a time of righteous, pious kings. Chronicles' presentation of King David, for example, omits the story of his infidelity with Bathsheba. Consistent with such changes, Chronicles rehabilitates the figure of Manasseh. According to 2 Chronicles, in response to Manasseh's iniquities, God sent the Assyrian army to capture him. The soldiers, showing slippage between two different enemies of Israel, brought him in chains to Babylon. There the wicked king sang a different tune— literally. 2 Chronicles 33:12–13 claims: "While he was in distress, he entreated the favor of the Lord his God.... He prayed to him and God received his entreaty, heard his plea, and restored him again to Jerusalem and to his kingdom. Then Manasseh knew that the Lord indeed was God." He was allowed to return to Jerusalem and his kingship was restored. Manasseh eagerly promoted the worship of God. He removed the pagan altars and idols he had previously supported. None of this is the account of Manasseh in 2 Kings.

2 Chronicles' account of Manasseh is not a depiction of actual events. It is better understood as a product of reflection on his portrayal in 2 Kings. The view in 2 Chronicles is that 2 Kings could not have told the full story about King Manasseh. If he were as horrible as 2 Kings describes him, he would have been punished. Since Manasseh wasn't punished, he must have changed his wicked ways

and been forgiven. Discernment of a textual problem in 2 Kings helped generate new stories about King Manasseh, transforming him into a repentant figure.

According to Chronicles' makeover of Manasseh, when he was in captivity in Babylon he prayed. 2 Chronicles leaves the words of his efficacious prayer unspoken. It states, however, that the prayer was written down: "His prayer, and how God received his entreaty, all his sin and his faithfulness . . . these are written in the records of the seers" (33:19). Kings and Chronicles often cite written sources, such as the Annals of the Kings of Israel, in their accounts of kings. While Chronicles used Samuel-Kings as a source, it is not always clear if the other documents which these books mention constitute genuine historical records that are now lost. Chronicles' appeal to such texts may simply be mimicking Kings' literary style. In any case, 2 Chronicles, by stating that Manasseh's prayer is preserved in writing without providing its content, laid the groundwork for the creation of new texts in antiquity: psalms attributed to Manasseh.

The Prayer of Manasseh: A Sinner Petitions God for Mercy

The Prayer of Manasseh was likely written in Greek. It begins, as many psalms do, by praising God. He can inflict great harm on sinners but, the speaker reminds the deity, his mercy is abundant. Repentance is construed as a right that God has established, which sinners can invoke. The speaker emphasizes that his many transgressions have justly provoked God's wrath. He abases himself before God: "And now I bend the knee of my heart, imploring you for your kindness." At the end the speaker repeats his entreaty that God not destroy him, but rather demonstrate his mercy; in response he pledges to praise the deity for the rest of his life.

The Prayer of Manasseh does not stress the moral transformation of the speaker's state of mind, but rather his profoundly asymmetrical relationship with God. By emphasizing his transgressions, he lowers himself before God, whom he hails as the supreme lord of the world. The speaker petitions the deity, as one would before a king in the ancient world, to spare him. Revoking justified punishment is a royal prerogative. By relenting his wrath against a sinner, the psalm implores, God demonstrates his dominion.

The Prayer of Manasseh is in the first person. Its speaker never identifies himself as Manasseh or even that he is a king. But elements of the text resonate with the biblical accounts of this king, especially 2 Chronicles. The speaker is weighed down with chains; 2 Chronicles 33 describes Manasseh as being brought to Babylon in chains. The speaker in the Prayer claims that he set up idols, which accords with the king's offenses according to Kings and Chronicles.

Understanding Manasseh as the speaker allows the Prayer to be understood as uttered by the king while suffering in Babylon, a point stressed in 2 Chronicles 33:12. This is similar to the three men of Daniel 3 who pray when thrown into a fiery furnace in Babylon. Rabbinic literature depicts Manasseh as likewise praying in a situation of extreme duress. The Babylonians, according to rabbinic tradition, placed Manasseh inside a hollow bronze bull, under which they started a fire—and he cried out to God from inside (e.g., *Targum of 2 Chronicles*; this legend is also attested in the heading of one version of the Prayer in Syriac). Understanding 2 Chronicles 33 as providing the Prayer's narrative context also conveys that its plea for divine mercy was successful.

The Dead Sea Scrolls support the view that 2 Chronicles' reference to a written record of Manasseh's prayer generated literary creativity. A collection of hymns discovered at Qumran, which scholars have unceremoniously entitled *Non-Canonical Psalms B*, includes a hymn attributed to King Manasseh (4Q381). It is not *the* Prayer of Manasseh. But it is *a* prayer of Manasseh. Its heading identifies it as a "Prayer of Manasseh, king of Judah, when the king of Assyria imprisoned him," which resonates with 2 Chronicles

33:11. In the poorly preserved poem, the speaker admits his transgressions and appeals to God for mercy, as in the Prayer: "I wait for your saving presence, and I cringe before you because of my sins." There are multiple prayers attributed to Manasseh from antiquity which resonate with his plea to God in 2 Chronicles 33.

The Prayer of Manasseh resonates with a literary phenomenon that is amply attested in the Dead Sea Scrolls—the revision of a text by adding direct speech. The account of Abram and Sarai in Egypt in Genesis 12 asserts that the members of the pharaoh's court praised her beauty. But it doesn't recount what they said. But in a version of this episode in a text from Qumran (the *Genesis Apocryphon*), the Egyptian courtiers utter an extensive poem about her beauty. The addition of prayers to older texts is also attested with respect to the prayers of Mordecai and Esther (Addition C) and the Prayer of Azariah (Daniel 3). Expansionist literary production of this sort was abundant during the second and first centuries BCE, providing a rationale to date the Prayer of Manasseh to this period. A precise moment of composition, however, cannot be recovered.

The Unusual Biblical Career of a Prayer

The history of the Prayer of Manasseh as a biblical text is rather odd. Jerome (fourth century) did not include it in his translation of the scriptures into Latin. The Greek Vaticanus and Sinaiticus codices of the Septuagint (both fourth century) do not include the prayer. It is in the other major early Christian biblical manuscript, Codex Alexandrinus (fifth century)—but not as a distinct book. Alexandrinus, unlike Bibles today, includes after the Psalter a book entitled Odes (sometimes called Canticles). It compiles a range of biblical songs and psalms from the Old and New Testaments. The Odes in Alexandrinus includes fourteen texts; the Prayer of Manasseh is the eighth, between Isaiah 38:10–20 (a prayer of

Hezekiah) and the Prayer of Azariah. The Prayer of Manasseh is the only text in Odes that is not excerpted from elsewhere in the Bible.

The Prayer's inclusion in Alexandrinus's Odes likely speaks to its importance in early Christianity. It was often included in "Books of Hours," that is, books of prayers for fixed times of the day, a common devotional practice in late antiquity and the Middle Ages. Its recitation is a long-standing feature of Compline services (prayers at the end of the day). The third-century CE *Didascalia Apostolorum* offers an expanded account of King Manasseh that includes the Prayer; this is the earliest evidence for its use. The *Didascalia* utilizes the hymn to convey to bishops the importance of repentance. Reflecting some Jewish interest in the Prayer in the medieval period, it was translated into Hebrew in the tenth century; a Hebrew version of the Prayer was discovered in a collection of prayers from the Cairo Genizah.

In the West, the Prayer of Manasseh is a late addition to Bible. It began to be included in the Vulgate Bible in the thirteenth century, hundreds of years after Jerome's translation project. It was often placed after 2 Chronicles. This editorial tradition, which became common, reflects the view that the Prayer constitutes the written prayer mentioned in 2 Chronicles 33:18–19. The Prayer of Manasseh is printed after 2 Chronicles in the Gutenberg Bible of 1455, the first book made by a printing press. This is also the case in the Geneva Bible (1560), an important early English translation, as well as in Eastern Orthodox Bibles.

Since the Reformation, the Prayer of Manasseh has not fared well in Western Christendom. Regarding the Prayer, Luther and his Catholic opponents were in rare agreement—they both weakened its canonical status. Luther placed it in the Apocrypha of his Wittenberg Bible (1534), and the Council of Trent (1545–1563), in its official pronouncement of the canon of scripture for the Catholic Church, left it out. In both instances, the rationale for not including the Prayer in the Old Testament is likely that it was a relatively late addition to the Vulgate. The Prayer of Manasseh, along with 1 and 2

Esdras, was included in the Sixto-Clementine Vulgate (1592), in an appendix after the New Testament, an edition of the Bible that is no longer used in Catholicism (see Chapter 2).

Conclusion

The Prayer of Manasseh is a hymnic expression of the power of repentance—that even a figure as horrible as Manasseh can ask God for forgiveness and receive it. The work also sheds light on ancient Jewish textual practices. The scribes who produced 2 Chronicles likely found the account of Manasseh in 2 Kings problematic, since there he is a wicked king who goes unpunished. Thus 2 Chronicles depicts Manasseh as changing his ways, presumably to explain why God did not punish him. Its terse depiction of Manasseh praying for forgiveness led in turn to the production of even more texts, forms of the king's prayer. The Prayer of Manasseh is a product of an ongoing process of textual interpretation and literary creativity that took place across centuries during the Second Temple period.

Guide for Further Reading

Horst, Pieter W. van der, and Judith H. Newman. *Early Jewish Prayers in Greek*. Berlin: de Gruyter, 2008 (pp. 147–80).
Schuller, Eileen. "4Q380 and 4Q381: Non-Canonical Psalms from Qumran." Pages 90–100 in *The Dead Sea Scrolls: Forty Years of Research*. Edited by Devorah Dimant and Uriel Rappaport. Leiden: Brill, 1992.

12

It's Hammer Time

1 Maccabees

1 Maccabees covers an important period of the history of Israel that many readers of scripture are not familiar with—the second century BCE. The Seleucid Empire, founded by a Macedonian general of Alexander the Great (Seleucus I), was based in Syria and ruled much of the ancient Near East from the fourth to the first centuries BCE. The Seleucids acquired control of Palestine in 198 BCE. In response to the cruel and oppressive policies of the Seleucid king Antiochus IV Epiphanes (r. 175–164 BCE), a Jewish rebel movement formed, led by a family known as the Maccabees. "Maccabee" is likely a nickname derived from the Hebrew word for "hammer," denoting their militant stance against the Seleucid state. The Maccabean revolt was successful and resulted in the establishment of the Hasmonean dynasty, which ruled Judah as an independent Jewish state from 142 BCE until 63 BCE, when the region was conquered by Rome. It is a rare period of Jewish control of Palestine in the Hellenistic age. The Jewish festival Hanukkah commemorates the military successes of the Maccabees.

1 Maccabees is also a form of propaganda. It attempts to legitimize the Hasmonean dynasty, which was unpopular when the text was composed in the early first century BCE, by highlighting its origins in the Maccabean revolt. The book offers a triumphalist story of victory, of Jews standing up and successfully fighting against oppressive forces. The book justifies the violence and brutality of the Maccabees as divinely sanctioned.

The Apocrypha: A Guide. Matthew Goff, Oxford University Press. © Oxford University Press 2024. DOI: 10.1093/9780190060770.003.0012

The Hasmoneans and Their Violent, Dangerous World

The sixteen chapters of 1 Maccabees cover a broad range of history, from Alexander the Great (fourth century BCE) to the Hasmonean ruler John Hyrcanus (r. 135–104 BCE). The book focuses on political and military affairs in Palestine from roughly 175 to 135 BCE. The book relates the catastrophic policies of Antiochus IV, the corresponding Maccabean revolt, and the first rulers of the Hasmonean dynasty. The revolt begins with Mattathias. After his death (ch. 2), his five sons (John, Simon, Judas, Eleazar, and Jonathan) lead the rebel movement and secure Judah's independence. The Maccabean brothers became the ruling Hasmonean dynasty. The origin of the name "Hasmonean" is obscure. According to the Jewish historian Josephus (first century CE), who produced an extensive account of Hasmonean history that paraphrases 1 Maccabees, the term derives from the name of an earlier ancestor of Mattathias.

After Mattathias, 1 Maccabees highlights Judas as a glorious hero who wins victory after victory against the Seleucids until he dies in battle (3:1–9:22; r. 164–161 BCE). In 1 Maccabees the term "Maccabee" refers only to Judas, but it comes to signify his brothers as well and their successful revolt. After Judas, the composition focuses on the rule of Jonathan (9:23–12:53; r. 161–143 BCE), and then Simon (13:1–16:3; r. 143–135 BCE). The book ends with brief treatment of the reign of Simon's son, John Hyrcanus.

1 Maccabees frames its narrative as a story of good versus evil, of Jewish rebels against an overbearing Gentile kingdom, the Seleucids. While Antiochus's tactics are undeniably cruel (discussed below), so are those of the Maccabees. According to 1 Maccabees 2, when Mattathias's army would conquer an area, they "forcibly circumcised all the uncircumcised boys"—a disturbing way to force Jewish customs upon Gentiles. When Judas learns that the Roman Empire decimated native peoples in Gaul (France) and Spain, he is not repulsed but rather develops a "bromance" with

Rome (ch. 8). He wants the Maccabees and Rome to become allies; 1 Maccabees claims that Rome sends them a treaty of friendship, written on bronze tablets. (There's no other evidence supporting this assertion, although the alliance is presumed in 2 Maccabees.) The Maccabees also identify with the Spartans, a Greek people famous in antiquity for their military rigor and discipline (ch. 12). These claims portray the Maccabees as strong and powerful, by having aggressive, militaristic states like Sparta and Rome recognize the Maccabees as a kindred people.

The violence and aspirations for power evident in the Maccabees makes them similar to other leaders in the ancient Near East, including their Seleucid enemies. 1 Maccabees situates the Hasmoneans within a larger world of politics, warfare, and upheaval. The book recounts many large battles, often involving elephants, and a great deal of treachery. The key difference regarding the Maccabees is that they are favored by God. But they seem just as brutal as everyone else.

A summary of political events recounted in 1 Maccabees can provide an impression of the violent and dangerous world in which the Hasmoneans thrive and become a regional power. When Antiochus IV is dying, after attacking a temple in Iran, he rules that his young son Antiochus V should become king. But soon Demetrius I, Antiochus IV's nephew, arrives from Rome and declares himself king, killing the boy Antiochus V. Another claimant to the throne emerges, Alexander Balas (who asserted he was Antiochus IV's son), and a kind of Seleucid civil war begins between him and Demetrius I. Both men compete against each other for Jonathan's support, the leading Maccabee at the time (ca. 152 BCE). He sides with Alexander, who attempts to solidify his royal credentials by asking the Egyptian king, Ptolemy VI Philometor, for permission to marry his daughter, Cleopatra Thea (an ancestor of the more famous Cleopatra). Ptolemy agrees and becomes Alexander's father-in-law. But he turns on him and tries to conquer Palestine for himself, forcing Alexander to flee to Arabia. One of Ptolemy's Arabian allies, named Zabdiel, cuts off Alexander's head and sends it to him. A few days later, Ptolemy dies in a battle. Another claimant to the Seleucid throne emerges, Trypho (also called Diodotus). After luring Jonathan's favor with many gifts, Trypho captures him in an ambush and eventually has him killed. When Simon is the ruling Hasmonean, Antiochus VII Sidetes seeks to become the Seleucid king. He assures Simon that he will remain friendly with him and defeats Trypho. But Antiochus VII, who reigned 138–129 BCE, breaks his promise. A Seleucid army commanded by Cendebeus attacks Judah and is defeated by Simon's son John Hyrcanus. Simon and his two other sons are killed at a banquet held by the Seleucid governor of Jericho, Ptolemy son of Abubus, who is also Simon's son-in-law, leaving Hyrcanus as Simon's last surviving son. The Hasmoneans lived in a perilous world.

From the standpoint of the Maccabean family, some key "headlines" of 1 Maccabees are:

- In his hometown of Modein, Mattathias refuses to sacrifice to a pagan idol, and when a fellow Jew does, he kills him. Mattathias heads to the hills, forming a rebel movement. This is the beginning of the Maccabean revolt (ca. 167 BCE).
- Judas removes a pagan idol Antiochus IV installed in the temple (the "desolating sacrilege"); the festival Hanukkah, which 1 Maccabees promotes, commemorates Judas's purification of the temple (164 BCE).
- Jonathan becomes the first Maccabean to assume the office of high priest, granted to him by Alexander Balas (152 BCE). The position is retained within the Hasmonean family as a framework for dynastic rule.
- Under Simon, Judah becomes an independent state (142 BCE). Shortly thereafter, soldiers leave the last vestige of Seleucid authority in Jerusalem, the fortress Akra.

206 THE APOCRYPHA: A GUIDE

1 Maccabees as a Scriptural Text

1–4 Maccabees are four distinct texts; a chapter is dedicated to each in this volume. 2 Maccabees offers an extended presentation of events recounted in 1 Maccabees 1–7, often in a very different way. 3 Maccabees does not focus on the Maccabees at all, but on Jews in Egypt. 4 Maccabees praises the Torah and Jewish traditions in ways that reformulate material in 2 Maccabees. 1–4 Maccabees were grouped together because they were understood as similar and thus numbered sequentially, like 1–2 Kings or 1–2 Samuel.

1 Maccabees was not written as a book entitled "1 Maccabees." This is the title given to the book in the two major early Septuagint manuscripts in which it appears, the Sinaiticus and Alexandrinus codices (fourth–fifth centuries CE). Early Christian authors such as Tertullian and Hippolytus (second–third centuries CE) cite 1 Maccabees and positively invoke the Maccabean brothers. The story of the Maccabees became popular in early Christianity because they were associated with martyrdom, a willingness to die for one's faith. This theme is prominent in 2 Maccabees. 1 Maccabees stresses not martyrdom, but rather that dying in battle is heroic. According to chapter 9, this is how Judas's life ends.

1 Maccabees is a book of the Old Testament in the Catholic and Orthodox traditions. The early Protestant reformers relocated 1 Maccabees to the Apocrypha. There was also reflection on 1 Maccabees' scriptural status in antiquity. Origen's list of books of the Old Testament preserved in Eusebius's *Ecclesiastical History* concludes by saying "outside of these" texts is a Maccabean book, probably 1 Maccabees (more on this below). This statement may mean the book is "outside" the canon in the Jewish Bible, which is the case. Jerome, while he drew on 1 Maccabees for his commentary on Daniel, diminished the status of the book, listing it among the books of the Septuagint that should not be used for church doctrine but are nevertheless good to read (see Chapter 1).

While no Maccabean book is in the Jewish Bible, the Maccabean revolt is important in Judaism. 1 and 2 Maccabees both emphasize that Judas's purification of the temple should be commemorated. This is the origin story of Hanukkah, which has long been a major Jewish holiday. 1 and 2 Maccabees also urge that Judas's defeat of a Seleucid general named Nicanor be honored annually. The Day of Nicanor used to be a Jewish festal day but long ago fell out of the tradition (see the next chapter).

1 Maccabees as Hasmonean, Hebrew Propaganda

1 Maccabees was written in Hebrew and in antiquity translated into Greek. No ancient Hebrew version of 1 Maccabees has been discovered. Analysis of the Greek text, however, indicates it was translated from Hebrew. Jerome, in his famous Helmeted Preface (discussed in Chapter 1), claims to know of a Hebrew 1 Maccabees. In the canon list of Origen mentioned above, he correlates books of the Christian Old Testament with books in the Jewish Bible, according to their Hebrew titles. Writing in Greek, he wants his non-Hebrew-speaking readers to know, for example, that the Jews call Genesis "Bresith." This is indeed the Hebrew name of Genesis (*be-reshit*), meaning "In (the) beginning," the book's well-known opening phrase. He also gives the Hebrew title of a Maccabean book, suggesting that at issue is an actual book, as with Genesis. He says the Maccabean text is called in Hebrew *Sarbethsabanaiel*. 2–4 Maccabees were written in Greek, not Hebrew. *Sarbethsabanaiel* is most likely the title of the lost Hebrew 1 Maccabees. Unfortunately, the phrase is corrupt, so scholars must emend the word to translate it. One possible option is "A Prince of the House of Israel." Another is the "Book of the Dynasty of God's Resisters." While the meaning of the title is unclear, it suggests that 1 Maccabees was written in Hebrew, even though our oldest form of the text is in Greek.

Understanding 1 Maccabees as written in Hebrew helps us understand the milieu in which it was composed. The book's presentation of historical events reflects a pro-Hasmonean perspective. The coinage of the Hasmonean state utilized Hebrew (and Greek); their official use of Hebrew accords with the Jewish nationalism and push for independence promoted by 1 Maccabees. While it cannot be conclusively proven, 1 Maccabees' unrelentingly positive portrayal of the Hasmoneans suggests it was likely written by scribes in their court, as a kind of royal propaganda that depicts the origins of the dynasty in glowing terms.

The book depicts the Maccabean brothers as mighty heroes favored by God. Judas wins every battle he fights, despite often being outnumbered, except for the one at which he valiantly dies, fighting with 800 men against 20,000 soldiers and 2,000 calvary (the Battle of Elasa; ch. 9). 1 Maccabees 9 also claims that the deeds of Judas are *not* recorded elsewhere. The book presents its preservation of knowledge about Judas's valiant exploits as a unique and important task. The only other military loss during Judas's leadership happens because of two men not in the Maccabean line, Joseph and Azariah, who went into battle against his orders. 1 Maccabees emphasizes that they "did not belong to the family of those men through whom deliverance was given to Israel" (ch. 5), referring to the Maccabees. Also, while the Maccabees despise some Jews ("renegades" who reject the covenant, more on them below), the book gives no indication that any Jewish group challenged or disrespected their authority.

The memorialization of the Maccabean brothers is an explicit theme of 1 Maccabees. The curation of this heritage is associated not with Judas but Simon. Chapter 14 praises his short reign (143–135 BCE) as a golden age. Israel had peace. The fruit trees were abundant. Old men relaxedly conversed with each other in the streets. Simon also builds an elaborate tomb for his family; it has seven pyramids and several columns. He enshrines his family's legacy. He is the last of the five Maccabean brothers. This explains why he is associated with the commemoration of their legacy. Continuation of Hasmonean rule goes through him (Hyrcanus being his son).

1 Maccabees covers Hasmonean history up to events early in the reign of John Hyrcanus (r. 135–104 BCE). The text mentions at the end of chapter 16 "the rest" of his deeds, suggesting the text was written or revised after his reign was over, thus likely during the rule of his son, Alexander Jannaeus (103–76 BCE). Since Rome conquered Palestine in 63 BCE, 1 Maccabees' positive treatment of Rome would make more sense before it occupied Palestine. Some form of 1 Maccabees akin to the form we have it was likely composed between approximately 135–63 BCE. The book's highly positive treatment of Simon suggests that part of the work may have been composed during his reign.

In terms of Hasmonean history, 1 Maccabees takes great interest in Mattathias and his sons, but once the following generation assumes rule (John Hyrcanus), it trails off. The composition wishes to emphasize the glorious past of the Maccabean brothers. It says relatively little about contemporary Hasmonean rulers, aside from making clear they are heirs to a revered Maccabean legacy.

The Dead Sea Scrolls help us understand why a pro-Hasmonean text would want in the early first century BCE to promote the dynasty by stressing the Maccabean glory days rather than more recent events. As mentioned above, 1 Maccabees was produced during the reign of Hyrcanus and/or his son Jannaeus. During this period there was widespread resentment against the Hasmoneans, especially during Jannaeus's rule. While one text from Qumran may praise Jannaeus (4Q448), the Dead Sea Scrolls in general show disdain toward the Hasmoneans. The Dead Sea sect flourished in the early first century BCE, the same general time frame when 1 Maccabees was written. No text written by the sect stresses or even mentions the Maccabean revolt. Compared to 1 Maccabees, this is a loud silence. One composition written by the Dead Sea sect known as the *Habakkuk Pesher* (an interpretation of that prophetic text) derisively refers to a Hasmonean ruler as "the Wicked Priest," a pun on "High Priest" (the two phrases are similar in Hebrew). Which Hasmonean leader (or leaders) is intended by the phrase is debated, but the epithet expresses anti-Hasmonean sentiment that is roughly contemporary with 1 Maccabees. The *Habakkuk Pesher* describes the Wicked Priest as a corrupt ruler who took money from the poor and used it for his own personal gain. It also claims that the Wicked Priest died by means of treachery, which accords with 1 Maccabees' portrayal of the demise of both Jonathan and Simon.

Although not a point the *Habakkuk Pesher* emphasizes, the Dead Sea sect may have considered the Hasmoneans the wrong family line to rule Judah. While the Hasmoneans starting with Jonathan assumed the office of high priesthood, it was traditionally held by the Zadokites, who are in the line of Zadok, high priest under King David. The Zadokites were a different lineage from the Hasmoneans, and Zadokites were important in the leadership structure of the Dead Sea sect. In 1 Maccabees the Hasmoneans act as virtual kings, but they are not in the royal line of David. The first Hasmonean to claim the title of king was Aristobulus I, who died soon after assuming power (r. 104–103 BCE). The first to have a lengthy reign as both king and high priest was his brother Jannaeus. But there were grounds at the time for considering him invalid to hold either office. One of the few texts from the period available before the discovery of the Dead Sea Scrolls bitterly derides the Hasmoneans as illegitimate kings. The *Psalms of Solomon*, a collection of eighteen psalms, is likely from the first century BCE. Its seventeenth psalm calls the Hasmoneans "sinners" and asserts that "with pomp they set up a monarchy because of their arrogance; they despoiled the throne of David with arrogant shouting."

Jannaeus was moreover a breathtakingly cruel king, even by 1 Maccabees' standards. As high priest he would lead the celebration of the Feast of Tabernacles (or Booths; Sukkot). In antiquity, Jews would travel to Jerusalem for this festival to attend a ceremony led by the high priest for which they would carry ethrogs, a kind of lemon, and palm fronds (*lulavin*). According to Josephus and some rabbinic texts, once when Jannaeus was officiating this event, the people began to throw their lemons at him, a clear indication of what they thought of him. In response he had 6,000 people killed. Josephus also relates that Jannaeus suppressed another popular uprising by holding one of the largest mass crucifixions ever held in Judah. He crucified eight hundred men and made them watch, while suffering on their crosses, their families being murdered. Jannaeus delighted viewing the spectacle, dining with his concubines. A Qumran text known as the *Nahum Pesher* (an interpretation of that prophetic book) gives a different but still bloody account of this horrific event, suggesting it has some basis in fact. Rabbinic literature likewise presents Jannaeus as a wicked king, stressing that he clashed with the Pharisees.

As mentioned above, 1 Maccabees could have been written during Jannaeus's reign. Even if one holds that it was written earlier, during the time of Hyrcanus, the book was transmitted during Jannaeus's rule, and it was not updated to include that period. Jannaeus's brutal, unpopular reign helps explain why a pro-Hasmonean text like 1 Maccabees would not cover more contemporary history from the early first century BCE. The text endorses the Hasmonean rulers of its time not by stressing their recent accomplishments, but rather their continuity with the Maccabees and the glory days of the revolt.

The Maccabean Revolt as the Birth of a Dynasty

According to 1 Maccabees 1, Antiochus IV's reign was astonishingly disastrous for Judah. Stressing a dichotomy between Jews and Gentiles, the text is irate that some Jews are more interested in adopting Gentile customs than adhering to Jewish traditions. A gymnasium, a traditional center of Greek education, is constructed in Jerusalem. Certain "renegade" Jews petition

Antiochus to build one, and he agrees. The book does not stress that the gymnasium is a problem because it promotes Greek philosophy or Hellenistic culture. The Maccabees embrace their affinity with Rome and Sparta. The problem with the gymnasium, according to 1 Maccabees, is that its Jewish male students are not circumcised. In antiquity a traditional element of the curriculum at a gymnasium was young men (*ephebes*) doing physical exercise, typically in the nude. In this context, not being circumcised is public knowledge. Any Jewish male participant must have at some level found that acceptable. The gymnasium, in the mindset of the text, discourages circumcision, a symbolic marker of being a member of the covenant community. 1 Maccabees 1 may imply that males removed the marks of their circumcisions via epispasm, an ancient medical procedure that would restore the foreskin of the phallus. It may simply be that the Jewish students had never been circumcised.

But the policies of Antiochus IV go far beyond a gymnasium or disputes among Jews regarding circumcision. The king launches a wide-ranging attack against Jerusalem and Jewish tradition. He sends an army to attack the city. It plunders Jerusalem and burns it with fire. Antiochus issues a decree that all the peoples of his vast kingdom should abandon their particular customs and become "one people." He forces regular sacrifices at the Jerusalem temple to cease and makes Jews sacrifice pigs, an unclean animal according to Jewish law. Copies of the Torah are burned. If families have their infant boys circumcised, the babies are killed and their mothers forced to hang them from their necks. If that wasn't bad enough, the king installs a "desolating sacrilege" in the Jerusalem temple or, as the King James Bible puts it, an "abomination of desolation." In the New Testament this expression, which it gets from Daniel, becomes a sign that the end-times are at hand. In 1 Maccabees it refers to a statue of a god, perhaps Baal or Zeus, or maybe of Antiochus himself to be revered as a god, in the temple. Antiochus's oppressive policies trigger the Maccabean revolt.

Other texts recount events pertaining to Antiochus and the Maccabean revolt in ways very different from 1 Maccabees. This is especially the case with 2 Maccabees. It ascribes many of the religious reforms in Jerusalem to two Jews, Jason and Menelaus, who each ascend to the high priesthood through corruption. But 1 Maccabees never mentions these men. The book's account of the symbolic beginning of the Maccabean revolt, Mattathias's murder of an idol-worshipping Jew, is not in 2 Maccabees. Antiochus also never distributes in 2 Maccabees an empire-wide decree that all peoples must cease their traditional customs, whereas this draconian law is foundational in 1 Maccabees' presentation of the king.

The visions of Daniel 7–12 also offer a very different perspective on Antiochus IV. They cryptically allude to the upheaval and destructiveness of his reign, and this coheres with 1 Maccabees. But the visions' imagery and mode of expression are entirely different. Daniel 7, for example, is a vision of four strange beasts, such as a lion with wings. The vision emphasizes that the fourth beast, which has iron teeth and ten horns, is the worst and most violent among them. One horn arises from it which has a mouth and eyes. The little horn fights against the people of God and attacks the laws and set times of God. An angel interprets this vision to mean that the beasts represent a historical sequence of four kingdoms and the horns of the fourth beast represent specific kings. While Daniel 7 has been understood in various ways throughout history, the fourth beast was originally intended as an indirect reference to the Seleucid (Greek) kingdom, and the little horn to Antiochus IV. The amount of time the little horn is to be in power, "a time, two times, and half a time," is a cryptic allusion to three and a half years ("time" = year), and this roughly accords with the length of time Antiochus's "desolating sacrilege" was in the temple, according to 1 Maccabees. Daniel 9 uses this same expression when saying that sacrifice will cease for half a week of years (= three and a half years). The little horn's attacks against Israel, the Torah, and regular sacrifices at the temple ("set times") accord with Antiochus's anti-Jewish policies.

Unlike 1 Maccabees, Daniel 7–12 construes Antiochus's brutal reign as preceding the final judgment. The Animal Apocalypse of *1 Enoch* likewise situates the Maccabean revolt as the advent of an eschatological scenario (see Chapter 17). Daniel 7–12's framing of Antiochus's destructiveness as an eschatological event leads to a different political stance than 1 Maccabees. The Danielic visions do not recommend taking up arms against the evil king. Rather, since it will all end soon, people should endure his cruelty a bit longer ("a time, two times, and half a time") and wait for God to fix everything. Daniel 11 may even allude negatively to the Maccabees, saying that those who are being killed or captured by the evil king before the final judgment "shall receive a little help, and many shall join them insincerely."

Rabbinic literature, which does not often refer to Antiochus or the Maccabean revolt, offers still other accounts of these issues. The late antique text *Megillat Antiochus* (the *Scroll of Antiochus*) stresses that when the Hasmoneans purified the temple (1 Maccabees credits Judas alone with this act), the lights of the menorah (a lamp) in the temple burned for eight days, although it only had enough oil for one day. This miraculous event is important today in the Jewish observance of Hanukkah. It is never mentioned in 1 Maccabees (it is, however, in Josephus). In *Megillat Antiochus*, Johnathan kills Nicanor, whereas in 1 and 2 Maccabees, Judas does. Greco-Roman historians offer their own accounts of the days of Antiochus. Polybius (second century BCE), for example, depicts Antiochus not as a cruel tyrant, but rather as an odd king. The historian relates, for example, that he would show up at parties unannounced with a fife (a kind of flute) and a band, and randomly give incredibly expensive gifts to complete strangers on the street.

Attesting the popularity of the tale, there is an even wider range of Maccabean literature. In addition to Josephus's detailed account of the Maccabean revolt and Hasmonean history, there is also an account of these events in Arabic, often called 5 Maccabees. There is also a 6 Maccabees, a text in Syriac (a Christian form of Aramaic), which offers a version of the story of the martyrdom of a mother and her seven sons found in 2 Maccabees 6–7 and 4 Maccabees. Three indigenous Ethiopian Maccabean books, 1–3 Maqebeyan (Maccabees), tell stories that are similar but often unrelated to 1–2 Maccabees. They focus on an evil king, Sirusayedan, who is opposed by a man named Maqabeyos and his three sons. A later Jewish iteration of Maccabean events, the *Hanukkah-nāmah* (the *Book of Hanukkah*), a Judeo-Persian epic written in the sixteenth century, poetically reworks the story of 1 Maccabees, primarily using *Megillat Antiochus*.

The diversity and extent of our sources regarding Antiochus IV and the Maccabean revolt problematize the task of determining what happened. That is not the goal of this chapter. It is rather to understand 1 Maccabees' iteration of events. By not highlighting Jason and Menelaus (who are perhaps among the unnamed "renegade" Jews who want a gymnasium in Jerusalem), the text presents Antiochus Epiphanes as the only major villain. This casts the Maccabees as heroes and defenders of the faith against an incredible foe. Their militarism, so framed, is morally just and a legitimate response to an evil king.

1 Maccabees depicts the Maccabees as restorers of the traditional religion of Israel. This is above all evident in Judas's removal of the "desolating sacrilege" from the temple. The book presents the Maccabees, especially Judas, as men of great piety who respect the Torah. Judas studies the law before battle. He inspires his troops before battle by invoking famous examples of God delivering Israel, such as the Exodus. He follows Torah regulations regarding warfare. According to Deuteronomy 20, before a battle a priest should address the troops and say that anyone who is building a house, engaged to be married, or even just too afraid to fight, can leave. Letting soldiers go away just before the fighting starts does not seem like a good military strategy. In the Hebrew Bible there is not a single example of an army following this commandment. In 1 Maccabees, however, Judas does (ch. 3). The logic of this law

is that victory is achieved not by having more troops than your enemy, but with God on your side. So understood, winning when outnumbered proves God is with you. Relatedly, as a show of piety, 1 Maccabees at times avoids using the name of God, referring to him instead as "Heaven."

Judas often wins battles despite being outnumbered, as previously mentioned. The trope of going into battle with fewer troops than your opponent is prominent in the biblical book of Judges. The leadership model of the judges also resonates with the Maccabean rulers. The judges were not kings but rose to power to save Israel from oppressive rulers, as do the Maccabees vis-à-vis Antiochus IV. In this way, 1 Maccabees presents the Maccabean family as in continuity with the scriptural heritage of ancient Israel. The text also does this by writing about the Hasmoneans, even though they were not kings, in a style that echoes the narration of the reigns of ancient kings of Judah in 1–2 Kings; like these books, 1 Maccabees moves chronologically from reign to reign, often giving the year (according to the Seleucid calendar) when events occur, and referring the reader to annals that provide fuller accounts of their rule (compare, for example, 2 Kgs 15:6 and 1 Macc 16:23). The Maccabeans are presented in monarchic terms without calling them kings. 1 Maccabees 13 states that when Simon began to rule, people in Judah started dating their documents as the "first year" of his reign—even though he was never king—in continuity with how years are counted when there is a new king in 1–2 Kings. 1 Maccabees valorizes the Maccabean family and their successful revolt as the birth of the Hasmonean dynasty.

The Inspiring and Dangerous Legacy of the Maccabean Revolt

1 Maccabees, with its stories about pious warriors achieving victory against tyrannical forces, can be inspiring. The *Africana Bible*

endorses the book as a potential resource for African Americans, arguing that the Maccabees' fight against oppression can be a model for their struggles against discrimination and racism. As we have seen, in 1 Maccabees the conviction that you are fighting with God on your side can also legitimate horrific violence. This is evident in the reception of the Maccabean brothers. Even though Martin Luther took the book out of the Old Testament, the composition's militant zeal fired him up. He says in his preface to 1 Maccabees that Christians should wield the gospel as a sword to attack the Antichrist (in the context of early Protestant polemic, this is a reference to the Pope), as Judas fought with a sword in his own day. The social movement Luther helped foment, in part with Maccabean rhetoric, unleashed extremism, violence, and peasant revolts throughout Europe, even though he personally opposed these developments.

The power of the story of the Maccabees is also evident in modern Israel. The Maccabees are often regarded there with a sense of pride, as Jewish warriors who defended Israel and pushed out its enemies. A leading Israeli beer is named "Maccabee." A Zionist iteration of the Olympics (for Jewish and Israeli athletes) is called the Maccabiah Games; the opening ceremonies are often held at Modein, the city of Mattathias. Early Zionists hailed the Maccabean brothers as a model for Jews that would encourage them to be strong, militant, and willing to fight. They believed that a Maccabean-style aggressive posture was needed in their struggles against the British, who exerted colonialist control over Palestine in the early twentieth century, and in their efforts to displace native Arabs. At the end of his 1896 book *The Jewish State*, Theodor Herzl, the founder of modern Zionism, asserts: "The Maccabees will rise again."

The ideology of Zionism, bolstered in part by its appropriation of the Maccabean legacy, has justified a great deal of violence, often against Palestinian Arabs. The Jewish Defense League (JDL), founded in the late 1960s by Rabbi Meir Kahane, is officially designated as a hate group, and it supports the forced removal of all

Arabs from Palestine. One possible precursor to the JDL is a group that was based in Brooklyn called the Maccabees. The Maccabean revolt, particularly as iterated in 1 Maccabees, raises issues that are often discussed today in terms of Islamic terrorism or the Christian nationalism of the American far right. Being convinced that you are fighting a war in the name of God can justify horrendous acts. 1 Maccabees is an inspiring but dangerous book.

Conclusion

1 Maccabees offers a detailed account of political and military events in the Hellenistic Near East during the second century BCE from a decidedly pro-Hasmonean perspective. It is reasonable to understand the text as a kind of court Hasmonean propaganda written in the early first century BCE. While it may have been produced in the time of John Hyrcanus, the composition, and the whole idea of wanting to produce a pro-Hasmonean text in the first place, likely reflects the backdrop of the unpopularity and upheaval of the reign of Hyrcanus's son, Alexander Jannaeus. The book presents the Hasmoneans as powerful and legitimate rulers not by stressing their recent achievements, but rather their genealogical connection to the earlier Maccabean brothers and their legendary revolt against Antiochus IV, which the book extols as the origin story of the Hasmonean dynasty.

Guide for Further Reading

Harrington, Daniel J. *The Maccabean Revolt: Anatomy of a Biblical Revolution.* Eugene, OR: Wipf & Stock, 2009.

Noam, Vered. *Shifting Images of the Hasmoneans: Second Temple Legends and Their Reception in Josephus and Rabbinic Literature.* New York: Oxford University Press, 2018.

Schwartz, Daniel R. *1 Maccabees.* New Haven, CT: Yale University Press, 2022.

13

Dying for Judaism Prompts God's Mercy

2 Maccabees

2 Maccabees is an interesting book. It has stories of political corruption, warfare, and divine deliverance. A man named Razis
rips out his own guts and throws them at soldiers about to arrest
him. The composition tells the history of the Maccabean revolt,
covering much of the same material in 1 Maccabees 1–7, often in
a completely different way. While 1 Maccabees, as discussed in
the previous chapter, portrays the revolt as the origin story of the
Hasmonean dynasty, 2 Maccabees strives to show that the historical episode illustrates a theological principle—that when the Jews
are loyal to God and the covenant, he will come to their rescue
in a time of need, and if they are not, he will not intervene when
disasters befall them. Scholars often call this Deuteronomistic historical theology since the same idea animates the presentation of
Israelite history in the book of Deuteronomy. For 2 Maccabees,
honoring the temple and observing traditional forms of worship
are critical for maintaining the covenant between God and Israel.
2 Maccabees highlights Jews who would rather die than forsake
their traditions (like Razis). Such acts of bravery, the composition
emphasizes, compels God to act favorably on behalf of the Jewish
people.

The Apocrypha: A Guide. Matthew Goff, Oxford University Press. © Oxford University Press 2024.
DOI: 10.1093/9780190060770.003.0013

2 Maccabees as a Scriptural Text

"2 Maccabees" was not the original title of the book. Clement of Alexandria (early third century) called it "the epitome of the Maccabeans." The term "epitome" denotes in antiquity an abridged summary of a separate, longer text. The bulk of 2 Maccabees is an epitome in exactly that sense (more on this below). In terms of the earliest manuscript evidence for the Christian Bible, of the three major manuscripts (Vaticanus, Sinaiticus, and Alexandrinus), only the third attests 2 Maccabees—with the title "2 Maccabees."

2 Maccabees has long been a book of the Old Testament in the Orthodox and Catholic traditions. It is not in the Jewish Bible. In antiquity some Christian authors disparaged the book's scriptural status while also using it as a scriptural text. Origen's canon list preserved in Eusebius, while likely mentioning a Hebrew form of 1 Maccabees (see Chapter 12), does not include 2 Maccabees. Origen, however, does cite the work in his *On First Principles*. 2 Maccabees was written in Greek. For this reason the composition had for Jerome a diminished status (see Chapter 1). He probably did not translate it into Latin, although the book has long been in the Latin Bible of Catholic tradition. Jerome uses the book, however, in his commentary on Daniel. 2 Maccabees' account of Jews being tortured to death was a persistent topic of interest in early Christianity and later Judaism (discussed below).

The Protestants moved 2 Maccabees from the Old Testament into the Apocrypha. Martin Luther, as recounted in his *Table Talk*, declared himself an enemy of the book. He ranked it with Esther among the biblical texts he despised most. 2 Maccabees 12 in particular attracted Luther's ire. There Judas Maccabee raises money for offerings for Jewish soldiers who died wearing images of other gods, to atone for their sins after death. A common Catholic interpretation in Luther's day was to understand this passage as scriptural justification for indulgences. This was a Catholic penitential practice that became associated with paying money to remove sins, a custom that could be easily abused. Luther and other Reformers were bitterly critical of indulgences. There is also a Catholic tradition that 2 Maccabees 12 supports the doctrine of purgatory, a state after death in which removal of sins is possible. Luther attacked both this interpretation of the passage and the concept of purgatory itself.

2 Maccabees as a Compilation of Texts: The Two Initial Letters

2 Maccabees is a collection of three distinct texts. The main body of the composition (2:19–15:39) is an iteration of Judean history from ca. 180 to 161 BCE, written in a verbose style that reflects extensive education in Greek rhetoric. It begins with two letters (1:1–9; 1:10–2:18), addressed to the Jews in Egypt. It is not clear if they are fictive or authentic documents that were sent to Egypt. The first, which purports to be from the people of Jerusalem and Judah, is dated to the year 188 according to the Seleucid calendar, which 2 Maccabees uses throughout, or 124 BCE. It cites an earlier letter sent to Egyptian Jews in 143 BCE. It states that the Jews in Judah suffered during the Maccabean-era crisis and have commemorated it.

The second letter is undated. It also relates to Maccabean events. An indication of his fame, this document is attributed to Judas Maccabee, and also the people of Jerusalem, Judea, and the senate, a Judean governmental body in the Hellenistic era. The letter is addressed to the Jews of Egypt and a man named Aristobulus. Aristobulus was a highly learned Jewish exegete in Alexandria, Egypt (second century BCE), some of whose philosophical writings are extant. His designation as an addressee indicates 2 Maccabees' interest in appealing to Jews who are in elite, intellectual circles in Egypt.

Both letters encourage Jews in Egypt to know about Maccabean events and honor Hanukkah. Still a major Jewish holiday,

Hanukkah commemorates how Judas Maccabee cleansed the temple circa 164 BCE, in the days of Antiochus IV Epiphanes, king of the Seleucid Empire which ruled Judah at the time. The letters' interest in Hanukkah may explain why a lengthy Maccabean history was appended to them—to recount the origins of the festival they promote.

The second letter contains several narratives that are unique in ancient Judaism. It relates Antiochus's death in Persia, at a temple of a goddess named Nanea (2 Maccabees 9 gives a different account of his death). She was associated with a Persian fertility goddess Anahit who was also worshipped in Armenia. In another story in the second letter, priests who were sent into exile hid the fire of the altar of the Jerusalem temple in a remote cave in Persia. Chapter 2 suggests that it was Jeremiah who commanded the exiles to take some of the temple fire with them. A form of this latter legend is attested in the *Chronicles of Jerahmeel*, a medieval Jewish compilation of biblical traditions.

As 2 Maccabees 1 recounts, amazingly, the fire survives, transformed into a flammable liquid. With it, Nehemiah reignites the ancient fire preserved from the Solomonic temple. The chapter calls this liquid "naphtha" (and "nephthar"). This is an early reference to petroleum, which is indeed abundant in Iran, where the story is set (the modern word for "oil" in Arabic and Persian is similar to "naphtha": *naft*). The story emphasizes that the second temple which Judas purified continues the vitality of the destroyed first temple.

Stressing continuity with older scriptural traditions, the second letter claims that Nehemiah founded a library that collected books about kings, prophets, and Davidic writings, texts which sound similar to but are not necessarily the same as the books of the Hebrew Bible. Judas likewise assembles books lost during his wars. The second letter also describes Jeremiah encouraging Jews to observe the Torah in exile.

Likely reflecting an early stage in the history of Hanukkah, both letters describe it as a festival of booths. This expression evokes a separate festival, Sukkot, that memorializes Israel's wandering in the wilderness. 2 Maccabees 10 asserts that Hanukkah should be honored like Sukkot since Judas and his men fled into the wilderness to escape unrest in Jerusalem. The composition legitimizes Hanukkah, a new festival it promotes, by connecting it to the more established festival of booths.

The second letter also likens the purification festival (Hanukkah) to a "festival of fire." This probably explains why it includes the story about Nehemiah rekindling the flame of the first temple. Hanukkah became revered in Judaism as the festival of lights. According to Jewish tradition, the flame of the menorah (lamp) burned in the temple for eight days, despite having enough oil only for one (a story in neither 1 nor 2 Maccabees). The second letter gives an early account of Hanukkah that associates it with the fire of the temple (and its oil!) but not yet with a menorah.

The two letters urge Egyptian Jews to worship according to directives from the temple establishment in Jerusalem. A concern in Judah about how Jews in Egypt observe religious traditions is historically documented. The Elephantine papyri, a horde of Aramaic documents from the fifth century BCE found at a military colony in Egypt, attest forms of veneration that are different from anything endorsed by the Hebrew Bible. One Elephantine text, for example, is a list of funds collected to support the worship of Yahweh and two other deities, named Ashim-Bethel and Anat-Bethel, without any sense that one must revere God alone. A man named Hananiah arrived there, presumably from Judah; the papyri include a letter from him, addressed to the entire garrison, dated to 419 BCE. It stipulates that its inhabitants are to honor Passover and the feast of unleavened bread, and on which days they should do so. The end of the Greek book of Esther claims that a letter regarding Purim was brought from Jerusalem to Egypt (see Chapter 6); Esther relates

224 THE APOCRYPHA: A GUIDE

the origins of Purim and promotes its observance. These texts construe Jerusalem and its temple establishment as the arbiter of proper worship among Jews in Egypt. There was in the second and first centuries BCE a large Jewish community in Egypt, particularly in the coastal city of Alexandria. The Jerusalem temple was interested in supervising the worship of Jews in that country perhaps because there was a Jewish temple in the Egyptian city of Leontopolis, probably founded by Onias IV, the son of the high priest Onias III. Although 2 Maccabees never mentions this temple, which ceased functioning in the first century CE, concern that the Leontopolis temple was exercising influence over Egyptian Jews perhaps explains why the letters in 2 Maccabees 1–2, with their emphasis on Jerusalem guiding Jewish religious observance in Egypt, were written.

The first letter, dated to 124 BCE, is important for establishing the date of 2 Maccabees as a whole. This date suggests that the two letters and the main body of the composition were compiled together during or after 124 BCE. The main section of 2 Maccabees is not dated. The composition has a positive or at least not hostile view toward Rome, which suggests it was written before 63 BCE, when Rome conquered Palestine. The compilation of an early form of 2 Maccabees, with its historical bloc appended to the two letters, likely took place between 124–63 BCE. This would make 2 Maccabees contemporary with or even slightly older than 1 Maccabees. 2 Maccabees is not a reworking of 1 Maccabees; they are distinct reformulations of a common body of Maccabean traditions.

2 Maccabees' Epitome of a Lost Maccabean History

The preface to the main body of 2 Maccabees (2:19–32) explains that what follows is an abridgement or "epitome" of a five-volume work by a historian named Jason of Cyrene. He was likely an actual person who wrote such a book, the only evidence for which is 2 Maccabees. Cyrene was a coastal city in what is now eastern Libya (north Africa), which had in antiquity a large Jewish community. The content of 2 Maccabees suggests that Jason's history focused on Judah. He may have been a Cyrenian Jew living in Judah. That Jews from Cyrene were living in Palestine is presupposed in the New Testament ("Simon of Cyrene" carries Jesus's cross). Moreover, the preface's claim that an author (or better, "epitomator") produced a shorter version of a longer composition accords with established scribal practices of the time. In an era in which texts had to be copied by hand, a laborious process, an abridging mode of rewriting made sense.

In the preface and at the end of 2 Maccabees, the epitomator reflects on his literary creation. He likens himself not to one who builds a house from the ground up, but rather one who paints and decorates it. His chief concern is with aesthetic design and ornamentation, not engaging every detail. He hopes that reading his epitome is an enjoyable experience, comparing it to drinking wine mixed with water, a popular way to imbibe alcohol at the time. The epitomator reworked and selected details from Jason of Cyrene's history so that his own iteration of events would illustrate how and when God intervenes during the course of history on behalf of the Jews.

Judah's Golden Age: The High Priesthood of Onias III

The history of 2 Maccabees begins (ch. 3) with Jerusalem enjoying a golden age of piety. The city is at peace and traditional forms of worship are observed. The text attributes this pinnacle of devotion to Jerusalem's exemplary high priest, Onias III; by contrast, he is a minor character in 1 Maccabees. The temple's devout leadership filters down to produce a high level of observance among the populace. The king, Seleucus IV Philopator (r. 187–175 BCE), respects Jewish tradition. He personally covers the costs related to sacrifices at the temple.

Problems begin when a temple official named Simon has a disagreement with Onias III regarding the administration of the city market (2 Maccabees does not divulge the nature of their dispute). This Simon is not Simon Maccabee who, while prominent in 1 Maccabees, barely appears in 2 Maccabees. Frustrated with Onias, Simon tells Apollonius, the governor of the region, that the temple is filled with treasure. Upon learning this, Seleucus IV changes his benevolent attitude toward the temple. He appoints an official named Heliodorus to seize temple funds. His insistence on entering the sanctuary causes great consternation, resulting in a scene reminiscent of 3 Maccabees 1, in which the Egyptian king Ptolemy IV likewise attempts to go into the temple. The epitomator writes in a style of Hellenistic historiography known as "pathetic" because it appeals to readers' emotions (Gk. *pathos*). They are to empathize with the plight of Jerusalem. The anguish of Onias III is melodramatically described and, as in 3 Maccabees 1, distraught women fill the streets, wearing sackcloth and asking God for help. They get it. A rider on a horse and two men appear from heaven. They beat Heliodorus severely and he is removed from the temple. The experience transforms him. Heliodorus now understands the power of God and offers sacrifices to him.

This construal of events is noticeably different from 1 Maccabees. There the crisis begins with the oppressive mandates of Antiochus IV. Here the problems start with a dispute between two Jewish leaders of Jerusalem *before* Antiochus becomes king. Antiochus is less of a focus than in 1 Maccabees. Instead the history of 2 Maccabees starts with a civics lesson about the fragility of good government. Immoral leaders, even in minor positions, can cause major crises, demonstrating that a city should be run by ethical people. This concern accords with a classic Greek interest in the democratic administration of cities. Also in keeping with a Hellenistic concern for cities, the epitome is often focused on Jerusalem rather than Judah as a whole.

2 Maccabees' golden age of peace and piety under Onias III takes place during Seleucid rule. The composition does not endorse, in striking contrast to 1 Maccabees, Jewish independence from the Seleucid Empire. Similarly, the end of 2 Maccabees, after Judas's army defeats and kills the general Nicanor (a battle also in 1 Maccabees 7), asserts that "from that time the city has been in the possession of the Hebrews." But Judah is still part of the Seleucid kingdom. In 1 Maccabees, Nicanor's death is only one major step toward full independence from the Seleucids, which happens later. 2 Maccabees promotes instead an idealized relationship between the Hellenistic king and the cities under his domain. Such a ruler endorses local autonomy and allows ethnic groups to follow their ancestral customs, as Seleucus IV does at first. Consistent with this perspective, while 2 Maccabees presents Judas Maccabee as a military hero, the composition shows little to no interest in his brothers or his family line. Unlike 1 Maccabees, 2 Maccabees does not promote the Hasmonean dynasty.

The Heliodorus episode illustrates an important lesson—that God will reward the Jews' devotion by delivering them if a crisis arises. That he sends warrior-angels to rebuff the Seleucid official should be understood in the context of Onias III's piety.

A Greek inscription first published in 2007 is of direct relevance to the Heliodorus scene in 2 Maccabees 3. It is called the Heliodorus stele. One part of it, dated to 178 BCE, is from King Seleucus IV and is addressed to a Seleucid official named Heliodorus. In addition to having the same names and time frame as 2 Maccabees 3, the stele also addresses the same basic issue of that chapter—imperial control over temples within the empire. Someone, the inscription states, must be appointed to oversee sanctuaries in Coele-Syria and Phoenicia, a Seleucid designation for the region that includes Judah, which 2 Maccabees also employs. The stele raises an issue that is at the heart of the Heliodorus episode in 2 Maccabees: who has ultimate jurisdiction over the Jerusalem temple—God or the Seleucid king? 2 Maccabees advocates passionately for the former, whereas the Heliodorus stele presumes the latter. There could have been an actual confrontation at the temple involving an official named Heliodorus, which 2 Maccabees and/or his source (Jason of Cyrene) richly embellished, to emphasize that God, not the king, controls the temple.

Jason and Menelaus Ruin Jerusalem

Things get worse when Antiochus IV becomes king, but not simply because of him. Onias III loses the high priesthood when his brother Jason (different from Jason of Cyrene) bribes Antiochus to acquire the office. Jason successfully petitions Antiochus to build a gymnasium, a center of Greek culture and education, in Jerusalem. The gymnasium is also a topic in 1 Maccabees. Additionally, Jason lobbies the king to register the men of Jerusalem "as citizens of Antioch." Jason, perhaps motivated by a desire to "modernize" his city, wants to transform Jerusalem into a *polis*, so that it would have features common in Greek cities, such as a gymnasium, and its men regarded as citizens with various rights and responsibilities important in the conduct of public life. That the men of Jerusalem become citizens of "Antioch" may mean that Jerusalem was to be renamed or that Jason's urban model is Antioch, the capital of the Seleucid Empire. Given the similarity of the name to the king's, a degree of flattery can perhaps be detected as well.

While a high level of piety is associated with the leadership of Onias III, the opposite happens under Jason. His introduction of "the Greek way of life" to Jerusalem causes a decline in the observance of religious traditions. Priests neglect to carry out their sacrifices at the temple. They prefer to watch wrestling matches or discus throwing, classic Greek forms of athletic competition. This has often been framed as an inherent conflict between Judaism and

Hellenism. But in 2 Maccabees, Hellenistic culture is a problem only insofar as it disrupts Jewish worship. Despite the crisis that befalls Jerusalem in 2 Maccabees, Jews and Gentiles in the work often have common views and interact peaceably. The composition describes the Jerusalem temple as world-famous, renowned among Jews and Gentiles alike. Even Judas and his enemy Nicanor have moments of friendship. According to chapter 14, Judas gets married and has children (which never happens in 1 Maccabees) after Nicanor recommends it.

Moreover, the Judaism which 2 Maccabees espouses is itself richly imbued with Hellenistic culture. This is not only evident in the fact that the composition was written in Greek. The preface extols "those who fought bravely for Judaism" against the "barbarian hordes." "Barbarian" is a classic derogatory Greek term for non-Greeks. The composition adapts a Greek trope to describe the conflict, as if the Jews are the cultured Greeks and their Greek-speaking Seleucid enemies are the uncouth barbarians. 2 Maccabees 15 praises Onias III as a "noble and good" man who could speak well and was trained from childhood "in all that belongs to excellence." The phrase "noble and good" (*kalon kai agathon*) conveyed in Greek culture a meaning similar to "gentleman"—denoting a man from an elite class with a distinguished education, whose demeanor and way of speaking impress people. 2 Maccabees praises Onias III according to classic ideals of Greek education, instilled in institutions such as the gymnasium. The composition utilizes tropes from Greek culture in its valorization of Judaism.

2 Maccabees promotes a way of life characterized by the observance of ancestral customs, loyalty to the covenant, and respect for the temple. Jews are defined not as an ethnic group in a racial or biological sense, but rather in terms of their ancestral customs. The composition is the oldest known text that uses the term "Judaism" to describe their way of life; it derives from Greek (*ioudaismos*).

Jason loses his position as high priest to an even worse figure, Menelaus, the brother of Simon who had earlier sparred with Onias III. He offers Antiochus a larger bribe than Jason did. With Menelaus in power, Jason goes into hiding. Onias escapes as well, but Menelaus has him murdered. He steals treasure from the temple, a heinous act never carried out by Jason. Neither Menelaus nor Jason appears in 1 Maccabees. Their centrality here underscores the consequences of bad leadership in the temple. As 2 Maccabees 5 observes, God does not send warrior-angels to expel Menelaus when he enters the temple to steal from it, whereas the deity did stop Heliodorus from doing the same thing. God does not intervene with regard to Menelaus because with such leaders the covenant relationship is out of balance.

Things continue to get worse. When a false rumor spreads that Antiochus is dead (which the composition connects to his military excursions in Egypt), Jason raises an army and launches an assault to retake Jerusalem from Menelaus. The city is wrought by a civil war between two corrupt priestly factions. Jason is unsuccessful and retreats, eventually dying in exile without a funeral. Antiochus concludes from the violence that Jerusalem is in revolt. His armies crush the nonexistent uprising, shedding a great deal of blood. Judas Maccabee is at this point introduced in the narrative, escaping into the wilderness during the city's turmoil.

Antiochus becomes increasingly emboldened. He launches a full-scale assault against Jewish traditions. Like Menelaus, the king carries off extensive treasures from the temple, again without God preventing him. As in 1 Maccabees, sacrifices at the temple are halted and circumcision is banned. Greek religion is imposed on Jerusalem. The temple is to be rededicated to Zeus, and Jews are forced to venerate Dionysus. Jews are also compelled to worship Dionysus in 3 Maccabees (for more on this issue, see Chapter 15). In 1 Maccabees the crisis begins with Antiochus's heinous anti-Jewish laws. Here they occur later in the story, as a response to intra-Jewish violence. The king's invasion of Jerusalem is not part of a grand plan to eradicate the Jewish religion, but rather an understandable, if not justifiable, effort to restore public order. His actions then become increasingly aggressive. His anti-Jewish policies stem from his growing arrogance and conviction of his own god-like power. Antiochus's actions represent the end result of the corruption and policies initiated by Jason and Menelaus. 2 Maccabees 6 explains that the reader should recognize that with these catastrophic events, God intended "to discipline our people." The term "discipline" is a translation of *paideia*, the Greek word for "education." Education in antiquity could be harsh. Teachers would beat their students, as the book of Proverbs heartily endorses. For 2 Maccabees, the disasters that struck Jerusalem comprise a "teaching moment" about the covenant and traditional worship—that God will deliver them from crisis when Jews are following their religious traditions and have pious leadership, as with Onias, and that he will not if they abandon their traditions and have corrupt leaders, like Jason and Menelaus.

Dying for Judaism Turns the Tide

The horrible situation wrought by Antiochus lays the groundwork for his demise. 2 Maccabees 6–7 contains a gripping account of the torture and death of an elderly scribe (Eleazar), a mother, and her seven sons. This story is not in 1 Maccabees. Eleazar, who should be treated with honor, is forced to either eat pig meat, which is forbidden in the Torah, or be killed. He chooses death. The mother and her sons, all unnamed, are likewise arrested and coerced to consume pork. They too refuse and bravely face torture to the point of death. 2 Maccabees describes their ordeals, one by one. The first brother, for example, has his tongue cut out, his head scalped, and his hands and feet cut off, and then, while still alive, his body is cooked in a large pan. They face torture and death with courage because, as they explain to their torturers, by dying for their ancestral traditions they shall receive a form of eternal existence that is far better than their present life in a physical body. 2 Maccabees describes the post-mortem life they await as accompanied by a form of resurrection, a trope that is common in the Jewish literature of the second and first centuries BCE.

Antiochus is present and actively involved in the torture of the mother and her sons. This is incongruent with the rest of the narrative. Prior to the torture accounts, the king leaves Jerusalem for Antioch, and afterward (in chapter 9) he is in Persia. The focus of the narrative when the torture occurs is Jerusalem, and one could reasonably suppose that is where it takes place, although 2 Maccabees never states this directly. The story of the mother and her sons was perhaps adapted from a source different from Jason of Cyrene's history, in which Antiochus is in Jerusalem (or perhaps Antioch).

There is another gruesome account of a Jew choosing death at the end of 2 Maccabees (ch. 14). Nicanor, eager to punish the people of Jerusalem, seeks to arrest a highly esteemed elder named Razis. He prefers death to capture and runs himself through with a sword. Still alive, when the army breaks the doors of his courtyard, he throws himself down from a tower into the crowd of soldiers. Showing incredible defiance and a dismissive attitude toward his own body, "he tore out his entrails, took them in both hands, and hurled them" at them.

The torture scenes are important in 2 Maccabees' theological construction of history. Judas defeats Nicanor in battle twice, once at the midpoint of the book and again at its end (chs. 8, 15). Each victory comes after an account of torture victims choosing to die. As 2 Maccabees 8 explains, shortly after the death of the mother and her sons, Judas is victorious "for the wrath of the Lord had turned to mercy." Judah's suffering at the hands of Antiochus, Jason, and Menelaus illustrates God's "wrath." He punished the Jews for their impiety by allowing those disasters to happen. The victims, by choosing death and torture rather than abandon their ancestral traditions, obliged God to show instead "mercy" and act in favor of Israel. Their deaths are efficacious. All of Judah benefits from their self-sacrifice. Judas's military successes, in a manner that has no parallel in 1 Maccabees, are attributed to divine favor triggered by the noble deaths of torture victims.

A consequence of God's "mercy," Antiochus dies in a ghastly way that is recompense for his cruelty. God, one can say, tortures the torturer. In chapter 9, the deity strikes him with a painful disease in his bowels. Antiochus, rushing in his chariot from Persia back to Jerusalem, fuming over Judas's successes, falls out of the vehicle. His mangled, diseased body rots, becomes filled with worms, and emits a horrible stench. Consistent with 2 Maccabees' emphasis that the suffering of Judah constitutes divine "discipline" (education), Antiochus learns from his afflictions that there is no greater sovereign than God. He loses his arrogance. He even wants to become a Jew and promises to extol the power of God throughout the world. But there is no redemption for Antiochus. He dies, as do Jason and Menelaus, in a foreign land without a dignified burial.

The Maccabean Torture Victims in Judaism and Christianity

The torture victims and their deaths in 2 Maccabees 6–7 have been a focal point of interest in the book. The tale's themes of bodily suffering and efficacious death resonate powerfully with Christianity. Early Christian literature is filled with stories about martyrs— people who were tortured and killed because of their faith. Numerous early Christian authors, such as Cyprian and Origen, invoked Eleazar, the mother, and her sons as models that Christian martyrs should follow. Augustine (fourth century) gave a homily on a feast day devoted to the Maccabean martyrs. He asserts in his sermon that there is a basilica (a large church) in Antioch devoted to the "Holy Maccabees." This basilica may have earlier been a synagogue. The bodies of the Maccabean martyrs were, according to tradition, buried there. The relics, as John Chrysostom (fourth century) relates, were revered in Antioch and the surrounding area. 6 Maccabees, a later Syriac Christian text that draws on Jewish traditions, likewise offers an expansive account of the nine victims. A long-standing interest in these martyrs in an eastern Christian milieu explains why the Orthodox tradition retains in its liturgical calendar a day devoted to them (August 1). Their relics, according to tradition, were relocated over the centuries, from Antioch to Constantinople to Rome, where they were kept in the Basilica of St. Peter's Chains. In the twelfth century they were allegedly moved to Cologne, Germany, where they remain to this day, in a golden reliquary in a medieval church in that city (St. Andrews).

The mother and her sons, and Eleazar, are also important in Jewish tradition. 4 Maccabees, a Jewish text from the first or early second century CE, is an extended meditation on these figures (see Chapter 16). The torture and death of the mother and her sons also appear in later Jewish tradition. Their stories are often situated not in the Maccabean era, but rather to a time of persecution that is important in rabbinic Judaism, during the reign of Emperor Hadrian (r. 117–138 CE), when Rome suppressed the Bar Kochba revolt in the 130s CE. *Lamentations Rabbah*, a compilation of midrash (interpretation) on the book of Lamentations, describes the ordeal of the woman (here named Miriam) and her sons, who have been incarcerated by the Romans. There are also medieval *piyyutim* (liturgical poems) in which the speaker is overcome by their ordeal. One for example begins: "It is over Hannah that my heart is torn. I clothe myself in sackcloth because of the evil day that she had to face" (the mother is often named Hannah in Jewish sources). There are also Jewish accounts of the torture and deaths of rabbis that evoke the gruesome stories in 2 and 4 Maccabees (an issue treated in more detail in Chapter 16).

Most Jewish texts engage only the story about the victims, not 2 Maccabees as a whole. The story of their deaths had a life independent of this composition. The tale was popular and spread widely. It worked its way into both 2 Maccabees and later Jewish literature, most importantly 4 Maccabees. The epitomator perhaps did not take this story from Jason of Cyrene's history, but rather incorporated it from another source. This possibility accords with the point mentioned above, that 2 Maccabees 6–7 is incongruous with the rest of the narrative.

Hanukkah, the Day of Mordecai, and the Day of Nicanor

The end of 2 Maccabees does not promote Hanukkah, but rather a festival memorializing Judas's defeat of Nicanor: "they all decreed by public vote never to let this day go unobserved, but to celebrate the thirteenth day of the twelfth month—which is called Adar in the Aramaic language—the day before Mordecai's day" (ch. 15). 1 Maccabees also affirms that this event should be commemorated on Adar 13. "Mordecai's day" is an early reference to Purim, which remains a major holiday, celebrated on Adar 14, going by the traditional Jewish calendar. The book of Esther, in which the figure of Mordecai is paramount, recounts the origins of the festival. The epitomator of 2 Maccabees perhaps sought to connect the commemoration of a day of Nicanor to Purim as a way to legitimize this new holiday. The goal was perhaps to construe Nicanor's unsuccessful efforts to subjugate the Jews as similar to the Persian Empire's failed effort to destroy them, which Purim celebrates. As discussed in Chapter 6, in the book of Esther Adar 13 is the "purge day" when the Jews slaughter their enemies. 2 Maccabees perhaps attempted to connect this day's celebration of Jewish violence to Judas's defeat of Nicanor.

While not part of Jewish worship today, the Day of Nicanor was observed in antiquity. *Megillat Ta'anit*, an early rabbinic text (first century CE) written in Aramaic, stipulates days on which one is not permitted to fast. It states that Adar 13 is one such day, and that it is none other than the Day of Nicanor. Fasting was not considered congruent with a day of celebration. *Megillat Ta'anit* also says this day is followed by Purim. The Day of Nicanor fell out of the Jewish worship, most likely due to the expansion of Purim observance. Adar 13 became in the medieval period a day of fasting (the Fast of Esther), before the celebration of Purim.

Maccabean military success against the Seleucids resulted in two Jewish holidays, one that became important and the other forgotten—Hanukkah and the Day of Nicanor. The end of 2 Maccabees never mentions Hanukkah, and the two opening letters never stress the Day of Nicanor. An earlier version of 2 Maccabees' epitome of Jason of Cyrene's history may have endorsed only the Day of Nicanor. The single reference to Hanukkah in the historical section of 2 Maccabees (10:1–8) awkwardly interrupts an iteration of the death of Antiochus (compare 9:29 and 10:9). This unit was perhaps added later, to make its account of Maccabean history accord more clearly with the two letters and their emphasis on Hanukkah.

Conclusion

2 Maccabees endorses a harmonious relationship between the Seleucid king and Jerusalem, in which the imperial state gives the city the freedom to follow its ancestral customs. This political model is consistent with the composition's commitment to Jewish tradition and its deep immersion in Hellenistic culture. But for this benevolent relationship between the empire and the city to materialize, 2 Maccabees teaches, both must have enlightened leadership. The temple should be led by a reverent high priest because he sets the tone for the piety and observance of the Jewish people as a whole. The catastrophes that led to the Maccabean revolt illustrate a key historical principle—that God will deliver the Jews

from turmoil if they remain steadfast to their ancestral traditions, and that he won't save them if they don't. Maccabean history, 2 Maccabees suggests, has a lesson for the Jews reading about it: that they should honor God and his temple, and observe their traditional forms of worship, which, the two letters appended to the composition stress, include Hanukkah.

Guide for Further Reading

Doran, Robert. *2 Maccabees: A Critical Commentary.* Minneapolis: Fortress Press, 2012.

Himmelfarb, Martha. "Judaism and Hellenism in 2 Maccabees." *Poetics Today* 19 (1998): 19–40.

Schwartz, Daniel R. *2 Maccabees.* Berlin: de Gruyter, 2008.

14

David Singing at the End
of the Psalter

Psalm 151

The Bible that most Jews and Christians read today includes a book of Psalms (also called the Psalter) which has 150 psalms. There is a long-standing Christian tradition that it is important for the Bible to have this number of psalms. Saint Augustine (fourth century) in his *Expositions on the Psalms*, for example, writes that it is appropriate for the Christian Bible to have 150 psalms since, being fifty three times, the number signifies the Trinity.

But one should not conclude that the biblical canon always had 150 psalms. At the time Augustine was praising the 150-format of the Psalter, it was actually common for the book to have 151 psalms. The earliest Septuagint manuscripts, even though they assert that the proper number of psalms is 150, all include Psalm 151. Psalm 151 is both beyond and within the Psalter. The surprising persistence of this psalm is undoubtedly because of its Davidic character. It is a poem attributed to David that focuses on key moments early in his life, such as his battle with Goliath.

Psalm 151 is in the Psalter of the Greek Septuagint tradition. The Eastern Orthodox tradition relies on the Septuagint as their Bible and thus a 151-psalm Psalter is the norm in that tradition. In Syriac Christianity, which still exists in the Middle East today, there is a tradition of appending after a Psalter with 150 psalms five additional ones, including Psalm 151 (Pss 151–155). The poem is not

The Apocrypha: A Guide. Matthew Goff, Oxford University Press. © Oxford University Press 2024.
DOI: 10.1093/9780190060770.003.0014

in the Vulgate Bible. Jerome translated the psalms from the Hebrew, and the Jewish Bible does not include Psalm 151. He did, however, produce a Latin version of the Psalter that he translated from the Greek, which therefore includes Psalm 151 (the Gallican Psalter). Thus, while not generally included in the Psalter of the Catholic Old Testament, Psalm 151 appears in some medieval Latin manuscripts, such as the beautifully illustrated twelfth-century Eadwine Psalter from England. The psalm's general absence from the Catholic Bible explains why Luther did not relegate it to the Apocrypha.

An event in 1956 transformed our understanding of Psalm 151. In that year, scholars learned that a Bedouin tribe had recently found a large scroll of psalms in Hebrew, from Cave 11 of Qumran (11Q5), the site of the Dead Sea Scrolls. The scroll is ancient, produced in the first century CE. It is large, containing over forty psalms. Most of them are also found in the biblical Psalter, although often not in the same order. The scroll includes several compositions which are not in the book of Psalms, such as Sirach 51:13–30 (discussed in Chapter 8) and others that were unknown until the scroll was discovered. The Cave 11 Psalms Scroll made available, for the first time, an ancient Hebrew version of Psalm 151 (and also Pss 154 and 155). The collection concludes with this psalm, although it does not enumerate it as the 151st (none of the psalms in 11Q5 are numbered). On the scroll's last column (col. 28), there is a blank line between this psalm and the preceding one (Psalm 134), signaling that Psalm 151 was demarcated as a separate composition (Figure 14.1). That the poem ended the collection is suggested by the blank page following the psalm. A precise date of the psalm's composition cannot be established, but it is older than the first century CE. The psalm is likely Hebrew poetry from the Hellenistic age (323–31 BCE).

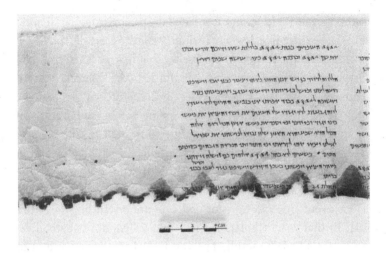

Figure 14.1 The end of the large Psalms Scroll from Qumran (11Q5).
Courtesy of the Leon Levy Dead Sea Scrolls Digital Library, IAA. Photo: Najib Anton Albina.

As a Young Shepherd David Would Sing Alone

Psalm 151 is a hymnic recitation of key events in David's life, as recounted in 1 Samuel. The Hebrew version of the poem is substantially longer than the Greek (Septuagint), which is generally the basis of modern translations of it. Both versions are below, with the Greek form arranged to show its correspondences with the Qumran version. The versification of the Hebrew here reflects the psalm's poetic structure and is not equivalent to its line numbering in the column.

Hebrew (Qumran)	Greek
Hallelujah of David, son of Jesse	This psalm was written by David—it is outside the number—after he fought Goliath singlehandedly.

[1]Smaller I was than my brothers,
    and younger than the sons of my father
so he made me the shepherd of his flock,
    and ruler over his kid goats.
	[1]I was small among my brothers,
	    and the youngest in my father's house;
	I tended my father's sheep.

Hebrew (Qumran)	Greek

²My hands made a flute,
   my fingers a harp,
   and I rendered glory to the Lord;
 I said within myself:
   ³"The mountains cannot bear witness
     for me,
   nor can the hills declare anything on my
     behalf, nor can the trees declare my
     words,
   nor the flock my works of praise.
	²My hands made a harp;
	   my fingers fashioned a lyre.

⁴For who will declare, who will speak,
   who will recount my works?"
 The Lord of all saw,
   God of all, he heard
   and gave ear.
	³And who will tell my lord?
	   The Lord himself; it is he who hears.

⁵He sent his prophet to anoint me,
   Samuel to exalt me;
 my brothers went forth toward him,
 beautiful of form, beautiful of appearance,
 ⁶lofty with their height,
   beautiful with their hair,
 but the Lord God
   did not choose them.
 ⁷He sent word and took me from behind
 the flock,
   and anointed me with holy oil;
 and made me leader for his people,
   ruler over the children of his covenant.
	⁴It was he who sent his messenger
	   and took me from my father's sheep,
	   and anointed me with his anointing
	     oil.
	 ⁵My brothers were handsome and tall,
	
	 but the Lord was not pleased with
	   them.

At the beginning of David's power, after the prophet of God anointed him.	

¹Then I saw a Philistine
   uttering reproach from the r[anks of the
     Philistines.]
	⁶I went out to meet the Philistine in battle,
	   and he cursed me with his idols.

².. . I . . . (too fragmentary to read)	⁷But I drew his sword;
	   I beheaded him and took away
	     disgrace from the people of Israel.

The two texts are similar enough to be considered versions of the
same poem. Both stress that David was smaller than his brothers

and that God chose him, not them, despite their height and physical attractiveness. They both stress that Samuel (named in the Hebrew, not the Greek) was sent to anoint him when he was a shepherd. These points accord with the depiction of David as a young man in 1 Samuel 16.

There are striking differences between the two versions. The "Hallelujah" heading of the Hebrew, though not in the Greek, is found in the final psalms of the biblical psalter (Pss 146–150). The claim in the Greek heading that the poem is "outside the number" is highly significant and discussed in the following section. The Greek heading also suggests that David wrote the psalm after he defeated Goliath. This claim is consistent with several psalms in the Psalter, each of which has a heading that correlates it to a specific moment in David's life (e.g., Pss 56–60). The opening of the Hebrew version, by contrast, never mentions Goliath. As is evident from the accompanying image from the Cave 11 Psalms Scroll, the phrase "his covenant" is on a line by itself, followed by a long space. This suggests that this phrase ended the psalm. Then follows a brief two-line poem that is fragmentarily preserved. It is about David's encounter with Goliath. It correlates with verses 6–7 of the Greek version of the psalm. Column 28 of the Psalms Scroll contains not one Davidic psalm but two. The first is about how David was chosen and anointed to be king; it accords with 1 Samuel 16. The second covers when David fought Goliath, soon after he was anointed; this resonates with 1 Samuel 17. Scholars refer to these poems as Psalm 151A and 151B. They form a sequential pair since Psalm 151A recounts his anointing and Psalm 151B, as its heading establishes, describes the beginning of David's power after he was anointed, exemplified by his defeat of Goliath. The Greek form of Psalm 151 is a product of the view that these two psalms comprise a single text. It is an issue of scholarly debate, but this suggests that the Hebrew reflects an older version of the text(s) than the form evident in the Greek.

Both versions of Psalm 151, the Hebrew and the Greek, deserve to be interpreted in their own right. The Hebrew version engages God's selection of David to be anointed and become the chosen king of Israel. After David fashions musical instruments, he recalls that neither the mountains, the hills, the trees, nor the flock can recount his words. God, however, who hears everything, can. The statement in verse 3 ("The mountains cannot bear . . .") can be reasonably understood as something David said (or thought) as a young shepherd, which he later recalls when he is king, remembering as a kind of nostalgia that he would sing while tending sheep alone. Because God heard him sing, the Hebrew poem suggests, the deity concluded that David should be the king of Israel. In 1 Samuel 16, young David is brought to the court of King Saul because of his musical abilities, which are to help soothe the tormented king. But 1 Samuel never describes the young David playing music or singing as a shepherd. The Hebrew of Psalm 151 answers a key question— *why* God chose David to be king. 1 Samuel 16 states, when explaining that his taller and handsome brothers were not chosen, that humans "look on the outward appearance but the Lord looks on the heart." Psalm 151 suggests that God discerned what was in David's heart by listening to his music and realized he would be a loyal, pious king. The ethos of the Hebrew psalm accords well with opening lines of the famous song "Hallelujah" by Leonard Cohen:

> Now I've heard there was a secret chord
> that David played and it pleased the Lord

In the Greek form of Psalm 151, God also chooses David, but the theme of kingship is not as prominent as in the Hebrew. A central issue is how King Saul knew to select the young David to play music for him at court. This is particularly the case if verse 3 plays on the word "lord," as recent scholarship has suggested. The first instance ("my lord") can be read as a reference to King Saul.

In this case the question "who will tell my lord" (Saul) is answered in verse 3b, with the second instance of the word "Lord," that is, God (thus capitalized). So understood, the deity heard David's music and told Saul, so that he would have David anointed. Also, the Greek heading suggests that David wrote the psalm after defeating Goliath, when he was a young man. The Hebrew, however, suggests that David wrote it later as king, remembering his days as a shepherd before he became king.

Psalm 151 Within and Beyond the Psalter

Psalm 151 (A and B) concludes, as mentioned above, the collection of psalms in the Cave 11 Psalms Scroll. This scroll, in another hymn previously unknown, called "David's Compositions," asserts that David composed a massive number of psalms, no less than 4,050. There was an ancient tradition that David was a prolific hymnographer, which is the basis of the widespread view that he wrote the biblical Psalter. But by attributing so many psalms to David, this Qumran text does more than that. "David's Compositions" strives not to establish a canonical number of 150 psalms, but rather to convey David's wide-ranging and vibrant hymnody. The Qumran poem establishes that it was easy for scribes to imagine his literary production as more extensive than 150 psalms.

The major early Greek manuscripts of the Christian Old Testament from the fourth century all include Psalm 151 as the last poem of the Psalter. The placement of the psalm is consistent with an older, pre-Christian tradition of concluding psalm collections with this poem, as is evident from the Cave 11 Psalms Scroll.

In ancient Christian Bibles, Psalm 151 is, oddly, both "beyond the number" of the psalms and the ending of the collection. At the end of its Psalter, Codex Alexandrinus has a colophon which reads, "150 psalms and the *idiograph*." The Greek word *idiograph* (lit. "one's own writing") refers to Psalm 151 and conveys that David wrote it. Psalm 151 serves in this manuscript as a supernumerary supplement to the Psalter. But Alexandrinus also lists its psalms, from 1 to 151, in numbered sequence, suggesting that the view that 150 psalms form the canonical boundary of the Psalter was not yet universally observed. Reflecting a different scribal attitude toward Bibles than today, the Psalter in Alexandrinus also includes an excerpt from a letter (*Letter to Marcellinus*) from the bishop Athanasius (fourth century) which extols Psalm 151, among other psalms. Codex Sinaiticus gives numerical headings to all the psalms except Psalm 151, but then includes a colophon at the end of the book, "the 151 psalms of David." Codex Vaticanus likewise stops numbering the Psalms at 150 and has a colophon that reads "the Book of 150 Psalms"—and then after this concluding statement provides Psalm 151 without any enumeration. In Vaticanus the psalm is quite literally "beyond the number." These manuscripts express the importance of the 150-format while including, with surprising variety, Psalm 151.

Psalms 151, as a Davidic poem at the end of the Psalter, should be understood not as an appendix, which would suggest it is an addition loosely related to the text preceding it. It is better understood, as one of my students once suggested, as a kind of "author-memoir" that tells us more about the life of the person who produced the collection, in particular that he was a gifted musician. The psalm's placement at the end of the Psalms imbues the entire collection with an impression of Davidic authorship.

Conclusion

The dominance of the view that the Psalter is a book of 150 psalms led Psalm 151 to become for many a kind of forgotten scripture. The discovery of an ancient Hebrew form of the poem among the Dead Sea Scrolls renewed interest in the composition. The presentation of Psalm 151 in early Christian Bibles testifies to the antiquity of the view that a hymn can be "outside the number" of biblical psalms but still considered an authentic composition written by David.

Guide for Further Reading

Mroczek, Eva. *The Literary Imagination in Jewish Antiquity.* New York: Oxford University Press, 2016 (pp. 171–83).

Reymond, Eric D. *New Idioms within Old: Poetry and Parallelism in the Non-Masoretic Poems of 11Q5 (= 11QPs^a).* Atlanta: Society of Biblical Literature, 2011 (pp. 51–74) (the translation of Psalm 151 is from this source, with modification; the Greek relies on the NOAB translation).

15

God Saves the Jews from Drunk Elephants

3 Maccabees

3 Maccabees is a strange and entertaining story about an Egyptian king, Ptolemy IV Philopater (r. 221–204 BCE), who unsuccessfully tries to kill the Jews in his country by having them trampled by drunk elephants. God saves them, and Jews in Egypt commemorate this deliverance with an annual festival.

The title of 3 Maccabees reflects its placement in ancient manuscripts of the Bible, especially Codex Alexandrinus. There it is located after 1 and 2 Maccabees and before 4 Maccabees. The title was presumably added to frame the composition as a biblical text, emphasizing that it is similar to 1–2 Maccabees. 3 Maccabees does indeed have affinities with these texts. They also focus on the anti-Jewish actions of a Gentile king that are ultimately unsuccessful. 3 Maccabees has much in common with 2 Maccabees, as discussed below. The Maccabean revolt against the Seleucid king Antiochus IV, however, is not a subject of 3 Maccabees. Its story takes place in the late third century BCE, fifty years before the Maccabean crisis.

3 Maccabees has been over the centuries by and large on the fringes of the scriptural tradition. Rabbinic Judaism shows no knowledge of the story. Relatively few early or medieval Christian writers refer to it. It has never been a book of the Vulgate and hence is not in the Old Testament of the Catholic Church. For this reason, Luther and other Protestant Reformers did not relocate it to the Apocrypha. 3 Maccabees is in Codex Alexandrinus, not in

The Apocrypha: A Guide. Matthew Goff, Oxford University Press. © Oxford University Press 2024.
DOI: 10.1093/9780190060770.003.0015

the two other major early Greek biblical manuscripts, Vaticanus and Sinaiticus, suggesting that not all early Christians regarded 3 Maccabees as a scriptural text. In eastern Christianity knowledge of 3 Maccabees was retained more so than in the West. It is a book of the Old Testament in Syriac and Armenian, important languages of eastern Christianity. 3 Maccabees is today a book of the Old Testament in the Eastern Orthodox tradition.

3 Maccabees: An Overview

3 Maccabees begins with the Battle of Raphia. This was an actual military conflict, fought in southern Palestine near Gaza in June 217 BCE between two major Hellenistic kingdoms, the Ptolemaic (Egyptian) and Seleucid (Syrian) empires. They were led, respectively, by kings Ptolemy IV and Antiochus III. This battle, which Daniel 11 alludes to, is one event in a larger series of conflicts often called the Syrian Wars that were fought between the Ptolemaic and Seleucid empires. They vied against each other for control of Palestine. 3 Maccabees 1 recounts that a Ptolemaic official named Theodotus who had gone over to the Seleucid side attempts to assassinate Ptolemy, but his plot is thwarted by an apostate Jew named Dositheus, son of Drimylus. The Egyptian forces, inspired by the exhortations and a promise of gold by Arisnoë, Ptolemy's sister and later his wife (this kind of incest being a tradition in the Ptolemaic dynasty), defeat the Seleucid army. Ptolemy then embarks on a kind of victory tour. His royal entourage visits towns in Palestine, giving gifts to strengthen the loyalty of the local population to their Egyptian rulers.

During Ptolemy's visit to Jerusalem, the king offers sacrifices to God, as part of his efforts to solidify local support for Ptolemaic rule. This is when things begin to go awry. He is so impressed by the temple that he wants to enter the sanctuary. This is impossible, he is told; even the high priest, the leading official of the temple, may enter the Holy of Holies only once a year (on the Day of Atonement). The king nevertheless insists. The situation escalates quickly. Pandemonium fills the streets. The people of Jerusalem are enraged, for whom Ptolemy's decision represents the height of arrogance. At issue is who has ultimate authority over the temple—the king or God. Simon II, who was the high priest from 219 to 196 BCE (and praised in Ben Sira 50), offers a prayer which reminds the deity that he has throughout history punished the arrogant, including the giants who rampaged the earth before the flood and the men of Sodom. Simon's prayer prompts divine action. God shakes the king "as a reed is shaken by the wind" to prevent him from entering the sanctuary. In 2 Maccabees 3, angelic forces stop Heliodorus, a Seleucid official, from doing the same thing.

The king's embarrassment in Jerusalem is the catalyst for the rest of the story. Back home in Egypt, he seeks to humiliate the Jews. Ptolemy erects a stone pillar which states that they are restricted from entering their synagogues (in keeping with his own inability to enter the Jerusalem temple), unless they also make sacrifices to other gods. The Jews are to be registered in a census so that they can be reduced to the status of slaves; those who refuse are to be killed (2:28–30). They are also to be branded with an ivy leaf, the symbol of the god Dionysus. Jews, the stele declares, can avoid becoming slaves if they worship Dionysus.

While some Jews accept the king's arrangement, the vast majority refuse. This enrages Ptolemy, and his anti-Jewish policies become more extreme. He issues a decree, which in effect gaslights the people of Egypt, who as a result turn against the Jews. According to this royal proclamation, the episode at the Jerusalem temple is not a sign of the king's arrogance but rather that the Jews of Jerusalem, because of their own arrogance and malice, rejected his efforts to extend his benevolence to them. His proposal to mark the Jews with an ivy leaf and have them become devotees of Dionysus is evidence of the king's generosity and the Egyptian state's commitment to the equal treatment of the Jews, which they likewise rejected.

The Jews' refusal to accept the king's gifts, this royal text concludes, demonstrates their seditious and barbarous nature, which makes them incompatible with the Ptolemaic kingdom and its commitment to civic equality. Thus the people of Egypt are to bind in chains all Jews in their locales, including women and children, so that they will be arrested and face "the sure and shameful death" that enemies of the state deserve. Chapter 4 recounts an emotional scene in which the Jews throughout the country, dejected and distraught, are transported to a "hippodrome" (in Latin, *circus*), a large arena for chariot races and other forms of public entertainment, that is in Schedia, a town near Alexandria. The king's effort to bring all the Egyptian Jews to Schedia is unsuccessful. 3 Maccabees depicts the Jews of Egypt not as a small minority but, as in the beginning of the book of Exodus, a large community within Egypt. Registering them, a process now conducted to carry out their execution, becomes too onerous to complete; the scribes' writing materials run out after registering Jews for forty days, with the task unfinished.

Ptolemy commands an official named Hermon, the royal elephantarch (the person in charge of the king's elephants), to give an astounding number of elephants—five hundred—enough wine and frankincense on the following day to go into a drunken frenzy, so that they will trample the Jews to death at the hippodrome. 1 Maccabees 6:34 states that war elephants were readied for battle by giving them the juice of grapes and mulberries, suggesting that getting elephants drunk beforehand was thought to be a good military strategy. The incarcerated Jews are terrified and pray to God for deliverance. As with Simon's prayer, God responds to their plight. The deity ensures that the king oversleeps (an act facilitated by his drinking the day before). The planned spectacle does not take place.

The king orders Hermon to repeat the process for the following day. With the elephants again drunk and the crowds amassed at the hippodrome, the imprisoned Jews implore God for help a second time—and again he responds. He strikes the king with forgetfulness and, with the gruesome spectacle ready to go, Ptolemy has no recollection of it whatsoever. When Hermon and his advisors urge the king to approve the start of the elephantine slaughter, he retorts that he would rather make their own family members suffer that fate. Later that day, when the king is drunk once again, he chastises Hermon for not deploying the inebriated pachyderms against the Jews—even though Ptolemy had earlier that day rebuked him for wanting to do this very thing. Ptolemy commands him to get the elephants drunk a third time. The next day at the crowded hippodrome, a priest named Eleazar prays for God to rescue the Jews. God's concluding act of salvation is a spectacle greater than anything concocted by Ptolemy. Two angels of frightening appearance, who can be seen by everyone except the Jews, terrify the king's military forces and more importantly the hammered mammoths which, panicked, turn and crush Ptolemy's men instead of the Jews.

This display of heavenly power transforms the king. He now recognizes God's superiority. Ptolemy orders the Jews to be released and, in keeping with his arbitrary and cruel leadership style, blames the whole thing on his advisors. He prepares a seven-day banquet for the Jews. This becomes instituted as an annual festival in the Egyptian month of Epeiph (July–August), to commemorate God's deliverance. Highlighting their reversal of fortune, the Jews are now registered, over a period of forty days, as part of their petition to the king to return to their homes. Ptolemy grants their request in an edict, that, not unlike the second decree in Septuagint Esther, is a counterpoint to his earlier anti-Jewish one. In the second edict the king affirms his commitment to the Jewish people.

The Egyptian Jews ask the king for permission to murder those of their community who had agreed to his earlier request to venerate Dionysus. The king agrees and they kill over three hundred people, which they celebrate according to 3 Maccabees 7 with a "joyful festival." Here too the composition is like Esther. In Esther 9 on one day (Adar 13) the Jews kill an incredible number of people who hate them (75,000!), and on the next the Jews in the Persian city of Susa kill 300—the approximate number killed in 3 Maccabees—and Esther associates this victory, also like 3 Maccabees, with a festival (Purim). Also like the end of Esther, at the conclusion of 3 Maccabees the people of Egypt regard the Jews with reverence and fear—a complete reversal of how they had earlier reviled them.

History, Historical Fiction, and Greek Education in Egyptian Judaism

3 Maccabees is a work of ancient Jewish fiction. That its narrative is set during the reign of an actual king suggests it is a kind of historical fiction. Modern examples of historical fiction would be contemporary films or novels about the Civil War or World War II that depict figures such as Abraham Lincoln or Franklin Roosevelt having conversations or in situations that are made up but seem authentic, as a way to give narrative expression to actual historical events. Understanding 3 Maccabees as historical fiction had led some scholars to liken the work to a genre of ancient Greek literature often called "romance." Greek romances, an ancient precursor of the novel, often tell a fictional story that relates a series of adventures set in the context of historical events, as does 3 Maccabees.

Understanding 3 Maccabees, however, as historical fiction or romance in a sense misses the point. While 3 Maccabees includes obviously made-up details, such as angels scaring tipsy elephants, it is not presented as a work of creative writing in which historical figures are characters. As discussed below, evidence from the Jewish historian Josephus (first century CE) suggests that the festival described in 3 Maccabees was an actual event once celebrated by Jews in Egypt, at least in the city in the Alexandria. If the festival did exist, then the episode it was intended to commemorate was thought to have taken place. In that case, even though we can easily identify 3 Maccabees as historical fiction, the composition presents itself as narrating an event that happened earlier in history—God's deliverance of the Jews from a king who sought to have them crushed by elephants. 3 Maccabees may have been written to place this event, well-known because of the festival that memorializes it, in its proper historical context (the reign of Ptolemy IV; more on this below).

3 Maccabees' focus on the Jews of Egypt suggests it is a product of that community. There was in antiquity a long and venerable history of Jews as a minority people in Egypt, particularly in Alexandria. Numerous Jewish texts from the Hellenistic period are the product of Egyptian Judaism. The Wisdom of Solomon is an important example. The ancient translation of the Hebrew scriptures into Greek (the Septuagint) was originally produced by and for Egyptian Jews. 3 Maccabees cites the Greek scriptures. The story may have drawn extensively from the Septuagint form of Esther; some scholars argue for the reverse position, that Esther uses 3 Maccabees. Either way, Greek Esther and 3 Maccabees have much in common.

It is instructive, however, to understand 3 Maccabees not simply against the backdrop of other Jewish texts. It was written likely by an Egyptian Jew who had received a kind of education called in Greek *paideia*, in which this individual acquired extensive familiarity with Greek cultural and literary traditions. Such education is a hallmark of Hellenistic-Roman Jewish texts from Egypt. Given 3 Maccabees' interest in historical events, it is helpful to understand the composition as written by someone who had read and studied Greek historiography. Knowledge of Mediterranean history, for example, is evident when the work likens Ptolemy IV to Phalaris, a ruler in Sicily from the sixth century BCE who was renowned for his cruelty.

The literary style of 3 Maccabees reflects familiarity with rhetorical techniques practiced by Greek historians. Aristotle in his *Rhetoric* writes that arousing emotion (in Greek, *pathos*) in readers can be an effective form of persuasion. Ancient historians would do this typically by emphasizing or exaggerating descriptions of suffering. The historian Polybius (200–118 BCE), for example, criticizes another historian named Phylarchus, by declaring that the latter's description (which does not survive) of the fall of a city in Greece (Mantinea) in 223 BCE was excessive in its efforts to elicit pity, as it vividly recounts the women of the city, clinging together with their hair disheveled, crying and wailing as they are led away.

If Polybius had read 3 Maccabees (and below I suggest it was probably the other way around), he would have reached a similar conclusion. 3 Maccabees strives intensely to make the reader feel pity for the plight of the Jews. Like Phylarchus, chapter 1 of the composition uses images of distraught women to achieve this effect. Shocked and angry over Ptolemy's planned entrance of the temple, mothers and wet nurses set down their babies wherever they were when they first heard the news and brides abandoned their weddings, to fill the streets in protest, moaning and crying. There is similar pathos involving frantic women in 2 Maccabees 3 as a reaction to Heliodorus's intent to go inside the sanctuary. The account in 3 Maccabees of the Jews being rounded up is likewise intended to prompt empathy in the reader, as does the description of them being distraught when the frenzied elephants enter the hippodrome.

Hellenistic Historiography and Ptolemaic Royal Propaganda

Whoever wrote 3 Maccabees was likely familiar with the language of the Ptolemaic bureaucracy. The author can be understood as living in Ptolemaic Egypt or after the Roman Empire brought the Ptolemaic kingdom to an end and began to rule the country in 31 BCE. Either way, the author was a student of Ptolemaic history. The language of the decrees of Ptolemy in 3 Maccabees (chs. 3 and 7) accords with actual documents promulgated by the Ptolemaic kingdom, some of which survive today. The royal edicts of 3 Maccabees evoke a kind of verisimilitude, composed so that they would have sounded to an Egyptian audience like authentic statements from the Ptolemaic kingdom. Use of the epithet of the king (Philopator), which the decrees of 3 Maccabees employ, is not attested in Ptolemaic royal pronouncements and correspondence until approximately 100 BCE. Eleazar's prayer alludes to the Prayer of Azariah, one of the "Additions" to Daniel. This Greek scriptural text is likewise often dated to around 100 BCE. This suggests that 3 Maccabees was written after this date, long after the days of Ptolemy IV.

3 Maccabees is helpfully interpreted against the backdrop of Ptolemaic royal propaganda. The Battle of Raphia was well-known in Egypt long after the event itself. The historical Ptolemy IV, like many kings throughout history, publicized his military victories. He issued a proclamation which scholars call the Raphia Decree. It was recorded on stelae (stone pillars) written in hieroglyphics, demotic (an Egyptian scribal language), and Greek. The decree recounts Ptolemy's victory at Raphia. It visually depicts him as a powerful king of Egypt, wearing a crown in the style of a pharaoh of old, astride a horse attacking Antiochus III with a spear. Arisnoë stands behind him. The stele accentuates their divinity, declaring that statues of them both should be erected in every temple in Egypt. The king's victory in Palestine, it also states, is to be commemorated annually with a festival. The decree portrays Ptolemy as a defender and restorer of traditional religion, in both Egypt and Palestine. It claims that he entered temples there, making offerings and libations, restoring shrines that Antiochus III had defiled. It asserts that people in Palestine welcomed him warmly and even built a temple in his honor. As scholarship has emphasized, key details of 3 Maccabees, such as the king getting a hostile reception in Jerusalem and God rejecting his efforts to enter

the temple, may have developed as rejections and inversions of the royal propaganda widely disseminated in the Raphia Decree.

Whoever wrote 3 Maccabees had probably also studied Hellenistic historians' accounts of the Battle of Raphia. An important account of the battle and the reign of Ptolemy IV is by the aforementioned Polybius. By the first century BCE he was widely read among educated circles. Key details in 3 Maccabees 1 regarding the conflict are also found in Polybius. His account of Ptolemaic history also mentions the failed plot of a deserter named Theodotus, but not that it was prevented by Dositheus son of Drimylus. Polybius states that Arisnoë encouraged the troops. In Polybius she does this together with Ptolemy at the beginning of the battle, and in 3 Maccabees she does so by herself during the fight. The overlaps between the two suggest that whoever wrote 3 Maccabees had read Polybius or some other historical work, now lost, with similar material.

An Egyptian Jewish Festival in 3 Maccabees and Josephus

In Josephus's *Against Apion*, in which the Jewish historian counters the anti-Jewish opinions of an Egyptian intellectual named Apion, we find a story strikingly similar to 3 Maccabees: a Ptolemaic king arrests the Jews of Alexandria and arranges for them to be trampled by intoxicated elephants. This act was unsuccessful, Josephus relates, in part because the king's favorite concubine (in some versions of the story she is named Ithaca, in others Irene) urges him to relent; this deliverance is commemorated by the Jews of that city with a festival. While 3 Maccabees never emphasizes a royal concubine, the core stories in 3 Maccabees and *Against Apion* are similar enough to be considered different iterations of the same legend. Josephus, however, places these events not during the reign of Ptolemy IV (late third century BCE) but Ptolemy VIII Euergetes, who was king in the second century BCE (he is mentioned by Ben Sira's grandson in that book's prologue). This suggests that a tale about a failed attempt by the king to have Jews in Egypt killed by drunk elephants was well-known, and that there actually was, or at least some ancient writers thought there was, an annual Jewish festival celebrating God's deliverance from this cruel act. The fact that 3 Maccabees and Josephus provide different historical settings to iterations of the same basic story of crisis and deliverance suggests that people did not know when it was to have taken place. Some learned Jews, such as the author of 3 Maccabees or Josephus, considered this a problem they should solve—and they did so in different ways, each giving a different historical context to the legend.

In the Shadow of the God of Wine: Drunk King, Drunk Elephants, Drunk Jews

3 Maccabees is the booziest text of the scriptural tradition. When readers first encounter the story, it is easy for them to speculate, as my students eagerly do, how many gallons of wine would be required to make five hundred elephants drunk to the point of frenzy. Then one should multiply that figure by three to estimate the amount of wine quaffed by elephants in 3 Maccabees. But it's not just pachyderms imbibing. The king and his advisors are often drunk. At the end of the book he shows favor to the Jews by giving them vast quantities of wine—enough, along with food, for a week-long banquet. In 3 Maccabees the wine does not just flow. The reader veritably drowns in it.

Ptolemy, it will be recalled, encourages the Jews to worship Dionysus. He is the god of wine. The prominence of wine in the story can be profitably understood against the backdrop of Dionysus in Ptolemaic culture. This god was important for the Ptolemaic dynasty. In the ancient Mediterranean world, Dionysus was associated with India. It was believed that he conquered India and had triumphantly returned. Alexander the Great, whose military excursions in Asia extended as far as India, became associated with Dionysus. The Ptolemaic rulers, in order to emphasize the legitimacy of their rule, connected themselves to Alexander's legacy. The body of Alexander was interred in Alexandria in a splendid mausoleum, and the proclaimed divinity of the Ptolemaic rulers was based on the deification of Alexander. This state-sanctioned promotion of Alexander made Dionysus important to the Ptolemaic kingdom.

One papyrological source indicates that the historical Ptolemy IV did indeed have an interest in Dionysus. This record states that this king required initiates of Dionysus in Egypt to be registered—an intriguing parallel to 3 Maccabees 2:28–30. Some ancient writers, such as Plutarch (first–second century CE), portray Ptolemy as a lush and connect his debauched lifestyle to his devotion to the god of wine. Familiarity with such historical accounts may explain why whoever wrote 3 Maccabees concluded that the cruel and erratic king memorialized by the festival was none other than the drunkard Ptolemy IV.

Moreover, the fact that Ptolemy uses elephants to vent his anger against the Jews can be considered both a Dionysiac and a Ptolemaic trope. Some Ptolemaic rulers had royal processions that included elephants. This animal was associated in antiquity with India, and thus evoked the return of Dionysus from India, which, as we have seen, was incorporated into Ptolemaic royal ideology. 3 Maccabees' emphasis on Ptolemy IV's elephants as powerful but ultimately unsuccessful also accords with Polybius's account of the Battle of Raphia. While Egypt won the battle, according to this historian one of the most disappointing outcomes of the fight for Ptolemy involved elephants. His army had recently built up its first cadre of war elephants, to counter their Seleucid foes, who had a long-established tradition of highly trained military elephants. Raphia was the first test of Ptolemy's war elephants. But they declined to fight. The historical Ptolemy IV tried to demonstrate his power via elephants and failed. This may have been another reason 3 Maccabees situates its story, about a king who tries but fails to kill the Jews with elephants, during the reign of this king. Also, according to Polybius, Ptolemy put seventy-three elephants on the battlefield at Raphia—far fewer than the five hundred he worked into a drunken stupor in the hippodrome.

3 Maccabees' presentation of Dionysus as a false alternative to the God of Israel also resonates with conceptions of the god of wine in the Hellenistic and Roman eras. 2 Maccabees asserts that during the Maccabean crisis the Jews were forced to stop observing their traditional rites and instead wear ivy wreaths and venerate Dionysus. That 2 and 3 Maccabees oppose God and Dionysus is probably a Jewish reaction to what was apparently a common view, or at least one Jews could encounter—that Judaism is inherently similarly to or even equivalent to Dionysiac worship. In Plutarch's *Table Talk*, a banquet companion asserts that the god of the Jews is in fact Dionysus. This is evident, the person relates, for several reasons, including that Jews during a festival enter the temple carrying a thyrsus, a staff with ivy leaves associated with Dionysus (a claim perhaps based on the Jewish practice of waving *lulavin*—palm fronds— during the festival of Sukkot). Plutarch even suggests that the Levites derive their name from epithets of Dionysus, such as *Lysios* ("Releaser") or *Evius* ("God of the Cry"). According to a contemporary of Plutarch, the Roman historian Tacitus, some contend that the Jews worship Liber, a Romanized name of Dionysus, because their priests wear garlands of ivy and chant to the accompaniment of pipe and drum music (perhaps another reference to the Levites). Another name for Dionysus was Sabazios (based on the identification of this Greek god with a deity of the Phrygian and Thracian peoples). Some equated the name Sabazios with Sabaoth, part of a major Hebrew epithet for God (the "Lord of Hosts [Sabaoth]"). That people identified the God of the Jews with Dionysus may explain why Jewish texts present these deities as two opposed options.

Strangers in a Strange Land: Jews and Anti-Judaism in 3 Maccabees and Hellenistic-Roman Egypt

3 Maccabees' chilling depiction of the Egyptians turning against the Jews, with the notable exception of the Greeks of Alexandria, is not presented as an inevitable consequence of Gentile animosity. Rather, the king uses his influence to sway a wide swath of the populace against them. Anti-Jewish sentiment is manufactured at the top and filtered down. At the end of the book the Jews are respected throughout Egypt; this is likewise a result of the king's ability to dictate public opinion, since he gives a full-throated endorsement of the Jewish people.

The claim in Ptolemy's decree that the Jews are traitors to the kingdom, an assertion likewise expressed by the Persian king Xerxes (Ahasuerus) in Esther, resonates with a viewpoint that was widespread throughout the Diaspora but particularly acute in Egypt—that even though the Jews had been there a long time, they were essentially foreigners and thus not entitled to the same rights held by other native-born peoples. The Jews of Egypt are, as Eleazar puts it in 3 Maccabees 6, "strangers in a strange land." Life could be difficult for Jews in Ptolemaic Egypt. The *Letter of Aristeas*, another important Jewish Egyptian text (second century BCE), claims that Ptolemy I enslaved many Jews and brought them to Egypt in the fourth century BCE. The decree of Ptolemy IV in 3 Maccabees 2:28–30 suggests that Jews will have the status of slaves, unless they worship the gods that other peoples do. Not all Jews in Egypt at the time were slaves, but Ptolemy's proposal in chapter 2 resonates with forms of discrimination that Jews historically encountered there. Being a member of society in the Hellenistic and Roman eras often involved honoring the local god(s) and a deified king. The anti-Jewish Egyptian intellectual Apion, according to Josephus, asked about the Jews of his country: "Why then, if they are citizens, do they not worship the same gods as the Alexandrians?"

When Rome took over Egypt in 31 BCE, their method of govern-
ance exacerbated ethnic tensions. The emperor Augustus levied a
poll tax in Egypt in 24/23 BCE. Such taxes are often highly unpopular. A poll tax means one pays not for a government service, but
to be listed among the inhabitants of the country. Many Greek citizens were exempt, but most Jews were not, along with other (non-
Greek) Egyptians. 3 Maccabees 3 depicts the Greeks in Alexandria
as sympathetic with the plight of the Jews; emphasizing common
cause with the Greeks, in particular elite, educated Greeks, accords
with Jewish resentment toward this tax. Although the nature of the
poll tax and who had to pay it are debated by scholars, it seems that
Jews, especially those who had received a Greek education, disliked
that the tax equated them not with the Greeks but with non-Greek
Egyptians, who were often uneducated peasants.

One leading scholarly opinion is that 3 Maccabees contains a
reference to Augustus's poll tax and should therefore be dated to
the early 20s BCE. The term for this tax is *laographia*. 3 Maccabees
2:28 uses this same word to denote the "registration" of the Jews
demanded by Ptolemy. Some translations of 3 Maccabees render
the term "poll tax." But the composition never presents onerous
taxation as a problem the Jews must deal with.

In any case, while the composition was not necessarily written in
Roman Egypt, ethnic tensions worsened at this time, and the book
would have been depressingly relevant. The Jewish philosopher
Philo lived in Alexandria at the time. According to him, Flaccus, the
Roman prefect of Egypt, promulgated a decree in the 30s CE which
asserted that the Jews were "aliens and foreigners" in Alexandria.
The property of Jews, including synagogues, was seized by the
state, and many Jews were killed by mobs. This is a historical ex-
ample of 3 Maccabees' basic point—that under the wrong leader,
Egypt can turn quickly against the Jews.

Even though anti-Jewish sentiment could reach vile heights in
Hellenistic-Roman Egypt, 3 Maccabees asserts the loyalty of Jews
to the Egyptian state. The composition depicts Ptolemy's maniacal

deployment of the powers of the state against Jewish Egyptians as an aberration. The commitment of Jews to Egypt has an important military dimension. 3 Maccabees 6 complains that many Jews forcibly taken to Schedia had been soldiers stationed in fortresses throughout Egypt and thus could no longer defend the country. Many Jews were in fact soldiers in Ptolemaic Egypt; there was also a military colony at an Egyptian island named Elephantine where many Judeans were stationed that was active when the Persians ruled Egypt (fifth century BCE); a horde of ancient Aramaic texts was discovered there (discussed in Chapter 4).

3 Maccabees' final portrait of Ptolemy IV, as a king who acknowledges the dominion of God, when read against the backdrop of anti-Jewish sentiment in Hellenistic-Roman Egypt, constitutes a sort of fantasy, a dream of recognition and support from the Ptolemaic court. The *Letter of Aristeas* expresses a similar dream in a different way. The composition presents a Ptolemaic king (Ptolemy II Philadelphus) as a patron of Jewish tradition. In this text he not only commissions the translation of the Torah into Greek, but also expresses deep reverence for Judaism in other ways. He sends, for example, generous gifts to the Temple and holds a sumptuous banquet that is fully kosher for the Jewish translators.

In a sense, 3 Maccabees undermines a distinction between Palestinian and Diaspora Judaism. The composition suggests, as does the *Letter of Aristeas*, that the temple in Jerusalem was a source of pride among Jews in Egypt. The two major prayers of the book, by the High Priest Simon and Eleazar, are uttered, respectively, in Jerusalem and Egypt. Both are effective. God responds, the book teaches, to the prayers of his people, whether they are in the land of Israel or not. The final verse of the book praises God as "the Deliverer of Israel." "Israel" here clearly denotes not a geographical locale, but rather the people Israel—including the Jews of Egypt.

Conclusion

3 Maccabees is a product of a kind of ancient Judaism that has been by and large forgotten. The written evidence for this kind of Judaism, of which Egypt was an important locale, is typically written in Greek and valorizes Jewish tradition in ways that reflect a deep and extensive engagement with Greek literary and intellectual traditions.

3 Maccabees exemplifies a key issue in the Jewish literature from the Diaspora that is also illustrated in texts such as Esther or Daniel—that when people turn against the Jews, the Jews should turn to God. 3 Maccabees illustrates this point not by stressing fidelity to the Torah, but rather the efficacy of prayer in a moment of crisis. Another message of the book which is unfortunately relevant is that a national leader can use his power to turn the populace against a particular ethnic group, to the point of becoming complicit in state-sanctioned violence against them.

Guide for Further Reading

Croy, N. Clayton. *3 Maccabees.* Leiden: Brill, 2006.

Johnson, Sara Raup. *Historical Fictions and Hellenistic Jewish Identity: Third Maccabees in its Cultural Context.* Berkeley: University of California Press, 2004.

Modrzejewski, Joseph Mélèze. *The Jews of Egypt: From Rameses II to Emperor Hadrian.* Princeton, NJ: Princeton University Press, 1995.

16

Judaism Offers the Best
Path to Reason

4 Maccabees

4 Maccabees has a singular focus: to demonstrate the supremacy of reason over the emotions, or in Greek, *logos* over *pathos*. *Logos* in Greek philosophy denotes reason but has a wide array of nuances. The term can signify, for example, the soul, the mind, and logic (a term which derives from the word *logos*). As for emotions, while the word today denotes moods and feelings, *pathos* can instead be rendered as "passions." The Greek term often signifies bodily desires, understood negatively. This is the case in 4 Maccabees, as in Greek philosophy. As with the Wisdom of Solomon, examining 4 Maccabees requires consideration of Greek intellectual traditions unfamiliar to many readers of scripture today.

4 Maccabees seeks to demonstrate that the superiority of reason over the emotions is evident from an extensive retelling of the gruesome story of the death and torture of Eleazar, a mother, and her seven sons, found in chapters 6–7 of 2 Maccabees, the subject of Chapter 13. Like this composition, 4 Maccabees extols these victims, who, when compelled under torture to abandon Jewish traditions, choose death instead. Unlike 2 Maccabees, 4 Maccabees seeks to show that this tale and others from the Torah illustrate that Judaism offers the best way to cultivate reason.

The Apocrypha: A Guide. Matthew Goff, Oxford University Press. © Oxford University Press 2024.
DOI: 10.1093/9780190060770.003.0016

4 Maccabees: Basic Issues

4 Maccabees was composed in Greek, in a rich, ornate style. The composition has eighteen chapters. It begins with an introduction that lays out the thesis that "devout reason is sovereign over the emotions." 4 Maccabees elaborates on this point in 1:13–3:18, in part by defining reason and the emotions. The bulk of the composition (3:19–17:6) provides an account of the torture and deaths of the nine victims. This large section can be subdivided into an account of the historical context of their plight during the reign of the Seleucid king Antiochus IV (3:20–4:26), and, in the same order as in 2 Maccabees, the ordeals of Eleazar (5:1–7:23), the seven sons (8:1–14:10), and the mother (14:11–17:6). The final section praises the nine victims and expounds on their significance, stressing in particular the mother (17:7–18:24).

Early biblical manuscripts include 4 Maccabees. Of the three oldest manuscripts of the Septuagint, two include 4 Maccabees (Sinaiticus and Alexandrinus). In these manuscripts it is titled 4 Maccabees. The early Christian authors Eusebius and Jerome knew the work by another title, *On the Supremacy of Reason*. This title fits the content of the text very well. Eusebius also states that the author of 4 Maccabees is none other than Josephus, the Jewish historian of the first century CE. This is unlikely because the style and content of Josephus's writings are substantially different from 4 Maccabees. The ascription of Josephan authorship to the composition, however, persisted for centuries. Several manuscripts of Josephus's writings, for example, include 4 Maccabees, as if it were another text written by Josephus. The author of the composition, if it was written by a single person, is unknown.

4 Maccabees gives the impression of an orator speaking, in the first person, to an audience. Chapter 3 begins the discussion of the nine victims by emphasizing that "the present occasion now invites us" to reflect on them. Chapter 17 imagines what the epitaph of

a memorial tomb of the torture victims would say. 4 Maccabees may have been produced as an oration delivered at a public event commemorating the Maccabean victims, perhaps at a synagogue on Hanukkah, a holiday inextricably connected to the Maccabean tradition. The composition could, alternatively, have been written to mimic the style of a public address.

As examined in Chapter 13, there was a basilica dedicated to the Maccabean victims in the Syrian city of Antioch. This establishes that Christian veneration of them was important in the eastern Roman Empire by the fourth century. The basilica may have earlier been a synagogue. 4 Maccabees may have originated as an address delivered there. In any case, the importance of commemoration of the Maccabean victims in Antioch suggests that 4 Maccabees was likely written there or its environs.

4 Maccabees is today not in the biblical canon of any confessional community. In the Greek Orthodox Church there is a tradition of including 4 Maccabees in the Bible as an appendix. Not being in the Catholic Old Testament, Protestant Reformers never removed 4 Maccabees from it. It never became a standard text of the Apocrypha. Although not in the Vulgate Bible, there is a loose, Christian reworking of 4 Maccabees in Latin, the *Passio Sanctorum Machabaeorum* (the *Suffering of the Maccabean Saints*). This text is a vestige of 4 Maccabees' earlier importance in Christianity.

4 Maccabees is often dated to the first century CE. It was written after 2 Maccabees, which is from the late second or early first century BCE. 4 Maccabees 4 describes the Seleucid governor Apollonius as in charge of "Syria, Phoenicia, and Cilicia," whereas in 2 Maccabees 3 he is the governor of Syria and Phoenicia, without mentioning Cilicia. This region, which is in southern Asia Minor (what is today Turkey), was placed by Rome under a single jurisdiction together with Syria and Phoenicia between 20–54 CE. 4 Maccabees' inclusion of Cilicia suggests it could have been written during this period. There is, however, no conclusive evidence to establish its date. 4 Maccabees may have been written in the late

first century or even the second. The composition has numerous affinities with the Second Sophistic (discussed below), which dates to this time frame.

Commemoration of the suffering and death of the Maccabean victims continued throughout the history of Judaism and Christianity. As discussed in Chapter 13, there is a Jewish tradition of lamenting the death of the mother and her sons. In rabbinic literature they are situated not in the Maccabean era (early second century BCE) but during the reign of the Roman emperor Hadrian (r. 117–138 CE). He oversaw the suppression of the Jewish revolt led by Bar Kochba in the 130s against Rome. Afterward, according to rabbinic tradition, Rome banned the study of the Torah. There are many legends about rabbis who were tortured and killed for studying the Torah. Their commitment to their ancestral traditions resonates with the older Maccabean tale.

The rabbis did not know 4 Maccabees. In Chapter 13 I suggested that the legend of the Maccabean torture victims may have circulated independently from the rest of 2 Maccabees. This tale did circulate in a Jewish milieu. It was perhaps utilized in the creation of narratives about early rabbis being tortured for their commitment to Torah. These stories can be as disturbing as those of 4 Maccabees. According to the Babylonian Talmud (tractate *Berakhot*), the famous rabbi Akiva recited the Shema prayer (which is still important in Judaism) while in prison, as the Romans scraped away his flesh with iron combs until he died.

The torture and death of ten rabbis, including Akiva, were memorialized in Jewish tradition. One good example is a medieval Hebrew poem called *Eleh Ezkerah* ("These Things I Remember"), which is still recited on Yom Kippur (the Day of Atonement) in some circles of Judaism. In that text, the Romans kill the rabbis in horrible ways. They, for example, murder one of them, Haninah ben Teradion, who openly studied the Torah after the practice was prohibited, by wrapping him in a Torah scroll which they set on fire. They first covered the rabbi with wet wool to prolong the burning.

In Christianity the nine victims were important in ways directly influenced by 4 Maccabees. Stories about martyrs, a Christian term for people killed because of their faith, are a foundational element of early Christianity. The earliest martyr texts have striking affinities with 4 Maccabees. In these works, such as the *Letters of Ignatius*, written by a patriarch of Antioch who was killed in the early second century CE, the martyr typically expresses an eagerness to be tortured to death in anticipation of receiving eternal life. They often encourage their tormentors to carry out their brutal work, as do the victims in 4 Maccabees. The *Martyrdom of Polycarp* (second century CE) describes the death of Polycarp, a bishop of Smyrna (a city now in Turkey) and disciple of the evangelist John, as a new birth, and his attainment of martyrdom as winning a "prize" and a "crown of immortality." 4 Maccabees deploys these same images to describe the death and post-mortem rewards of the Maccabean torture victims. Origen's *Exhortation to Martyrdom* (mid-third century) uses and cites 2 Maccabees to recount their story, referring to the first son as "that noblest athlete of piety." 4 Maccabees, however, not 2 Maccabees, describes the victims as athletes (a trope discussed below).

The similarities between 4 Maccabees and early Christian martyr stories may not indicate that their authors used 4 Maccabees as a source. 4 Maccabees, since it was written in the first or early second century CE, has the same basic time frame as the earliest Christian martyr texts. Perhaps all this literature reflects a common milieu. In this period, Christianity was not a distinct religion neatly separated from Judaism. Christianity and rabbinic Judaism both trace their origins to this period. Both describe this era as a time when their adherents were being killed and were willing to die for their traditions. Both sets of stories may reflect a common cultural background, likely shaped by the brutality of Roman rule.

By the fourth century, when commemoration of the Maccabean torture victims had become part of the Christian liturgical year (see Chapter 13), some authors were turning to 4 Maccabees to understand their significance. Gregory of Nazianzus, an archbishop of Constantinople, asserted in a homily dedicated to these victims that the book which recounts their ordeal promotes "the theory that reason is the absolute master of emotions"—the very thesis espoused by 4 Maccabees. Other fourth-century authors, such as Ambrose of Milan in his *On Jacob and the Blessed Life*, utilized 4 Maccabees to emphasize likewise that the dominance of reason over the emotions is critical to leading an ethical life.

An Exemplary and Rewritten Past: 4 Maccabees vis-à-vis 2 Maccabees and the Torah

In 4 Maccabees 18, the mother asserts that the father (both unnamed) of their sons taught them "the law and the prophets." In the Dead Sea Scrolls and the New Testament, which are roughly contemporary with the composition, this expression denotes scriptural texts. Her sons, the woman emphasizes, knew the Torah. 4 Maccabees frequently refers to the ancestral lore of Israel. The work brings up Joseph's refusal of the advances of Potiphar's wife (Genesis 39), arguing that he was able to overcome his sexual attraction toward her because of his possession of reason. The composition repeatedly invokes the Danielic story of the three men thrown into the fiery furnace. It appeals to God's command that Abraham sacrifice Isaac (Genesis 22) no less than four times. 4 Maccabees emphasizes Isaac's willingness to be killed by his father more than Abraham's to kill his son, as is also the case in rabbinic Judaism. In 4 Maccabees, Isaac and other scriptural patriarchs serve as exemplars for enduring pain and controlling the emotions. The seven sons were able to withstand torture because their father taught them the Torah.

4 Maccabees extensively engages 2 Maccabees. In the latter text the suffering and death of the nine victims compel God, who is moved by their courage and dedication to Jewish tradition, to act

on behalf of Israel, ensuring the victory of Judas Maccabee and the defeat of Antiochus. 4 Maccabees shows awareness of the political significance of the victims stressed by 2 Maccabees. Chapter 1, for example, affirms that they "became the cause of the downfall of tyranny over their nation."

But 4 Maccabees is a fun-house mirror reflection of 2 Maccabees. 4 Maccabees shows an almost obsessive interest in the nine victims. It shows relatively little concern for their historical context. This is an inversion of 2 Maccabees, where their story is one episode, one and half chapters out of fifteen (2 Macc 6:18–7:42). It is one part of a longer historical narrative about Judas Maccabee and his military victories against the Seleucid kingdom. In 4 Maccabees only one section, 3:19–4:26, places the torture accounts in their Maccabean context. The composition shows scant interest in political details that are crucial in 2 Maccabees. 4 Maccabees never even mentions Judas Maccabee. 2 Maccabees (ch. 3) begins its historical narrative during the reign of Seleucus IV Philopator (r. 187–175 BCE). In 4 Maccabees the story starts when Seleucus I Nicanor is king. This is most likely a mistake. Seleucus I ruled a hundred years prior to the Maccabean revolt (r. 305–281 BCE). The rest of the story is set in the same basic time frame as 2 Maccabees, with significant changes. For example, in the latter text Simon, the opponent of the high priest Onias, tells the governor Apollonius about the wealth of the temple, which results in the king dispatching Heliodorus there, who unsuccessfully attempts to commandeer temple monies. 4 Maccabees truncates this story so that it is Apollonius who goes to the temple and is rebuffed by angels. Heliodorus is written out of the narrative. 4 Maccabees also never mentions the corrupt high priest Menelaus. The composition shows minimal interest in Jason, the other wicked high priest in 2 Maccabees. These revisions highlight Antiochus as the sole villain of the tale.

While 2 Maccabees' description of the torture is explicit and unsettling, that of 4 Maccabees seems even more disturbing. In the latter text, for example, the first son is stretched out upon a wheel, a torture instrument common in 4 Maccabees that is never mentioned in 2 Maccabees. This wheel, when tightened, severs the ligaments from their bones. The torturers set a fire beneath the wheel as they tighten it, his body being simultaneously burned and contorted. As chapter 9 states, soon "the wheel was completely smeared with blood and the heap of coals was being quenched by the drippings of gore and pieces of flesh were falling off the axles of the machine." Regarding the third son, the torturers ripped his limbs out of their sockets, broke the bones in his arms and legs, and ripped off his scalp. Then they broke his back by putting him on the wheel and tightening it.

4 Maccabees, in comparison to 2 Maccabees, intensifies the willingness of the victims to accept their fate and embrace death. In the latter text the seventh son is tortured to death because Antiochus is frustrated that he is unable to break the sons to his will. In 4 Maccabees the seventh son takes his own life by jumping into fiery braziers. The mother likewise ends her life by leaping into flames. 2 Maccabees, by contrast, does not describe her death.

To appreciate how 4 Maccabees thematizes torture and death, it is important to understand how the composition relates them to philosophy. We now turn to that issue.

Is Not Philosophy the Study of Death?
The Philosophical Rhetoric of 4 Maccabees

While the narrative core of 4 Maccabees appropriates Jewish traditions, its genre and rhetorical format are drawn from Greek literary culture. The composition in terms of Greek rhetoric can be understood as epideictic discourse. This denotes a literary genre that seeks to promote knowledge of a topic, often by praising it (in this case, reason). The work's self-presentation as the words of a speaker praising people who have died also invites comparison with the funeral oration, another established type of Greco-Roman rhetoric.

4 Maccabees' interest in public oratory, rhetoric, and philosophy allows it to be profitably interpreted against the cultural backdrop of the Second Sophistic. This phrase denotes the period 60–230 CE, in which oratorical performances by sophists such as Dio Chrysostom and Maximus of Tyre became valued as an art form, especially in the eastern Roman Empire, where 4 Maccabees was likely produced. In their performances they often dealt with philosophical topics. Philostratus (second–third centuries CE), whose *Lives of the Sophists* chronicles this literary movement, describes their oratorical art as philosophical rhetoric.

Philostratus's characterization of the Second Sophistic accords well with 4 Maccabees. The first word of the text (in the Greek) is "most philosophical." In the mindset of the composition, philosophy and the Jewish traditions the Maccabean victims are dying for are virtual synonyms. For example, 4 Maccabees 5 presents Eleazar as a renowned philosopher (and a priest), whereas in 2 Maccabees 6 he is a scribe. The composition's correlation of philosophy and biblical traditions may seem odd to readers today. A merging of the two is more apparent in Greek since the word "philosophy" means in Greek "love of wisdom."

The "philosophizing" mode of Judaism evident in 4 Maccabees is one example of a more extensive phenomenon. Jews who were part of the ancient Greek-speaking Mediterranean world composed several texts which combine Jewish scriptural exegesis and Greek philosophy. Philo is a Jewish scholar from Alexandria, Egypt (first century CE), whose many writings seek to demonstrate that the Torah contains numerous hidden philosophical insights (this is often called an allegorical style of exegesis). The Wisdom of Solomon, as discussed in Chapter 7, engages both Jewish scriptural traditions and Greek philosophy. The philosophical Judaism evident in these texts is a product of authors steeped in Jewish traditions who also received a Greek education (*paideia*). They provide an iteration of ancient Judaism that is compatible with Greco-Roman cultural and intellectual values.

4 Maccabees' focus on a tale about death and suffering as a way to demonstrate the philosophical value of Judaism itself reflects the author's education in Greek philosophy. Socrates, in the Platonic dialogue the *Phaedo*, famously asks, "is not the study of philosophy the study of death?" Socrates accepted his own death with fortitude upon learning that he would be executed by the city of Athens around 400 BCE for "corrupting the youth." His provocative question underscores the task of philosophy as preparation for death. Awareness of death can be a catalyst for reflecting on how to live. The *Phaedo* stresses that philosophy, the cultivation of logical thinking, is important because at death, the soul (mind), which is immortal, will be released from the body. It no longer hinders the soul's pursuit of truth (which for Plato consists of ideal, rational Forms, of which things in this world are imperfect reflections). The cultivation of reason offered by philosophy prepares the soul for existence without the body. A philosopher, Socrates taught, should not fear death. In 4 Maccabees, the Maccabean torture victims are philosophers.

Their willingness to accept death is also connected to their expectation of a blessed afterlife. 4 Maccabees combines the classic Platonic idea of the immorality of the soul with the prospect of eternal life for the righteous, a common trope in the Jewish literature from the turn of the common era. Reason, being associated with the mind, is connected to what is spiritual and by extension what is heavenly. 4 Maccabees 13 portrays the victims as being welcomed by Abraham, Isaac, and Jacob after death, presumably in heaven. By following the example of Abraham and other patriarchs, one joins them after death. 2 Maccabees consistently frames the postmortem rewards of the nine victims in terms of resurrection and some sort of restoration of the body. Perhaps because 4 Maccabees' conception of reason is spiritual (non-physical), it never uses language of resurrection to describe their blessed afterlife.

4 Maccabees' Pathetic Praise of Reason

For a book that extols philosophy, 4 Maccabees is in a sense not that philosophical. The composition, as discussed above, resonates with the philosophical rhetoric of the Second Sophistic. This mode of exposition is quite different from that of classic Greek philosophy. The latter is often in the form of a debate or dialogue, led by a teacher like Socrates who poses questions. 4 Maccabees, unlike such writings, does not construct an argument, building point upon point, to reach a conclusion. Rather, it invokes one specific example after another, mostly drawn from the Torah and the Maccabean tradition, asserting virtually every time that it demonstrates that reason rules the emotions. The composition's thesis is repeated more than argued.

4 Maccabees shows the superiority of reason by appealing to the passions (*pathos*). The work, like 2 and 3 Maccabees, utilizes a rhetorical style that Aristotle described as pathetic; that is, such a text elicits the reader's support by appealing to their *pathos* (emotions), often by melodramatically recounting the pain of individuals whom the author wants the reader to feel sympathy with. As already described, 4 Maccabees recounts the suffering endured by the nine victims with an unsettling level of detail. The composition encourages an emotional (pathetic) response to their story. It even models how the audience is to experience listening to their ordeal. As chapter 14 states: "Even now, we ourselves shudder as we hear of the suffering of these young men." This is not a philosophical mode of argumentation. 4 Maccabees offers a pathetic praise of reason.

The Dominion of Supernatural Reason: The Jewish Stoicism of 4 Maccabees

While the rhetorical style of 4 Maccabees is quite different from that of classic philosophy, the composition utilizes specific tropes and ideas from the philosophical tradition. According to chapter 1, reason is "the mind that with sound logic prefers the life of wisdom." The composition conflates reason and wisdom (recall the literal meaning of philosophy, "love of wisdom"). It defines wisdom as "the knowledge of divine and human matters and the causes of these." This matches almost verbatim a definition of wisdom offered by the famous Roman statesman Cicero (first century BCE) in his *Tusculan Disputations*. Cicero's ideas were shaped by the Stoic tradition, a school of philosophy that arose in the Hellenistic era. This mode of Greek philosophy heavily influenced 4 Maccabees.

The composition's immersion in Greco-Roman learning is evident in its description of wisdom. After 4 Maccabees 1 states that wisdom is education in the Torah (a point Ben Sira is very much in agreement with), it asserts that there are four kinds of wisdom: rational judgment (prudence), justice, courage, and self-control (temperance). Plato in his *Republic* identifies four cardinal virtues essential to living an ethical life that are very similar to the ones in 4 Maccabees 1: wisdom, courage, temperance, and justice. Aristotle discusses in his *Nicomachean Ethics* several cardinal virtues, including the four in 4 Maccabees 1.

4 Maccabees' prioritization of reason and its stark dichotomy between reason and emotion were deeply influenced by the Stoic tradition. As discussed in Chapter 7 in relation to the Wisdom of Solomon, in Stoic thought, rationality is connected to the cosmos. The Stoics conceptualized reason (*logos*) as a breath or spirit that pervades the universe. It is equivalent to fate or providence. This comprehensive divine force explains the coherence and structure of reality.

The Stoic moral ideal is to live a life fully devoted to reason. Given the Stoic conception of reason as a cosmic principle, it is rational to accept one's fate, since whatever happens is in harmony with the universal *logos*. It is thus a sign of reason to accept adversity. Stoic ethics construes living as a challenge, a constant test of one's ability to remain rational without becoming shocked or angry (which would be examples of *pathos*); hence the meaning of the term "stoic" in modern parlance, denoting someone who remains calm or unmoved. Stoics called the ideal state of being human *apatheia* (the origin of the word "apathy"), that is, living without *pathos*. The Stoic philosopher (and former slave) Epictetus (first–second centuries CE) taught that "it is not things themselves that disturb people but their judgment about things." People should control with reason how they react to events, including difficult and painful ones. In keeping with the earlier teaching about death in Plato, death for Epictetus is not terrible. Rather, "what is terrible is the judgment that death is terrible." Stoic philosophers held that there are times when it is proper and rational to commit suicide. Diogenes Laertius (third century CE), who wrote a biography of ancient philosophers, explains that suicide is justified when a person experiences incredible pain or bodily mutilation—both situations when people choose death in 4 Maccabees.

There was no shortage of disagreements or debates within the Stoic school. 4 Maccabees was influenced by such disputes. Major early Stoic thinkers, such as Chrysippus (third century BCE), argued that the passions are not inherent or natural but the result of poor judgment; thus by living in accordance with reason, one can eliminate them. Other Stoics disagreed. Posidonius (first century BCE) disputed that the passions can be eradicated, arguing instead that the goal should be instead to keep them constantly under control. 4 Maccabees 3 argues for the exact position advocated by Posidonius against the earlier Stoics. To express the rule of reason over the passions, the composition likens reason to a king, as in chapter 14: "O reason, more royal than kings!" Chapter 1 similarly describes reason as a "master cultivator," a gardener who "tames the jungle of habits and emotions." The emotions, 4 Maccabees teaches, exist ideally as subject to the dominion of reason.

4 Maccabees' thematization of reason, however, diverges in an important way from Stoic thought. As discussed above, Stoicism holds that nature is defined by a universal principle of reason. In 4

Maccabees, by contrast, reason *opposes* what is natural. The work often praises not simply reason, but "divine" or "pious" reason. It is reason's opposition to natural desires that makes it divine and pious. In keeping with the book's emphasis on rationality, chapter 2 teaches that God gave the law to the mind, thus helping it subjugate the emotions. This is similar to how Platonic philosophy presents the soul (mind) as superior to the body. This intellectual background explains why, in the mindset of 4 Maccabees, reason and the Torah are conflated. Both are construed as divine or supernatural, in the sense that they are above and superior to the natural. 4 Maccabees provides a philosophical rationale for observing the commandments of the Torah. The first law it stresses involves food (*kashrut*). Chapter 1 acknowledges that Jews desire foods forbidden by the Torah but do not eat them because their reason is able to rule over their appetite. The law resonates with the Maccabean victims because they are tortured after refusing to eat pork. The composition's prioritization of the Torah transforms how it engages Stoic thought, in which the divine is immersed in the natural world, making reason instead akin to supernatural law. One can understand 4 Maccabees as articulating a Jewish Stoicism.

The Manly Mother

4 Maccabees presents desires for food and sex as natural components of the human experience that should be strictly curtailed by reason. It is also natural, chapter 14 emphasizes, that a mother, among both humans and "unreasoning" animals, protects her offspring from harm. Carrying them in the womb and giving birth to them gives her an inherent desire to see her offspring survive and thrive. The mother of 4 Maccabees does the opposite. She encourages her children to accept torture and even death. She exhorts them in chapter 16 "to die rather than violate God's commandment" and watches them die one by one. She feels intense

anguish watching her children suffer and die. For a mother, such pain is natural. But her commitment to Jewish law, and her own possession of reason which she received from the Torah, is greater than such *pathos*.

4 Maccabees' emphasis on the Maccabean mother should also be understood in terms of a widely held view among Greco-Roman intellectuals, who were overwhelmingly male, that women are more susceptible than men to being ruled by their emotions. The mother is a woman who embodies reason. The discourse culminates with her. This does not, I would argue, make 4 Maccabees a feminist text. Rather, Jewish law is so effective at cultivating reason that it can make *even a woman* a paragon of reason! As chapter 15 asserts, reason gave her "a man's courage." 4 Maccabees praises the mother because she is a woman, in a sense, with the mind of a man.

Reason and Victorious Torture

The Stoic prioritization of the dominion of reason over the emotions explains why 4 Maccabees presents the pinnacle of reason as the ability to withstand torture. Like Stoic sages, they accept pain, torture, and death with fortitude. The composition wants to show that the Maccabean victims' incredible endurance is a consequence of their extensive reason. They make long and elaborate speeches, a utilization of their rational minds, while being horribly tortured. Reason is construed as if it were a kind of super-power, giving them an astonishing ability to handle pain.

One contemporary Jewish author valorizes Judaism in a way quite similar to 4 Maccabees. Josephus discusses a Jewish sect called the Essenes. His account of them has several affinities with the literature of the sect described in the Dead Sea Scrolls. His description of the group was designed to appeal to an educated Greco-Roman reading public. Josephus asserts in his *Jewish War* (a history of Judah's failed revolt against Rome ca. 70 CE) that the Essenes never succumb to torture. The Romans would force them under torture to blaspheme or eat defiling foods. But they, Josephus writes, would just smile at their tormentors. For Josephus the Essenes' ability to withstand torture demonstrates the same core point which 4 Maccabees stresses—that Judaism is a noble philosophy that does an excellent job at cultivating reason.

4 Maccabees also highlights the power of reason to control the passions by likening the torture victims to athletes. Athletics was an important and popular element of ancient Greek culture. As a successful athlete pushes their physical limits to attain victory, so too the Maccabean victims' dedication to virtue was tested and they emerged victorious. 4 Maccabees 17 describes their ordeal as a "contest" that was divine "for on that day virtue gave the awards and tested them for their endurance." As victors, for them "the prize was immortality in endless life." Philo emphasizes the Essenes' all-encompassing dedication to righteousness by describing them as "athletes of virtue." Athletic metaphors are also common in roughly contemporary New Testament texts. In 1 Corinthians 9, for example, Paul compares himself to a boxer trained to endure pain, who will attain victory in the form of an eternal crown.

The Superiority of Jewish Law

4 Maccabees seeks to do more than portray Judaism as compatible with Greco-Roman culture. While being tortured, the eldest son in chapter 9 promotes an incredible thesis: "through all these tortures I will convince you that the children of the Hebrews alone are invincible where virtue is concerned." The Jews "alone" have unassailable means to cultivate reason—the Torah. It so construed is better than any other tradition at cultivating virtue. Judaism out-philosophizes the philosophers. A modern analogy would be a Muslim American author who argues that the Quran and Islamic tradition offer the best way to instill American values such as freedom and patriotism;

that is, Muslims, by staying true to their traditions, are the most American of Americans. 4 Maccabees plays a similar role for Jews in antiquity. It was written primarily for Jews who were part of a minority culture in the Diaspora that experienced various forms of discrimination. 4 Maccabees conveys that they deserve respect and are an integral part of the Greco-Roman world.

4 Maccabees is not a radical or militant book. It does not advocate that people embrace torture or die for the Torah. It does not encourage its readers to be martyrs, although there is a long-standing tradition of Christians understanding the book that way. The composition stresses that its Jewish audience should learn from the example of the Maccabean victims that they should keep the law, as the book stresses in its final chapter: "O Israelite children, offspring of the seed of Abraham, obey this law and exercise piety in every way."

4 Maccabees' praise of the Torah is quite different from that of other ancient Jewish texts written in Greek. The composition never offers allegorical exposition of Torah commandments, in sharp contrast to Philo's mode of exegesis. The Wisdom of Solomon utilizes stories from the Torah in its promotion of righteousness, an ethical value all people can support, while remaining silent on commandments that accentuate difference between Jews and non-Jews, such as circumcision or dietary restrictions. The latter, by contrast, is prominent in 4 Maccabees. That one should follow the commandments of the Torah is at best implicit in the Wisdom of Solomon, whereas it is explicit in 4 Maccabees.

Conclusion

4 Maccabees reformulates Jewish tradition in light of Greek philosophy, in particular Stoicism. This explains not only why it espouses reason, but also why it construes enduring torture and accepting death as the pinnacle of reason. The composition teaches

the importance of the rational soul for keeping the passions, often associated with the body, under control. To this end, 4 Maccabees extensively reworks the story found in 2 Maccabees 6–7 about the nine victims tortured and killed by Antiochus. They were able to show such courage and devotion, 4 Maccabees teaches, because they were educated in the Torah, which profoundly endowed them with reason. The composition provides a countervailing force to the discrimination that Jews in the Greco-Roman world could face. Jews, the text urges, should learn from the noble example of the Maccabean torture victims and follow the Torah. 4 Maccabees presents Judaism as a moral philosophy that is uniquely equipped to instill prestigious values of the Greco-Roman world—reason and virtue.

Guide for Further Reading

DeSilva, David A. *Fourth Maccabees*. Sheffield, UK: Sheffield Academic Press, 1998.

Rajak, Tessa. "Paideia in the Fourth Book of Maccabees." Pages 63–84 in *Jewish Education from Antiquity to the Middle Ages: Studies in Honour of Philip S. Alexander*. Edited by George J. Brooke and Renate Smithuis. Leiden: Brill, 2017.

Van Henten, Jan Willem. *The Maccabean Martyrs as Saviours of the Jewish People: A Study of 2 and 4 Maccabees*. Leiden: Brill, 1997.

17

Forgotten Scripture

1 Enoch and *Jubilees*

Martin Luther removed neither *1 Enoch* nor the *Book of Jubilees* from the Old Testament. By the time of the Reformation, most Christians had long forgotten about them. Both books, however, remain to this day in the Old Testament of one of the oldest forms of Christianity—the Ethiopian Orthodox Church, the traditional church of Ethiopia, in East Africa. Christianity was adopted by King Ezana of the Ethiopian kingdom of Axum in the fourth century. The retention of these two books in the Ethiopian Bible is a testament to the importance of these books in antiquity. *1 Enoch* and *Jubilees* are also important today for an unexpected group— the Rastafarians. The Rastafarians, best known for their reggae music and marijuana, began in Jamaica as a religious movement that venerates Ethiopia as the black Israel. Embracing all things Ethiopian, they adopted the Ethiopian version of the Bible. Not everyone forgot *1 Enoch* and *Jubilees*.

Over the past generation there has been a dramatic rise of interest among scholars in these two compositions. This is in no small part due to the Dead Sea Scrolls. They brought to light, for the first time, fragments of ancient Jewish manuscripts of both compositions. They demonstrate that books which comprise *1 Enoch* were written in Aramaic and that *Jubilees* was written in Hebrew. These texts survive in full only in Ge'ez, the classical language of Ethiopian Christianity. This chapter provides a brief introductory assessment of these two lengthy texts.

The Apocrypha: A Guide. Matthew Goff, Oxford University Press. © Oxford University Press 2024.
DOI: 10.1093/9780190060770.003.0017

The Sage from Before the Flood:
Enoch and His Books

The *Book of Enoch* (*1 Enoch*) is better understood as a macro-text than a single book. It is a compilation of five separate ancient Jewish texts:

The *Book of the Watchers* (*1 En.* 1–36)
The *Similitudes of Enoch* (*1 En.* 37–71)
The *Astronomical Book* (*1 En.* 72–82)
The *Dream Visions* (*1 En.* 83–90)
The *Epistle of Enoch* (*1 En.* 91–108)

These booklets are bound by the figure of Enoch, who is prominent in all of them. The book of Genesis offers a few brief but tantalizing details about Enoch. According to the genealogy in Genesis 5, he is from the seventh generation after Adam. Enoch also "walked with God" and he "took him." That first statement can instead be translated that Enoch "walked with the angels." The compositions in *1 Enoch* presuppose the latter view since they contain extensive accounts of Enoch interacting with angels. Enoch is above all associated with knowledge—exceptional, esoteric knowledge, revealed to him by angels—about the heavens and the earth, the distant past, and the eschatological future. No one else has seen what he has, as *1 Enoch* 19 says. He is a sage from the days before the flood who knew everything.

The Dead Sea Scrolls include fragments of at least eleven ancient manuscripts which together attest parts of every booklet of *1 Enoch* except the *Similitudes*. These scroll remnants demonstrate that the *Book of the Watchers* and the *Astronomical Book* are older than the other texts of *1 Enoch*, written in the third century BCE. These two texts comprise the core from which later Enochic traditions develop. The *Book of the Watchers* focuses on watchers (the Aramaic word for "angels") who desire women and descend from heaven to

have sex with them (*1 En.* 6–11). The book is silent as to whether
the women consented. The angels, shockingly, can be understood as rapists. *Watchers* treats the sexual union prompted by the
watchers as highly inappropriate. It is a violation of the boundary
between heaven and earth that produces horrifying monsters. The
women give birth to giants. They are incomprehensively large, over
3,000 cubits tall according to most manuscripts, or well over a mile
high. The crimes of the giants are startling. They eat the food of
humans, then the humans, and then, still hungry, each other (*1
En.* 7). In *Watchers*, God sends the flood to solve the crisis on earth
caused by the giants. The Enochic watchers myth resonates with
traditions in Genesis. Genesis 6:1–4 prefaces the flood story with
a brief and enigmatic tale in which the "sons of God" (a Hebrew
term for angels) have sex with women who bear sons, "mighty
men" (*gibborim*; NRSV: "heroes") or, according to the Septuagint,
"giants" (*gigantes*). *Watchers* provides a fuller story of this episode
than Genesis 6:1–4.

The misdeeds of the watchers are not only sexual. They disclose
heavenly secrets to the women. These revelations cover topics such
as astronomy, medicine, and metallurgy (*1 En.* 8). They teach humankind how to make metal weapons such as swords and armor,
and bracelets and other forms of adornment out of gold and silver.
This exacerbates the antediluvian crisis on earth. Knowing how to
craft objects out of metal expands the ability of humans to inflict
violence on each other and, in the mindset of the text, enhancing
female beauty with ornamentation increases sexual immorality.

The fallen angels, ashamed of their deeds, ask Enoch to intercede
on their behalf and ask God for forgiveness. Their request is unsuccessful and instead Enoch, like a prophet, chastises the watchers.
While the watchers are consigned to await the final judgment imprisoned in the netherworld, their gigantic offspring are incited by
the archangel Gabriel to destroy each other in a war. But while their
bodies are eliminated, their spirits remain. They are condemned
to harass and attack humankind. This is the oldest extant Jewish

etiology of demonic spirits. It was considered common knowledge at the time that malevolent spirits exist which attack humans. *Watchers* explains their origins—they are spirits of brutal giants who died in a war long ago, in the days before the flood.

In keeping with the view that Enoch "walked with angels," *1 Enoch* 17–36 offers an extensive travel narrative of Enoch in the company of angels. They take him around the world and show him its wonders and secrets. He is shown, for example, in the west, a mountain in which the spirits of the dead are gathered to await judgment (ch. 22) and, in the east, the Garden of Eden (ch. 33).

The *Astronomical Book*, the other third-century BCE Enochic text, is presented as a book written by Enoch that preserves astronomical knowledge disclosed to him by an angel. The work contains technical information about the movement of celestial bodies. The *Astronomical Book* espouses a solar calendar, whereas most in the ancient Near East at the time followed a lunar calendar (a tradition still followed today in Islam). Genesis 5:23, by stating that Enoch lived to the age of 365 years, may allude to this solar motif. The older Aramaic form of the composition found at Qumran is very different than the later Ethiopic version. The Aramaic text offers a sequence of fractions (fourteenths) that delineate the daily change of the portion of the disc of the moon that is visible. Almost nothing from this system is retained in the Ethiopic *Astronomical Book*.

Watchers and the *Astronomical Book* valorize Enoch as a scribe and exceptional conduit of heavenly knowledge, who preserves what he learned by writing it down. Genesis, by contrast, associates Enoch with neither supernatural revelation nor textuality. The portrayal of Enoch in the early Enoch literature accords with intellectual developments that were current in the Hellenistic Near East. The Hebrew Bible itself shows minimal interest in the far-flung past. The classic stories of Genesis 1–11 about primordial history, such as the flood and the Garden of Eden, are almost never engaged elsewhere in the Old Testament. The early Enochic literature is, however, driven by an intense curiosity about the deep past. During the

Hellenistic era, which began after the death of Alexander the Great in the fourth century BCE, ancient peoples such as the Egyptians, the Babylonians, and the Jews were ruled by Greeks, in the form of empires founded by Alexander's generals. The Greeks were widely regarded, even by themselves, as a much younger people than those of the Near East. At a time when age was equated with value, something seemed out of place with this status quo. The sons ruled the fathers, as it were. This led to a kind of cultural anxiety that encouraged the peoples under Greek hegemony to stress their own antiquity. In the third century BCE, when Jewish scribes were writing tales about Enoch's antediluvian exploits, Berossus and Manetho, priests from Babylon and Egypt, composed accounts of their respective cultures that chronicle their deep antiquity and articulate the origins of human civilization in a way that highlights their own cultures' traditions. Berossus, for example, writes that humans learned key types of knowledge, such as how to build cities and the development of writing, when a large fish-monster named Oannes came to shore and began to reveal secrets. This tale adapts the Mesopotamian mythic tradition of the *apkallu*, antediluvian sages who were often depicted as human-fish hybrids. There was a vibrant discourse in the Hellenistic age about the origins of civilization (a topic scholars sometimes call heurematology). The distant past was a highly valued and contested space in which intellectuals of various cultures sought to assert the importance of their own traditions.

The rise of interest in Enoch among Jewish scribes should be understood against the backdrop of Hellenistic cultural politics. Writing and astronomical knowledge, both prominent tropes in Enochic literature, are common topics in Hellenistic discourse about the origins of human civilization. *Jubilees* 4 praises Enoch as the first human to obtain both types of knowledge. *Watchers*' emphasis on unsanctioned forms of revelation via lustful angels may polemicize the older Mesopotamian tradition of the *apkallu*. So understood, *Watchers* acknowledges the venerable antiquity of Mesopotamian mythic lore, while denigrating it as providing an illegitimate and harmful form of antediluvian wisdom. The disclosures of the watchers serve as a foil to the revelations given to Enoch.

Interest in Enoch does not subside after the third century BCE. The three other booklets of *1 Enoch*, written in the second and first centuries BCE, along with numerous other references in ancient Judaism to Enoch and Enochic books, attest the contrary. The *Dream Visions* contain a lengthy vision given to Enoch in a dream known as the Animal Apocalypse (*1 En.* 85–90). It imagines the history of Israel, from Adam to the final judgment, as a kind of fable that depicts various ethnic groups as kinds of animals. The Egyptians are wolves, for example, and the Israelites are sheep. It offers a vivid depiction of the final judgment that, it teaches, was to occur soon after the Maccabean Revolt. The Animal Apocalypse's presentation of antediluvian history includes an extensive iteration of the watchers myth, depicting the giants as elephants, camels, and wild asses, as if it were part of the story told by Genesis (so too *Jubilees*). This suggests that the *Book of the Watchers* at the time had a form of authoritative status.

The *Epistle of Enoch* is, like the *Astronomical Book*, explicitly presented as a book written by Enoch. It contains extensive discourses about eschatological judgment. The work, showing development regarding traditions about Enoch, depicts him not as a recipient but a source of exceptional knowledge. The *Epistle* contains an intriguing story about the birth of Noah (another version of this story is in another text from Qumran, the *Genesis Apocryphon*). When he was born, according to *1 Enoch* 106, light beamed from his eyes and his body was snow white. His father Lamech, thinking that the infant resembles an angel, accuses his wife of having sex with one. An indication of the popularity of the watchers myth, sexual aggression from angels is presumed to be a problem women faced in the antediluvian age. Lamech's father Methuselah travels a great distance to seek answers from his father

Enoch, who knows the answer to any question. He proclaims that in the future there will be a great flood and that the baby Noah is destined to play an important role in it, thus explaining his unusual features.

The *Similitudes of Enoch* was likely written in the first century BCE, or perhaps in the early first century CE, making it later than the other booklets of *1 Enoch*. The *Similitudes* asserts that a messianic figure called the Son of Man will play a central role as judge in the eschatological judgment. The use of Son of Man as a title for Jesus in the later New Testament gospels draws on older traditions, especially Daniel 7, that are also attested in this Enochic text. The end of the *Similitudes* (*1 En.* 70–71) depicts Enoch's transformation into a heavenly figure. He becomes the Son of Man, who throughout the composition was a separate figure whom Enoch saw in his eschatological visions. The apotheosis of Enoch into a heavenly being is taken up and expanded in later Enochic texts (*2 Enoch, 3 Enoch*).

The Rise and Fall of Enochic Scripture

Early Christian literature presumes that Enochic literature is authoritative. The New Testament Letter of Jude quotes *1 Enoch* 1 to affirm that the final judgment is inevitable. Tertullian (second century), in his treatise *On the Apparel of Women*, asserts that believers in Christ should revere the "scripture of Enoch," citing 2 Timothy 3:16 to assert its "inspired" status (a verse commonly quoted by evangelicals today to assert that scripture is divinely inspired). He also derives a moralistic teaching from the Enochic tale of the watchers—that women should dress modestly (as if the sexual advances of the angels were their fault).

In the fourth century, when a Christian canon of scripture was becoming standardized, Enochic literature fell out of favor. As an orthodox form of Christianity began to develop, some Christian groups came to be seen as heretical. For some of them,

Enochic writings were important. When leading orthodox figures condemned those groups, they also impugned the Enochic texts they revered. The bishop Athanasius derided apocryphal writings as an "invention of heretics" and complained that people have been deluded to believe that Enoch wrote books, when, he insisted, no scriptures existed before Moses (this is also discussed in Chapter 1). Saint Augustine dismissed the book of Enoch as having spurious fables about angels fathering giants, considering its depiction of angels as sinful and incompatible with Christian scripture.

1 Enoch was never in the canon of rabbinic Judaism. While many older Second Jewish texts assert that Enoch ascended to heaven, the early rabbinic text *Genesis Rabbah* interprets the claim in Genesis 5 that "God took" Enoch to mean instead that the deity killed him. This constitutes an effort to delegitimize venerable Enochic traditions and purge them from rabbinic exegesis of Genesis. One motivating factor was likely the importance of Enochic literature in the emerging religion of Christianity, from which rabbis wanted to differentiate themselves. The production of stories about Enoch, however, continued in Judaism. A late antique text known as *3 Enoch* (also called the *Hebrew Book of Enoch*), for example, identifies Metatron, a powerful celestial figure who sits on a throne in heaven and dispenses revelation to Rabbi Ishmael when he ascends to heaven, as none other than the transfigured Enoch. There is also extensive lore about Enoch in Islam. Jews, Christians, and Muslims continued to read books attributed to and about Enoch, even though the booklets of *1 Enoch* were, outside of Ethiopia, not considered scripture.

The *Book of Jubilees*

The *Book of Jubilees* is a lengthy composition, comprising fifty chapters. A "jubilee" is a sabbath-based unit of time. The jubilee year comes after seven sabbaths of years, or 49 years (7 × 7). A jubilee, one can say, is sabbath squared. If the sabbath is holy, the jubilee is the holy of holies. Leviticus 25 emphasizes that the jubilee year is particularly holy, a time when debts are annulled and slaves liberated. *Jubilees* expands this Torah-based jubilee method of measuring years into a chronological system that serves as a framework for Torah stories.

Fragments of at least fourteen manuscripts of *Jubilees* were found at Qumran, a substantial number. The oldest manuscript of *Jubilees* (4Q216) was produced in the late second century BCE. The composition, in its strikingly positive account of Enoch, utilizes *Watchers* and the *Astronomical Book*, both from the third century BCE (*Jub.* 4:15–26). This suggests that *Jubilees* was written, like many texts treated in this volume, in the second century BCE.

The number of *Jubilees* manuscripts from Qumran suggests that at least some Jews in the second and first centuries BCE considered the composition to have a kind of authoritative status. One Qumran text, the *Damascus Document*, appeals to an early form of *Jubilees*, which it calls "the Book of the Division of the Times into their Jubilees and Weeks," as a work that helps one understand the Torah.

The presence of *Jubilees* in the Ethiopian Old Testament indicates that some early Christians regarded it as an authoritative text. *Jubilees*, however, is never cited in the New Testament. A few early Christian authors or texts know of the composition, such as Epiphanius and Jerome (both fourth century); they sometimes refer to it as "Little Genesis." There is no extensive evidence that early Christians disputed the status of *Jubilees* as an authoritative text. In rabbinic Judaism there is no explicit discussion of *Jubilees*, but the composition contains many tropes found in later rabbinic sources, such as the motif that God made Abraham endure ten tests. *Jubilees* indicates that some traditions attested in rabbinic literature pre-date rabbinic Judaism.

The *Book of Jubilees*: It Takes You
Inside the Cloud

Jubilees offers a version of scriptural narratives, from the creation of the world (Genesis 1) to Israel's liberation from slavery in Egypt and their subsequent journey into the wilderness (Exodus). The composition grounds its scripturesque content in a claim that is nothing short of incredible. In Exodus, God gives Moses the law at the summit of Mount Sinai, which is shrouded in a thick cloud. The people of Israel are not allowed to approach the mountain. They learn about the laws revealed to Moses only when he descends from it. *Jubilees* purports to reveal what Moses was told inside the cloud. Chapter 1 and the Prologue recount what Moses was shown "on this mountain," and the rest of *Jubilees* (chs. 2–50) proceeds with stories that accord with Genesis and Exodus. When reading *Jubilees* one is, in a sense, reading over the shoulder of Moses as he is given and writes down revelation. The composition offers a transcript of Moses's divine encounter on Sinai. The book thus claims to present a version of scriptural texts that is *prior* to the Torah itself, which Israel received after Moses came down from the mountain.

Jubilees presumes that the laws in the Torah are important and emphasizes their status as divinely revealed. But the scribes who produced *Jubilees* did not conceive of scripture the way the Bible is valorized in our own culture, as a fixed, unchanging text. Rather, the composition shows interest in stories in the Torah by offering its own version of them. *Jubilees* erases the distinction between the scriptural text and its interpretation.

The composition's Sinai-based framework enhances its ability to function as an authoritative interpretive lens through which the Torah should be understood. The Dead Sea Scrolls indicate that in the second and first centuries BCE, Jewish sectarian groups proliferated. This rise of sectarianism was at least in part generated by disputes regarding how to interpret the Torah. *Jubilees* develops within this cultural milieu. The composition presents itself not as taking sides in sectarian disagreements, but rather asserts that its own interpretations of Torah stories are literally from Sinai and thus beyond dispute. *Jubilees* 23 describes the rise of an evil generation during which there will be much sin, violence, and disagreements about the Torah. But then a new generation will arise to study the laws and turn to righteousness. This new generation is likely a reference to the scribal intellectuals who composed and transmitted *Jubilees*. They understood themselves as teaching the proper understanding of Torah when most of Israel has gone astray. While eschatology is not a major theme of *Jubilees* as a whole, chapter 23 claims that the turn of this new generation to righteousness will usher in a utopian epoch of peace, long life, and joy. This perspective explains why the scribes responsible for *Jubilees* understood their form of Torah interpretation to be important.

Jubilees, Scripture, and Judaism

The iteration of scriptural texts in *Jubilees* addresses a specific problem—how to relate the book of Genesis (and part of Exodus) to Judaism. The Dead Sea Scrolls establish that by the second century BCE, *halakha*, a central concern of later rabbinic Judaism, was an important if disputed aspect of Jewish identity and a key rationale for studying the Torah. The term *halakha*, derived from the Hebrew term "to walk," denotes practices and forms of conduct that are regarded as consistent with commandments in the Torah. Kinds of animals one cannot eat or types of activities one can or cannot do on the Sabbath are classic halakhic questions. In terms of the Torah's own presentation of events, the revelation of Sinai occurs surprisingly late. The whole of Genesis occurs before the Sinai event, which is recounted in Exodus. If Judaism is defined in terms of observing the commandments given to Moses on Sinai, what does the book of Genesis have to do with Judaism?

Jubilees answers this question by teaching that the way things are is the way they have always been. It tells stories about the patriarchs as if they were aware of and followed ordinances in the Torah. For example, according to *Jubilees* 7, when Noah plants his vineyard (Genesis 9), he does so in accordance with guidelines regarding agriculture stipulated in Leviticus 19. The patriarchs of Genesis are presented as originators of important festal days described later in the Torah. Abraham, according to *Jubilees*, is the first person to celebrate Sukkot, which is still a major Jewish holiday, commemorating Israel's wandering in the wilderness. In this construal, the revelation Moses received on Sinai does not constitute new knowledge. It is a renewal of traditions and practices developed by the earlier patriarchs of Israel. So understood, Genesis, which in Hebrew is entitled *be-reshit* ("In [the] beginning"), describes not only the beginning of the world but also the beginning of Judaism.

Jubilees was likely intended to be studied along with Genesis and parts of Exodus. The Christian nickname "Little Genesis" for the composition suggests that it was read in relation to Genesis. How it may have functioned can be gleaned from the above example regarding Noah's vineyard. If one accepts *Jubilees'* self-presentation as a more immediate account of the Sinai revelation than the Torah, one can presume when reading Genesis that Noah planted his vineyard in accordance with Torah guidelines—not because Genesis 9 says so, but because *Jubilees* 7 does.

Jubilees' concerns can often be discerned through comparison with Genesis. Depicting God in anthropomorphic terms, for example, is considered problematic. *Jubilees* omits the story of Jacob wrestling an angel in Genesis 32 or, as verse 30 suggests, God himself. *Jubilees'* anti-Gentile perspective can also be appreciated in relation to Genesis. Genesis espouses a kind of xenophobia, with parents teaching their sons not to marry outside of their kinship group (endogamy). *Jubilees* expands and emphasizes this theme. Not all themes of the composition, however, can be seen solely through comparison with the Torah. The work's emphasis on

Enoch as the first to learn writing and record astronomical knowledge is better understood, for example, in terms of Hellenistic discourse about the history of human civilization, as described above.

The Bible, as a canon of scripture for communities of faith, is often understood not simply as a collection of writings. Rather, its books are regarded as constituent parts of a single text that is coherent, logically consistent, and morally uplifting. *Jubilees* shows that by the second century BCE a conception of scripture akin to this view was emerging. The stories of Genesis involve sex, violence, and deceit. Jacob acquires the divine promise God gave to Abraham (a key pillar of the covenant between God and Israel) through treachery, by disguising himself as his brother Esau. Abraham gives his wife Sarah to the pharaoh of Egypt and receives wealth from him in exchange—a transaction which, as students in my classes like to point out, makes Abraham seem kind of like a pimp.

Jubilees recounts these stories in a way that undercuts the moral problems they raise. Now Abraham does not give Sarah to the pharaoh. He seizes her (ch. 13). Abraham is not a pimp but a victim; his wife has been kidnapped by a rogue royal court. In *Jubilees*, Jacob still acquires in the Abrahamic promise by disguising as Esau (ch. 26). But now Abraham articulates beforehand that the promise is supposed to go to Jacob. So understood, Jacob's deceit does not cheat Esau out of something he was entitled to; it rather constitutes a fulfillment of God's plan and Abraham's wishes.

Jubilees strives to present its stories as logically coherent and without contradictions. God famously warns Adam in Genesis 2:17 that he should not eat of the fruit "for in the day that you eat of it you shall die." Adam eats this fruit but lives to the ripe old age of 930. The scribes who produced *Jubilees* observed this contradiction and resolved it when recounting Adam's death, by asserting that "one thousand years are one day in the testimony of heaven." Thus from a divine perspective, Adam *did* die on the day he ate the fruit—with seventy years to spare! There are other instances of *Jubilees* changing or omitting details to avoid logical and textual problems. In Genesis 7, for example, Noah and his family enter the ark twice; in *Jubilees* 5 they do so only once. Attention to such details indicates that *Jubilees* is a kind of ancient textual scholarship, by scribes whose close study of the Torah resulted in the creation of new, Torah-esque texts.

Chronologizing Israel's Past

Jubilees gives Torah stories a chronological framework. This composition, unlike Genesis or Exodus, consistently specifies in what year a given event takes place, using its jubilee-based system. This format can seem cumbersome to readers today. *Jubilees* 12:9 offers an example of how the text's jubilee system works. The verse asserts that Abraham married Sarah "in the fortieth jubilee in the second week, it its seventh year." Thirty-nine jubilees have occurred, or 1,911 years (39 × 49 = 1,911), since a jubilee unit constitutes 49 years; they are in the fortieth. In this jubilee they have completed one week of years (7) and are in the seventh year of the second (7). Added together (1,911 + 7 + 7), Abraham married Sarah in the year 1925 A.M. (*anno mundi*, Latin for "year of the world"). That is not the year according to a particular calendar. They were married 1,925 years after God created the world. Some texts of *Jubilees* presume that a jubilee constitutes 50, not 49, years. Such evidence suggests that the composition is not the work of a single author, but rather a communal product written over time that occasionally incorporates different perspectives.

Jubilees' chronological framework presents a wide swath of stories, from Adam to Moses, as comprising a single narrative along a historical continuum. This is implicit in Genesis; it is explicit in *Jubilees*. The composition seeks to demonstrate that Israel's traditional stories about the patriarchs accord with a divine plan that orchestrates history. The end of *Jubilees* establishes that the "present moment" of the composition, when Moses is on the mountain, is during the year 2410 A.M. They will enter the promised land of Canaan in forty years. This is a period of punishment in the Bible, but here it is established as a time for Israel to study the Torah in preparation for their eventual entry into the land. This recapitulates a pattern found in the book of Deuteronomy, which depicts Moses recounting the laws of the covenant to Israel before the people cross into the Canaan. Israel is nine years into the forty-ninth jubilee, which began in 2401 A.M. (49 × 49). Thus according to *Jubilees'* chronology, Israel will enter the promised land in 2450 A.M. This is not a random number. It is the fiftieth jubilee (2401 + 49). It is a jubilee of jubilees. The jubilee year, according to Leviticus 25, is when Israelites are to return to their ancestral homes. The year 2450 is thus a unique period of holiness and a fitting time for Israel to enter the land.

To comprehend this key point, *Jubilees* asserts, one must perceive that the proper basis for measuring years is the sun, not the moon. The latter, which produces a year of 354 days, was the norm in the ancient Near East at the time. *Jubilees* teaches that a year should be defined as 52 weeks or 364 days. The composition endorses, like the *Astronomical Book* of *1 Enoch*, a solar calendar. The Dead Sea Scrolls indicate that it was a basis of sectarian disputes at the time. The form of calendar one uses impacts worship, in particular when festal days occur. An accurate understanding of the Torah, *Jubilees* teaches, is grounded in an accurate understanding of the cosmos and history.

Conclusion

1 Enoch and *Jubilees*, though long forgotten in the West, constitute important testimony for understanding ancient, pre-Christian Judaism. They shed light on issues that were important in the third through first centuries BCE. They betray an abiding concern for lore about patriarchs of old as a way to articulate a range of concerns, such as the origins of civilization, the calendar, and *halakha*. Enochic texts and *Jubilees* illustrate that texts considered to be authoritative, in the Second Temple period and even in the first centuries of the common era, encompassed a larger corpus of texts than the writings preserved in the Bible.

Guide for Further Reading

Goff, Matthew. "Jubilees." Pages 1–97 in *The Jewish Annotated Apocrypha: New Revised Standard Version*. Edited by Jonathan Klawans and Lawrence M. Wills. New York: Oxford University Press, 2020 (quotations of *Jubilees* are from this source).

Nickelsburg, George W. E., and James C. VanderKam. *1 Enoch: A Commentary on the Book of 1 Enoch*. 2 vols. Minneapolis: Fortress Press, 2001, 2011.

Reeves, John C., and Annette Yoshiko Reed. *Enoch from Antiquity to the Middle Ages*, Volume 1: *Sources from Judaism, Christianity, and Islam*. New York: Oxford University Press, 2018.

Yoshiko Reed, Annette. *Fallen Angels and the History of Judaism and Christianity: The Reception of Enochic Literature*. Cambridge: Cambridge University Press, 2005.

18

Read the Apocrypha

Readers of scripture often consider the Bible to be important because its writings connect them to the distant past. It is a story about remembering. But it is also a story about forgetting. Many people do not know that there are numerous books which were in the Old Testament for centuries, and for millions of Christians still are, that are not in their Bible. This is particularly the case in the United States. As discussed in Chapter 1, this is in no small part because Puritans and other Protestants who took a resolutely negative stance toward the Apocrypha played a foundational role in the history of scripture in North America. A Bible with an Apocrypha section, of lesser authority than the Old and New Testaments but scripture nonetheless, is, as we have seen, a venerable Protestant tradition. The original version of the King James Bible from 1611 includes an Apocrypha section. The books of the Apocrypha by and large fell out of the Protestant tradition. Many forgot they were ever there in the first place. This book was written to help people rediscover forgotten scripture.

The formation of the Apocrypha involved anthologizing into a single corpus several writings, each of which has its own characteristics, themes, and cultural context. It is important to highlight the distinctive character and perspective of each text, as this book has done. It is also helpful, after having examined each text, to identify recurring themes and motifs which occur throughout the books covered in this volume.

The Apocrypha: A Guide. Matthew Goff, Oxford University Press. © Oxford University Press 2024.
DOI: 10.1093/9780190060770.003.0018

A Common Milieu: The Hellenistic Age

The books examined in this volume were composed between the third century BCE and the second century CE. By and large they are products of the Hellenistic age. Accordingly, many of these texts existed in antiquity primarily in Greek, the lingua franca of the period. Much of the ancient Jewish literature in Greek is a product of scribes and intellectuals who lived in minority Jewish communities in the Mediterranean world. They were part of the Jewish Diaspora.

These Jews translated their ancestral writings from Hebrew into Greek, producing what became the Septuagint (LXX). Many of these books are Greek versions of well-known Hebrew texts, such as Genesis or Isaiah. Ancient manuscripts of the Septuagint, as we have seen, also include what would later become the classic Apocrypha, such as 1 Maccabees and Tobit, and writings not in the Catholic Old Testament (i.e., 3 and 4 Maccabees).

The Reception and Composition of Jewish Scripture in the Hellenistic Age

The texts covered in this book offer insights into conceptions of Jewish scripture and textuality in the Hellenistic age. They affirm that Jews in this era revered a corpus of older traditional writings. Some of these compositions, such as Tobit and 3 Maccabees, cite older scriptural texts. The instruction of Ben Sira depicts a teacher in the early second century BCE urging his students to study the Torah. 4 Maccabees praises the Maccabean martyrs to encourage Jews to keep the Torah and observe Jewish traditions.

But the Judaism of the Hellenistic era does not have a term equivalent to "Bible." The Apocrypha/Deuterocanonical writings indicate that scripture in the Hellenistic age was a dynamic and expansive textual category, a topic discussed in Chapter 1. There was a keen awareness of a corpus of older writings about ancient

Israel and important Jewish ancestors. Scribes did not regard them as a canon of fixed texts that they should only venerate and copy. They engaged the textual heritage of ancient Judaism to create new stories about Israel's past. The Wisdom of Solomon, for example, adapts in the first century CE the scriptural trope that Solomon was a legendary king of ancient Israel renowned for his wisdom by depicting him as delivering a lengthy exhortation about the virtues of wisdom. The Enochic book of the *Watchers* appropriates traditions attested in Genesis 6 to produce an extensive narrative about sexual transgression by angels before the flood. The versions of Daniel, Esther, and 1 Esdras in the Septuagint indicate that the scribes could be quite free and expansive when transmitting texts. They extensively revised older versions of these texts, effectively making new stories out of old ones.

Strangers in a Strange Land: The Babylonian Exile and the Jewish Diaspora

In terms of the distant past, one recurring motif in the Apocrypha/ Deuterocanonical literature is the Babylonian exile. Many of these texts, such as Baruch and the Danielic Bel and the Dragon, are set in the Jewish community exiled to Babylon after the Babylonians destroyed Jerusalem in the early sixth century BCE.

In these stories, some Jews achieve great success. Daniel attains a position of great power in the royal court of the Babylonians and later the Persians. They also contain stories about Gentiles launching extreme anti-Jewish measures. In Esther and 3 Maccabees, powerful men, in Persia and Egypt respectively, seek to eliminate Jews from the lands they rule. While Jews could achieve prominence in a Gentile world, things could quickly turn for the worse.

Relatedly, animosity between Jews and Gentiles is a common theme in this literature. The Letter of Jeremiah and Bel and the

Dragon transform Jeremiah and Daniel, respectively, into fierce critics of Babylonian religion. Their polemic is framed as a condemnation of idolatry, which is also an important motif in the Wisdom of Solomon. A frequent refrain is that Jews should worship God and not the deities revered by other peoples. In the Greek version of Esther, not in the Hebrew, she refuses Gentile food and proudly declares, when married to the Persian king, that she would never share a bed with an uncircumcised (Gentile) man.

Some of these texts do not focus on exceptional crises, but rather present life in exile as a whole as an alienating, difficult experience. Baruch and the Prayer of Azariah, for example, teach, as do some texts in the Hebrew Bible (e.g., Ezra 9), that the exile and the destruction of Jerusalem constitute punishment by God against the Jews for their sins. So understood, the harsh reality of exile can help them realize that they must re-establish their commitment to God. In Baruch this theological shift coincides with their departure from Babylon to Judah. Babylon, so understood, not only represents punishment, but also functions as a site of religious renewal.

The prominence of the Babylonian exile in the books examined in this volume suggests that some Jews in the Hellenistic era understood this earlier event to be relevant to their lives. Baruch in particular suggests that living in the Diaspora could be imagined as a sort of continuation of the Babylonian exile. It is as if it did not last seventy years, as the book of Jeremiah proclaims, but was considered an ongoing, present experience. Understanding the exile as a social context in which discrimination and outright oppression was an ever-present possibility became a creative catalyst that shaped how Jews engaged and expanded their literary heritage, as a way to make sense of life in the Greco-Roman world and its difficulties.

The social reality they faced as a minority people was a powerful incentive for Jews to assimilate, not to practice customs which accentuate ethnic difference, such as observing the Sabbath or keeping kosher. The texts examined in this book consistently push in the opposite direction. In various ways they emphasize that the response to such problems is for Jews to uphold, not abandon, their traditions. These texts teach that God will eventually deliver his people if they are loyal to him.

It is unfortunate that many readers of scripture are not familiar with the Apocrypha/Deuterocanonical books because they often promote a positive theological message—that while Jews can face discrimination and harassment for keeping their traditions, they should nevertheless do so because that is how they maintain their covenant with God, who can deliver them from any crisis they face.

A Noble Philosophy: A Forgotten Kind of Ancient Judaism

As products of the Hellenistic age, the Apocrypha and adjacent writings often demonstrate that their authors had attained a prodigious degree of Greek learning (*paideia*). Several of these texts, all written in Greek, can be reasonably understood as literary evidence for a lost form of Judaism that is characterized by *paideia* to an extent not attested in later rabbinic Judaism. These texts valorize Judaism in ways that would have appealed to intellectuals, Jewish and Gentile alike, during the Hellenistic age.

The Wisdom of Solomon, for example, praises Judaism as a kind of noble philosophy. The composition draws extensively on Hellenistic philosophy, in particular Stoic conceptions of the natural world, to depict the scriptural tradition as promoting righteousness in a way that is open in principle to all people. The composition engages the Torah, especially the Exodus story, to make this point, while avoiding particularities of Jewish law that highlight differences between Jews and Gentiles, such as circumcision and dietary restrictions. 4 Maccabees also draws on Stoicism, in particular Stoic ethics and its stress on accepting whatever fate brings, to praise Maccabean-era victims of torture (Eleazar, the seven sons, and their mother) as philosophers. Their extensive education in the Torah, the composition teaches, endowed them with a level of reason that allowed them to remain true to their traditions even to the point of death by torture.

Ancient Jewish engagement with Greek learning is not limited to philosophy. 3 Maccabees, for example, is a product of extensive study of Greek historiography. Its account of the Battle of Raphia (217 BCE) contains details, such as Theodotus's failed attempt to assassinate the Ptolemaic king (Ptolemy IV), which are also found in the description of the conflict by the Greek historian Polybius. His work was highly respected when 3 Maccabees was composed. While it cannot be proven conclusively, whoever wrote 3 Maccabees had likely studied Polybius.

The "Re-Judaification" of Christian Scripture

The compositions examined in this volume were written as ancient Jewish texts. They survived not among Jews, but Christians. Some motifs and themes found in these works do, however, appear in rabbinic literature. This is the case, for example, regarding the death and torture of the nine Maccabean victims. There is evidence that some Jews made robust efforts to reappropriate texts in the Christian Old Testament. Medieval Jewish scribes produced Hebrew and Aramaic manuscripts of Tobit, and there was a tradition that Jews should read the story during Shavuot (a Jewish holiday celebrated in the book by Tobit's family). The book of Judith likewise became associated with Hanukkah in the Middle Ages. The rabbi Nahmanides (thirteenth century), as we have seen, shows familiarity with Judith and the Wisdom of Solomon. *Sefer Yosippon* is a medieval Hebrew rendition of writings by the ancient Jewish historian Josephus, who wrote in Greek. The contents of *Yosippon* are, however, not limited to Josephus. It also includes stories found in the Old Testament that are not in the Hebrew Bible. It contains, for example, an account of Mordecai's dream, which is in Greek Esther

(Addition A), not its Hebrew version. Such evidence requires further study, but it suggests that in the Middle Ages some Jews realized that the Christian Old Testament preserves Jewish books which are not in the Jewish Bible—and that this discovery prompted various efforts, one can say, to make them Jewish again.

Read the Apocrypha

It is my hope that this book has convinced the reader of a single point—that people who have never heard of the Apocrypha/ Deuterocanonical writings, or any of the books examined in this volume, would enjoy reading them. They are stories about drunk elephants, apotropaic fish guts, and cannibalistic giants. Encouraging people to read these compositions is in a sense in continuity with what both Jerome and Luther, separated by a thousand years, asserted—that while these texts should not be used for church doctrine, it is good for people to read them. They are compelling, interesting, and engaging. It is good for anyone to read them, regardless of their confessional affiliation.

Index

For the benefit of digital users, indexed terms that span two pages (e.g., 52–53) may, on occasion, appear on only one of those pages.
Tables and figures are indicated by an italic t and f following the page number.